D1237066

South of Saigon

*A Secret Naval Mission
to Southeast Asia*

Martin Wilens

To order additional copies of this book, contact:
Xlibris Corporation
1-888-795-4274
www.Xlibris.com
Orders@Xlibris.com
106677

To all my friends and family, especially my late brother Mel, and late son Herbert, who have heard parts of this story over the past forty years and can now, in spirit, put it all together.

And to the men and women who have fallen in fighting for liberty and freedom.

Contents

Maps and Illustrations

---

[*] Maps obtain from the Naval Institute Press, Annapolis, Maryland. Referrence: Historical Atlas of the USN, by Craig L. Symonds. Current map of the Mekong Delta may contain modern-day designations of places and rivers that differ from 1966

[**] A series of detailed maps of NVN & SVN showing "city maps" of Hanoi, Saigon, and Vung Tau. .

Introduction

My story begins on a sultry summer day in 1966 at the US Navy think tank in Arlington, Virginia, known as CNA, where I was employed as an operations research engineer. I had just joined this group, moving from my previous job as deputy manager of the nuclear ship *Savannah* program at the US Atomic Energy Commission, a thirty-minute Beltway ride around Washington, DC, to Germantown, Maryland. I was hired to assist in conducting studies on nuclear naval forces for the then secretary of defense, Robert McNamara, at DDRE[*] in the Pentagon. It ends on a flight home from the Mekong Delta, South Vietnam, on New Year's Eve six months later, having spent my time initially testing three militarized air cushion vehicles (ACVs) in riverine patrol in the delta south of Saigon.

My mission gravitated from an "op. eval." of these three British-designed (Westland Aircraft) low flying boats that had operational speeds over calm waters in excess of fifty knots, to advising ADM Veth, deputy commander of naval forces in South Vietnam (ComNavForV)[**], on the conduct of Market Time and Game Warden, the coastal and riverine patrol missions in IV Corps Zone (south of Saigon). These crafts were unique because a cushion of air was trapped beneath four to six feet of flexible neoprene skirts completely surrounding the craft and could operate over any terrain that didn't present obstacles higher than that.

---

[*] Department of Defense Research and Engineering.
[**] Rear Admiral Norvell G. Ward was chief of the US Naval Advisory Group from April 1, 1966, until April 27, 1967, when Rear Admiral Kenneth Veth assumed that role. In the interim, Admiral Veth was deputy chief.

My mission became, as so many things in warfare, far different and vastly more important than originally intended.

Specifically, the good admiral merely wanted me to figure out how the Viet Cong and scattered units of the North Vietnamese Army were being supplied from the North, when our patrols along the coast and throughout the tributaries of the Mekong in the delta were finding nothing.

This is that story . . .

Junks on the upper Mekong River, Cambodian mountains, 1966

Montagnards, tribal warriors from highlands of III Corps,

VC avoided them

I

Arlington, Virginia – The Center for Naval Analyses (CNA)

The Center for Naval Analyses (CNA) occupied a twenty-story building overlooking the Potomac River, in a section of Arlington, Virginia, known as Rosslyn, and by many as Pentagon East. Looking out over the snarled rush-hour traffic fighting its way across Key Bridge to Georgetown. I was staying late, not to earn any points with the "think tank gamers" who were busy trying to figure out who to screw out of some posh foreign trip or steal one of their associates' work to use in the next useless study the US Navy would ignore. Having finished whatever paperwork I had ginned up for our study's leader, a buddy of mine named Dudley "Doc" Colladay walked into my office, while I was engaged in a phone call with my man on Wall Street. Being able to double as an operations research engineer and a stock picker, I was double dipping like most bureaucrats, playing the stock market in order to feed four kids on a government salary, despite my wife doing private-duty nursing on the side to make both ends meet.

Using "pattern recognition," a knowledge of how technical analysis worked in the world of the Street's vultures, I was plotting out tomorrow's market moves when our surface effect ship (SES) study leader, Doc, suggested we call Nancy, "his side squeeze," and sat down.

"You doing any good today?" he asked, and I shot back, "In the study or the market?"

Doc suggested that I had been at my desk too long, and as was our custom, we would retire to the roof lounge bar high above the clogged streets of Rosslyn and have "a few pops" with Nancy.

Doc and I were in no rush to get home or become entangled in our nation's capital's traffic—and Nancy was single.

Doc was from a place called China Lake, California, and a seasoned veteran of weapons evaluation study experience. He was typically Californian, laid-back, fun loving, smart as a whip, and getting as much as he could out of Nancy, who was nothing special to look at, but she turned Doc on. What can I tell you?

To this extent, he was no different than a number of my counterparts, as some of these think tank guys were so mathematically inclined, they could "game anything," including their wives.

At any rate, Doc and I had been assigned to the same study group, which had as its assignment, to find the "best mission" for a militarized ACV, often called hovercraft by the British, and not to be confused with hydrofoils, which were an entirely different animal. Over some tension-releasing vodka tonics in a terraced bar high above Rosslyn, or Pentagon East, Doc informed me that because of my knowledge of hull designs, maritime engines, and propellers, I had been tapped for a highly secret and potentially exciting job to go to England and study ACV technology, under the world's expert at Westland Aircraft, Mr. Stanton-Jones.

How British!

As was typical in matters such as this, my previous background with naval propulsion systems proved useless for this assignment, but as later events were to prove, the ability to "think for oneself" became useful.

CNA conducted studies to assist the chief of naval operations (CNO) in justifying to McNamara's Whiz Kids that the Navy's cut of the pie, that is for construction and operating funds for the upcoming budget fights on the Hill, were justified. McNamara was the last secretary of defense until Don Rumsfeld, who took the military establishment running the Pentagon as if it were a "cost effective" corporation.

He had turned the usual process of appeasing the joint chiefs of staff and pushing their pet projects on its head. All resource allocations had to be mathematically justified through modeling various combinations of force mixes, often partially nuclear, with no preconceived notions as to the correct outcome.

The military bigwigs hated him, and the three main military branches had their own think-tank organizations to assist them in their battle against him.

The most famous organizations being the Rand Corp., in southern California representing the Air Force; Planning Research Corp., representing the Army; and the Center for Naval Analyses (CNA), the US Navy and Marines.

Sure enough, Doc was right, as he was well connected to CNA, and I was not, having had a number of his buddies following him from China Lake. Our study project manager paid me a visit the next day to inform me that I had been picked to go to Europe—namely the Isle of Wight in the English Channel and study ACV technology under "the Master," Stanton-Jones, for about two weeks.

I didn't think of it at the time, but this assignment was a trap as the reasons being offered were flattering, and who was I to turn down an all-expense-paid visit to London and the Isle of Wight?

Within a few days, after arranging for passports and BOAC reservations were made through my friend Rita in travel and after bidding good-byes, I was off to see the Queen . . . whom I'm sure knew nothing about ACVs.

Located in the English Channel is the windswept barren Isle of Wight, a good isolated spot for testing hovercraft under varying maritime conditions. It was truly a desolate spot, but not surprisingly so, once I thought about it, with London located so close by. I first met Stanton-Jones at Westland's testing facilities there, and once again, not much to my surprise, besides being very intelligent and an accommodating fellow, he was stereotypically British! He was a very tall, angular man, about six foot four and reminded me of that splendid literary character, Ichabod Crane. Upon seeing him, it occurred to me that Englishmen don't fit their clothes well. Neither did he! They don't fit comfortably as their bodies seem to require adjusting to the fit, save the Prime Minister, of course, and perhaps led to the establishment of Savile Row clothiers in London.

After dutifully spending my time witnessing some testing and retrofitting the craft for shipment to the States, I got the impression that the Queen was unloading some "seriously deficient lemons" on Uncle. It was there I first noticed the serious degrading of performance of the craft in "sea states above #3" (4-6 ft. waves) and winds to match.

After it was all over, I had formed an initial impression, which later proved to be obvious, that the correct application or military mission for these ACVs were to be conducted in sheltered waters and relatively shallow depths.

I left for London and home via BOAC's courtesy lounge about ten days after my arrival as the ACVs and I separated, going our own ways. Leaving the raw channel weather despite it being midsummer with humid dog days in Washington was somewhat of an out-of-the-frying pan operation, but the attractive trip to England to see these swift small flying machines, dubbed the SK-5s by the British, had come to a welcomed end.

The three ACVs were shipped to Bell Aerosystems in Buffalo, New York. This was the home of Bell's helicopter division, and fittingly so, as air-cushion technology most closely resembled that of a low-flying helo, operating in the supporting cushion of air trapped between the aircraft and the surface acting as a plenum for the trapped air. Accordingly, our study adopted the American acronym for ACVs, SES, which stood for surface effect ship.

It is the same concept that causes conventional aircraft, when running low on fuel, to dump overboard any excess weight and to fly as low to the surface as possible in order to operate in the cushioning effect of the air trapped beneath the craft and the sea.

Before long, the brass at CNA led by Dr. Bothwell, a studious academic, ill-suited for the likes of "McNamara's boys," further set the trap on yours truly. I was asked, soon after arriving back in Arlington, to spend some time in Buffalo overseeing the retrofitting of the craft for ultimate deployment to South Vietnam. This was all news to unsuspecting me, but after all, it could have been worse. They could have sent me to Buffalo in the wintertime.

Once there, I watched, noted, and said very little as the craft were "battle hardened" with twin .50 caliber machine guns, Decca Radar, grenade launchers, enlarged fuel tanks, and some lightweight armor plating, mounted not around the personnel cabin, but just aft of it to protect the transmission system and gear boxes. These components were mounted to control and drive both the controllable-pitch propeller and a fan, which ingested air into the hard metal structure of the craft known as the plenum. A horizontally mounted centrifugal fan was upgraded and installed just aft of the gear box, and by twisting the pistol-grip throttle, the pilot could slow the forward speed of the craft, thereby diverting air ingested through the fan system into the perimeter-mounted flexible trunk system. This served the purpose of perfecting the seal around the entire perimeter of the craft, trapping the cushion of air beneath the boat to a greater extent and raising the hard structure of the vehicle a few feet more in elevation. There, in a nutshell, was the top-secret air-cushion vehicle technology of the mid-1960s.

From there on, the objective was simple: find a naval-based military mission for them. As amazing as it may seem, the US Navy was run by "fly boys," who were only interested in aircraft carriers and the protection of their mission and the planes that flew from them. Of course, then there was Admiral Rickover and his missile-launching nuclear submarines, but that was the extent of the USN's interest in those days, and as the famous Willie Sutton had so aptly put it when asked why he robbed banks: "That's where the money was!" As a result, there was no interest in high and important places for "the small-boat Navy" or counter-insurgency warfare, especially the type being fought in IV Corps Zone's Mekong Delta.

The Delta was a massive marshy alluvial plain formed by the Mekong and its main tributaries, the Bassac[*], My Tho, Ham Luong, and Saigon rivers that emptied the melting snows of the Himalayas into the South China Sea. The region was sometimes known as the rice bowl of prewar Indo-China as it fed the people of what we now know as Cambodia, Laos, and Vietnam; hence its strategic importance could not be overestimated.

At the mouths of both the Bassac and the Mekong rivers, daily tide changes of twenty-five to thirty feet were not uncommon. Hence it was an ideal place for a high-speed craft with zero draft capability. The fact that the Navy initially placed the ACVs off the coast in thirty or more fathoms of water, in a coastal patrol mission coded Market Time, came as no shock to me.

---

[*] These rivers were sometimes known as Hau Giang (Bassac) and Co Chien (Mekong). *See map 1*

MAP 1. USN coastal patrol patterns—Market Time

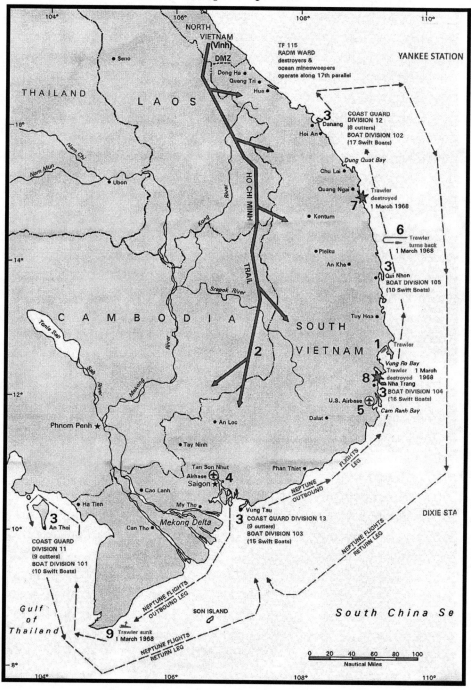

Having performed my unwanted mission in Buffalo, I returned to my desk in Arlington expecting to settle down to dutifully shuffling papers for our study group and having some evening pops with Doc. But to no surprise to some of my cohorts, who were aware how the gamers at CNA could place you in one of their mathematical models and figure out the probability of almost anything, especially human reactions, the trap was closed, and the door shut behind me. I was a thirty-two-year-old father of four with a house in the 'urbs, a German shepherd named Budweiser, and a wife doing private-duty nursing after she had found, at least daily, where the two boys and two girls, ages three through ten, were.

Matter of factly, I was called upstairs to the big boss's office to see Dr. Bothwell, only to be told that OP-93, our conduit to the secretary of defense's office and whom we worked for, had asked me to accompany the ACVs to the Mekong Delta. There was no one else available to ask as I was now "the Navy's expert on ACV technology." A setup from the beginning . . . I should have known better!

Typically for me, I immediately said, "I am sorry, but I couldn't go." Getting right to the point, I offered that I was a father of four, and there were bullets flying around the Delta. Hell, no! I wasn't going . . . Fire me if you wish.

Parenthetically I had successfully avoided the Korean War in the early fifties, first studying nuclear and civil engineering at Cornell University, in Ithaca, New York. When that excuse appeared to be wearing thin, I got married in 1956, my fourth and next to last year and had a child on the way. The CNA gamers asked me to speak to my wife and sleep on it! After all it was only a brief assignment, and I'd be back in the States in six to eight weeks. After thinking about it as they had asked me, I came to the only conclusion I could think of. Go see Doc!

Doc Colladay laughed when he heard the story and said he had suspected as much from the very beginning! When asked why he hadn't warned me, he laughed, saying, "It was all a game they play and probably wanted you off the study group for a myriad of reasons, as this is the way they do things at think tanks."

However, over a drink of course, Doc offered a way out as he said, "Let's game them back. Why don't you say you had changed your mind after a long discussion with your wife, and these were the conditions under which I will go?" Doc and I never had so much fun as we dreamed up a set of conditions that would have pissed off anyone, especially the Pentagon types. The session lasted for a couple of hours, and God knows how many vodkas. Even Nancy thought the whole process hilarious and classified the entire mess as "boys playing games."

On the back of a cocktail napkin, we developed a response:

The Wilens Laundry List

1. $100,000 of Lloyd's of London Life Insurance—good in the war zone. (This was 1966.)
2. $3,000 per month deposited at Chase Manhattan, Saigon—no questions asked.
3. Commercial flight tickets, routed through Hawaii, with a one-week stopover to brief CINCPACFLT[*] in Pearl Harbor.
4. Return tickets on a commercial flight through Hong Kong and Tokyo on the return eight weeks later.
5. Issue a noncombatant card in my name designating me with the rank of acting captain—USN, the nearest rank to an admiral in our Navy.

---

[*] Commander-in-Chief Pacific Fleet, stationed in Honolulu, Hawaii. CINCPAC commanded the US Seventh Fleet, on Yankee Station in the Gulf of Tonkin.

You should have seen their faces! Doc was a clever guy . . . What a beautiful way of getting out of a jam, and as Mel Brooks would say, "A genius!" CNA said this was preposterous and out of the question, but they would refer it to OP-93 in the Pentagon.

Within a week, I was on my way with everything I had asked for and more. I could take my time on the return trip through Hong Kong and Tokyo! The die had been cast! Saigon (now known as Ho Chi Minh City), here I come! How bad could it be for two months, tops?

Little was I to know . . . but once again, I should have known.

II

Pearl Harbor – I'm On My Way

My passport being current, and the series of shots only taking two days, and a last-minute useless briefing at OP-93, and kissing the family—except for the German shepherd Budweiser—I was off on my first leg of a trip halfway around the world through San Francisco and then Hawaii. Not so bad for starters.

I called my Cornell buddy, Chuck Rolles, who I had played guard with on the varsity basketball team for three years, living in the hills above Honolulu, and there was the little matter of my sixty-one-year-old Jewish mother, who we didn't dare tell. Chuck's freckle-faced wife Jean, who he met at Cornell, volunteered to mail my mother a series of postcards from Oahu, spacing them about ten days apart, telling Mom what a wonderful time I was having in Hawaii! Her nuclear-engineering, basketball-playing son . . . only in the Ivies, where I was on a full scholarship . . . $3,500 per year! (1952-'57), was in fact having the time of his life on the beaches of Hawaii . . . she thought.

United Airlines sure spun the hell out of the American public on Honolulu and Waikiki Beach. Notwithstanding all the Orientals with cameras swinging from their necks as they darted in and out of shopping centers, the whole visit to Oahu was a joke. Aside from Don Ho's singing and the military maps outlining World War II ops in the Pacific in the cemetery hills overlooking Pearl Harbor . . . the visit was a disappointment.

I was DOA[*] upon my arrival at Pearl Harbor!

The briefing of CINCPAC fleet involved telling them what I was up to one morning and spending the rest of my time there on the beaches and golf courses.

I was to return twenty years later to Maui and Kauai where I thoroughly enjoyed my visit. More exciting than my arrival and subsequent visit to Hawaii was my nerve-racking exit about one week later.

The flight schedule westward bound for Saigon via Okinawa and Manila wasn't competing with the East Coast shuttle service between New York and Washington. Flights left Honolulu twice a week, on Tuesdays and Thursdays. I approached the airport in my Hertz special, making the flight appear to be a "dead heat." Then as all things in war and peace, I couldn't find the rent-a-car return sign, and things quickly became dicey. Since my contact, CDR Bruce Bronson, was waiting for me at Tan Son Nhut airbase fifteen miles outside of Saigon, I wasn't going to miss this flight! The only thing to do was park the car in front of the airport, leave the keys in the ignition, and wish Hertz my best. As I approached the check-in counter, time was getting critical—as in ten minutes. After showing the pretty United Airlines agent my passport and being pointed in the right direction for the departure gate, I jumped over the ticket counter at the dismay of a few officials whose faces had turned a bright color. With one carry-on bag in hand and raincoat flying, I pulled an OJ[**] (running through airports that is), dashing down the terminal corridor to the exit gate and passenger way.

I couldn't have arrived at the plane door too soon as it was closed. Knocking as hard as I could muster yielded another piece of luck . . . It opened, and I flashed my Navy ID card . . . and it worked! As I got on board, "Let's go," an airline gal

---

[*]   Dead On Arrival
[**]   Famous pro football player, O.J. Simpson.

shouted. I was very happy to see the door locked quickly behind me, for I had no idea who I might have pissed off at the terminal, not to say the least the immigration boys and the Hertz crowd. After all, once airborne, they could chase me to Saigon if they wished.

Non-combatant ID card

Once on board and thanking all hands for their accommodations, my first thought was, this plane has got to go down. I recalled Snuffy Stirnweiss, a New York Yankee second baseman from one of Joe McCarthy's famous teams of the 1940s, running for a commuter train in suburban New Jersey. Because of his athleticism, he jumped aboard the last car of the train as it left the station. A few minutes later, it plunged three hundred feet into the Passaic River and his tragic death. Perhaps it was my anxiety complex, but inexplicably, the analogy haunted me for a long time afterward.

I'd like to say that my trip across the "belly of the Pacific" was an enjoyable one, but experiencing having two breakfasts in one day crossing the International Date Line, it's a long and exhausting flight. If one is in a rush, the great circle route through Alaska and Tokyo, which is the way I returned (yes, I made it back) was the way to traverse the Pacific.

Having had enough close calls and not wishing to push my luck, I didn't leave the plane when it stopped in either Okinawa or Manila. I also had been told, "A guy like you could get himself in trouble in Manila very easily."

A bit of an iconoclast, I always thought rules and policies were for people who couldn't think. Needless to say, this outlook didn't always pay dividends.

III

Saigon – Cholon District, Tu Do Street, and the Tunnels

Unnoticed by most of the passengers, the pilot's course into the Tan Son Nhut landing strip took a steep descent in an effort not to fly within the range of potential enemy gunfire near the airport.

Our plane came in hot with full flaps and props set at a high RPM, using the full length of the jet strip. Bedlam, it rained as I traversed the tarmac field leading to the main building, with body bags lying in neat rows, about a dozen in a line, ... filled. Army helos (UH-1Es, dubbed Hueys)[*] landing and taking off with breakneck rapidity, and a much larger Boeing-Vertol Chinook (CH-47) copter, and a C-130 cargo plane discharging or loading men and material headed for hotter places. We landed around noon, and it was about 100 degrees and humid and was told, "This isn't so bad today," it being about ten degrees north of the equator! Inside the main terminal, soldiers in heavy boots and camouflaged fatigues were racing every which way in an effort to catch a ride somewhere, going this way and that way, which appeared not to resemble any pattern or order. Periodically, one GI recognizing a friend clear across the expansive main floor of the terminal would shout, "Hey, Freddie, 21?" Fred would reply, "30," never breaking stride. I was to find out later, this was the number of days remaining in their one-year tours! There were some that re-upped for another one-year tour, as promotions came more quickly in the war zone, and some guys didn't want to

---

[*] Borrowed from the US Army by the Navy, often designated UH-1Bs and dubbed by the US Navy as Seawolves.

go back, but that's another story. The basic premise of one-year tours was flawed from the beginning and led to many a problem being left to their successors.

Now, among hundreds of military personnel lying on the terminal floor, sleeping or reading with their heads propped on their duffel bags, apparently waiting for someone or something (perhaps waiting for Godot), I looked for my contact from the local Navy research office to which I was assigned. After all, they had sent CDR Bruce Bronson, chief of the office, my itinerary from Pearl, but alas . . .

No Bronson!

My choice was simple: either sit on the floor with the GIs, with no duffel bag and talk to them and wait, or leave by cab to my hotel wherever that was. After about a one-hour wait, which seemed longer, I hailed a cab trying to look as if I knew what I was doing and being assured by the local intelligence it was only about a twenty-minute ride into town.

Nothing could have been further from the truth . . . with everything from armed-troop carriers (ATCs) and from jeeps to tanks thundering down ill-paved roads to and from the airport, the trip took almost an hour.

Once in downtown Saigon, I was greeted by the thundering cyclos, engine-powered bicycles with outdated French mufflers.

They expelled a bluish-gray smoke that choked the city. I was discharged at the Embassy Hotel, located on a suburban street that "teed into" the grounds of our Embassy one block away and my home for the next few months, I thought. I paid the "cabbie" in piastres, although he would have been more than happy to accept my green US dollars. I had bought piastres at the airport at the official rate (what a fool), but I learned quickly.

I approached the hotel front desk, presided over by a very appropriately dressed local man in his thirties. The hotel looked acceptable but not great, as I was expecting American engineering and construction, which didn't exist in Saigon except for military installations. Situated on a leafy residential street, about a ten-minute walk from the downtown action, it was only one block from the US embassy. This proved to be convenient for lots of visitors, but of course, not me. I reached the desk clerk after a short wait, but as he searched for my reservation, the line behind me began to lengthen considerably. I noticed he was a mixture of French and Vietnamese features and mannerisms. His brown-tinted sunglasses, gradient shaded from top to bottom, and pencil-thin mustache made him appear as if he had just stepped out of a Louis Vuitton ad—buying a handbag for his second wife. Surely, you would not designate him as an executor to your will or buy a used car from him. My impressions proved correct, as a green ten-dollar bill quickly caused my reservation to be located. "Ah, Mr. Wilens," here it is! I was starting to get "the hang of things" around here. Forget the advice and directions and *keep plenty of "green" handy.*

I proceeded, as George Carlin once so aptly joked about, to put my things away in this very austere-looking single hotel room and bathroom, overlooking nothing. I noticed a small lizard slithering its way across the ceiling but tried not to notice it. It turns out this was normal and safeguarded the premises against more dangerous and less desirable visitors.

There was a knock on the door; it was my floor maid. She asked me if I wanted some boiled water or needed more towels.

For a minute, I thought I was back in New York.

Upon having received both items, I asked her where the closest Chinese restaurant was, and she smiled and said, *"Sin loi,"* which I soon found out meant *"solly (sorry)* about that." My guess was, it avoided them having to tell you either they didn't speak English, or they didn't know. It was an often-heard retort.

Now, where the hell was Bronson? As I walked through the lobby headed for the street, map in hand, there was CDR Bronson standing in the lobby like a cigar store Indian. He recognized me quickly as I hadn't yet caught on how to become a chameleon in this town. He pronounced, "I see you made it," without any reference to why he hadn't met me at the airport. Having just made the trip from the airport myself, I sort of understood why, so I let it go. There was no sense getting off on the wrong foot with the commander. This could be a very long two months although technically I "outranked him" by quite a bit.

We proceeded by cab, a tiny two-seater only slightly larger in size than an early VW and built by Renault, the French car company, to the office about a mile away in the northwestern part of the city. It was then and there that, map in hand, I began my self-instruction on how to get around town and picked up conversational Vietnamese. "Git tong, bong lai, tai tri, tai mot" meaning, stop, proceed, turn left, turn right," respectively chattered Bronson to the driver as I sat oblivious to their meaning at first.

Darting in and out of the blue smoke-emitting cyclos, bikes, and standard rickshaw traffic that knew no lanes or courtesy as to "who had the right of way," we drove through, what clearly had been a decade or more before under French rule—a beautiful city.

The naval research office—or the Compound as it was soon to become known to me, was standard GI and unimpressive. No security, which after I pointed this out to CDR Bronson, replied, "Oh, we don't need any because no one knows it's here!" (No signs or military cars anywhere.)

Morning rush hour in downtown Saigon
USN Research Office on right

I immediately made up my mind that since this was a six—to eight-week tour, with a narrowly defined mission, there would be a "mental trash bin" in which to discard matters such as this for two very good reasons.

First and foremost, I didn't give a damn about trying to make the Navy operate more efficiently as it was a useless and impossible task, and secondly, it wasn't the mission I was assigned to . . . and my name would not be remembered by historians for a task such as this and other malfunctioning undertakings I was quickly to become familiar with.

At the end of the day, it being my first in the office, the boss offered to "wrap it up early," and "let's have dinner at Le Cave tonight." I quickly accepted as the last thing I wanted to do was go back to my room and discuss my evening plans with either the desk clerk or the maid.

31

As we neared the restaurant on Le Loi Street, a typical widely designed boulevard, treelined, with six lanes of traffic, three in each direction, and two islands, four lanes apart, separating two lanes of traffic from the third in each direction. What?

For the most part, the third lane, in each direction, was for parking and other nonvehicular traffic.

Fittingly, Le Cave was located down below street level and connected to the upper level and reception area by a series of dark and winding brick lined passageways. Monsieur Bernard, very properly dressed, and the apparent owner, greeted us in French and in an unusually formal manner for most restaurants in Saigon.

I think it was Bruce's rank and officer's uniform that did it. Over a drink at which Saigon's contractors, newsmen, and affluent conversed in cocktail chatter, there was a notable absence of the military.

When I pointed this out to Bruce, he very confidentially informed me there were two reasons for that. One was it was too expensive . . . certainly far more than the officers' clubs; and secondly, it was well-known that Mr. Bernard dutifully paid his "VC taxes" [*] so as avoid any bombing incidents and kept his politics to himself. The plot thickens quickly!

I was starting to think that between the hotel desk clerk and Mr. Bernard, this operation was taking on aspects of a triangular affair . . . and I didn't have a scorecard . . . yet . . . and this was my first day!

It became further complicated when Bronson explained to me, probably not at Le Cave, but at other places of business in Saigon, the people who were wearing their waiter's uniforms

---

[*] Viet Cong shakedown money something like—"no tickie, no shirtie."

during the day may don their black pajama-like uniforms and join the VC on some sort of raid later that night. Whoa! They didn't tell me anything like this back at CNA. Bruce offered, "Not to worry, you'll get used to it . . . It will not pose a problem." It later proved not to be entirely true. After a delightful dinner, Bruce dropped me off at my hotel, and I settled into "home," I thought, for the next two months. Once alone, and nine thousand miles away from Washington, DC, a funny feeling overcame me—"that I may have bitten off more than I could chew!" Like, did my hotel pay their VC taxes? Suddenly, priority number one of my mission became abundantly clear: Stay alive!

All that ACV testing bullshit quickly became secondary. This place may be quicker than Manhattan . . . but six to eight weeks wasn't a long time, I thought!

One balmy night, I was on my own and had heard about a nightclub on Le van Duet Street, not too far from the Compound. It had a reputation for good music, a hot dance floor, and women! Knowing a little about all three, I figured how bad it could be and proceeded to visit the club. It only took two minutes to see it was as advertised. After taking in the overall scene, I sat down at the bar to ease into the territory as they say, listened to this hot band from Paris that played too loudly but with a rhythm that one could easily dance to. Aside from the music and a dance floor comprised of a checkerboard of multicolored glass cubes, which flashed their brightly colored beams rhythmically to the music, a mosaic of flashing colors piercing a thin layer of piped-in smoke! Hot! Steamy . . . and a mixture of Asian and Eurasian women to match! Suddenly I started to feel at home. That was until Nadine sat down next to me and asked me to buy her a drink . . . Here we go again . . . Hadn't I seen this in the movies? She was a mixture of French and Vietnamese, an unusually tall, shapely fine-featured Eurasian in her late twenties . . . this far away from home. I bought her a drink of colored water . . . Saigon tea—I'm sure.

After admitting to be working for the house and why she needed to work two jobs to support her mother and little brother, I asked her to dance as I had heard this story before. She was a little surprised that a "round eye" could dance the way I did, and that moved me up a notch on the list on who was going home with Nadine tonight. A few hours and a few dances later, I was surprised to see her get into one of those Renault cabs for two and drive away into the night . . . so I did the same . . . After all, I had a meeting with some of the PACV boys in the morning, who were coming into town to see what all this testing was about. There would be time for Nadine later . . . She wasn't going anywhere.

The next morning, my rickshaw man fought his way through the fumes spewing away from the traffic headed downtown, just like any other rush hour, with hoards of commuters bound for the office.

Waiting for me was the CO of the PACVs[*] and his second in command. Over an initial round of GI coffee and the local equivalent of a Boston scone, we got down to the business of putting together the semblance of what the Navy called an operations evaluation or op. evil. Both men, Jack Fleming—the CO, a lieutenant commander; and LT Kip Kumler, were in their early twenties and a product of the NROTC[**] program at one of our fine institutions of learning. Jack from the University of Texas and Kip, a Cornell engineer, of all coincidences. After exchanging the usual "did you know, and did you see the Bowl game last year inanities," including some "far above Cayuga[***] stories," we got down to business.

---

[*]   PACV, USN's acronym for patrol air cushion vehicles in 'Nam.

[**]   Naval Reserve Officers Training Corps.

[***]   A forty mile long finger lake in upstate New York, - above which Cornell University is located at its southernmost end.

MAP 2. South Vietnam Corps Districts and Infiltration Routes

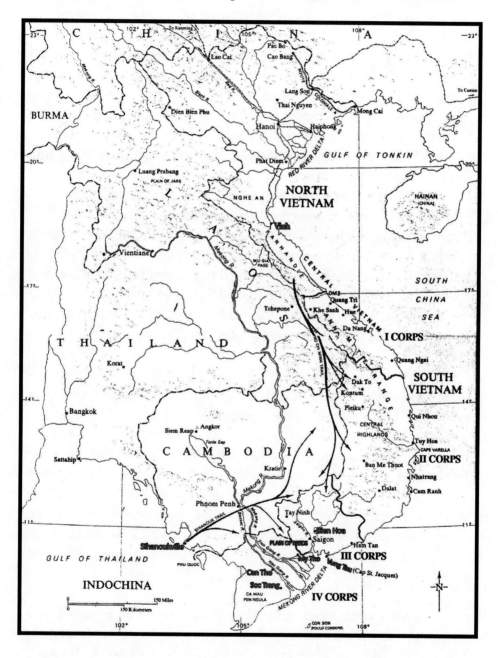

It didn't take long to realize that Kip, with his engineering background, was going to be of more use to me than Jack. We agreed to have him be the official link between myself and their group of about twenty-five men. Immediately, I broached the concept of bringing the patrols into the Delta, in shallow water applications along the Mekong, and the Game Warden (riverine patrol), brown-water environment. They seemed anxious to cooperate, in fact looking forward to a little relief after the boredom of uselessly patrolling the coast in an operation coded Market Time that had yielded absolutely nothing. The crafts were stationed about a forty-five minute helo ride south, southeast of Saigon on Vung Tao peninsula, a spit of land about thirty miles long, jutting out in a southwesterly direction into the South China Sea. The base had been named by the locals as Cat Lo and was an ideal location for embarking on patrols to the Delta's various tributaries. It also had the added feature that Vung Tao, a town located at the end of the peninsula, was off-limits to any fighting between the VC and our forces. It also was an agreed R&R sanctuary for both factions, complete with some of the most inviting beaches in the country.

No problems other than a few drunken brawls or arguments over a *cho am* (local single lady) were known to have ever occurred. Back in Washington, no one had ever heard of the place!

Seeing weekend work was optional, which meant no work for me nor anyone else in our compound, about six of us headed off for what turned out to be my favorite restaurant, Van Caan's on the Circle. Winding our way through the stench of the fermented fish sauce known as *nuoc ma'm*, used by the locals as cooking oil, we made our way downtown by rickshaw. The smell permeated the night air.

Van Caan's was located on the western edge of the downtown district at the end of the main east—west boulevard, Le Loi Street. Friday night came fast during my first week; between visiting the Navy's officers' club and seeing what the PX had to offer, time flew by.

Back at the PX in Saigon, aside from good cheap beer by the case, which came from across the Orient, the best liquor was available. Johnnie Walker—Black Label scotch, Beefeaters gin and vodka (the brands of the day) cost $1.50 and $1.00 respectively. Kirin and Asahi beer from Japan, San Miguel from the Philippines, Tiger Beer from Bangkok, Foster's from Australia, and the most frequently drank, "El Cheapo beer", Ba Muoi Ba (number 33 in Vietnamese), the local offering.

No wonder with these selections at your beck and call, costing next to nothing,—nobody drank the water.

Van Caan's was situated at the entrance to the Chinese part of town, known as the Cholon District. Perhaps twenty percent of Saigon's inhabitants were either Chinese or Malay and represented the more industrious and business-owner class of citizens.

As the meeting broke up, both Fleming and Kumler saluted me, at which point, I was thinking I'd better get this aspect of my tour straight right from the beginning. I told them to knock it off as that was the way I preferred it. I figured the less people knew, the better off I was going to be, and those that already knew my rank didn't have to advertise it. I realized this was contrary to most military thought, but then again, I wasn't military.

It was at this point I introduced the idea of my visiting the PACV base at Cat Lo. We agreed to give me a few days to design some tests and just how they could arrange for me to make the transit from Saigon to the Vung Tau peninsula where the base was located. Jack and Kip discussed that aspect of the meeting with Bronson privately, at which point I guessed the sensitive issue of safekeeping a superior officer in their care, and a "civilian" at that, was brought up. The last thing their careers needed was to lose me on some "half-assed trip" over the Rung

Sat Special Zone (RSSZ)[*], or anywhere else for that matter. They would be filing reports and making explanations to their next in command for the foreseeable future!

The RSSZ was a labyrinth of snake and crocodile infested swamps that lie directly in line with an air trip from Saigon to the peninsula. Its western boundary was the Saigon River, roughly rectangular in shape and about 500 square miles in area. The Soirap River fittingly wound its way through it in serpentine fashion. The VC owned it!

Only our highly trained naval commandos, known as the SEALS, were ever allowed to venture into the Rung Sat,—and then only on carefully planned raids designed to ambush the enemy at night, disrupt their command and control infrastructure,—kill as many as they could,—and "get the hell out" as soon as possible.

They worked in teams and would stand in chest-high, snake infested swamp water all night, linked together by a loosely tied rope system, used to signal each other of any unfriendly disturbances or infiltration.

The average age of a SEAL was about twenty-one, except for their senior officers, who might have been a few years older. I was to later make their acquaintance when they came to the compound in Saigon for a little R&R.

It was over this off-limits area, only twenty-five to thirty miles due south from Saigon, I was to fly over in order to transit my way to Cat Lo. Yet another battle site and a series of facts one never read about or heard in the hallways of the Pentagon.

There were isolated missions undertaken on the part of the SVN Navy, which were never of any particular consequence. In

---

[*] *See map 3*

1967, a relatively newly formed Army amphibious unit, known as the MRF, ventured into the Rung Sat.

At Van Caan's we started out being seated at a long table which resembled an oversized picnic table, which easily accommodated twenty people.

Starting out with a small triangular plastic prop for our chopsticks and a wet, steamy hot washcloth, we cleaned up at the table, asking that the "33 beers" keep coming and set up a revolving platter in the center of the table. Without asking, the platter began to fill with hot and cold prawns, shrimp rolls (not egg rolls for there were no chickens),—nor were there any dogs,—and spare ribs.

It was then, before I made an embarrassing mistake, I was asked not to order egg drop or wonton soup, as for the most part dog was substituted for chicken. I thought there was a marked absence of puppies around town.

I followed the crowd and ate hot and sour soup. A few weeks later, I was to graduate to shark's fin soup, truly a delicacy.

The remainder of dinner was scrumptious highlighted by my dancing with one of the locals to a sad attempt by the band to impersonate Vaughn Monroe's "Racing with the Moon," made famous by the popular blind English pianist of the day, George Shearing. (It's Shearing you're hearing.) The night was thoroughly enjoyable, and I knew that I would be returning to this place.

Besides, the Vietnamese food didn't hold a candle to this cuisine, and if you asked any of the locals, Chinese or otherwise, they would tell you so.

Van Caan's, on the circle leading to Cholon, was easily the best Chinese restaurant in Saigon, complete with its own totally outdated Americanized big band live music !

Midmorning markets, downtown Saigon. No shortage of food.

Some of Saigon's low-income apartments

IV

Game Warden and Market Time – On Patrol

Over the next few days, I successfully put together a series of tests for the boys at Cat Lo to run . . . but came to the conclusion that in order to conduct these tests properly, the amount and accuracy of the data to be collected would be of paramount importance. I had better supervise them. As a result, I informed CDR Bronson to arrange for my "virgin flight" down into the Delta, for what was going to turn out to be the time of my life, in more ways than one!

Outfitted in plain Jane unidentified (no insignia) fatigues, a pad and pencil, a baseball cap, and a pair of sunglasses, and armed with my noncombatant ID card issued by the Pentagon, I climbed aboard the Huey for my first copter flight over the Rung Sat to Cat Lo. If I had been captured by the VC . . . I was "toast." A picture of this card can be seen on *page 25*, the photo identifying me as an acting captain, USN (GS-15-civilian equivalent). If there was one of the enemy in the country who understood what that meant, I'll make you a watch. Hell! I didn't quite know what it meant, except to the VC, it wasn't going to be anything good! This was the card the OP-93 boys back at the Pentagon gave me to establish my rank and ensure my safety!

It accomplished very little of the former and none of the latter.

UH—1E Helo & Author

A UH-1E helicopter was the workhorse of the day, although for really large jobs, like picking up the 7.5 ton ACV, we would call in the much larger and less vulnerable Chinook, CH-47 helicopter. The first obstacle was to board the craft without getting decapitated as the props were already in motion when I bent over at the waist "to the max" to make sure of not losing my head. Once in the air, one didn't do much talking as the din of the engine and the rotation of the props combined in a symphony could put Wagner (mitt a V) to shame. I inquired about our safety from ground fire and was advised that as long as we maintained our altitude above 1,700 feet, things would be okay. Consequently, I immediately learned where the altimeter was before takeoff.

It wasn't on my first trip to Cat Lo, but I might as well get this experience out of the way now. On one of the trips, the pilot advised us to make sure we were securely buckled into our seats. Since there was no air-conditioning aboard, we flew with the doors wide open.

Without so much as a warning, and as far as I was concerned a vote, the pilot turned the chopper over on its side, so that the passengers, which included me, were looking straight down through the open door at the VC or the crocodiles—take your pick. Later, the pilot explained he just wanted to go down around treetop level "for a look-see!" He scared the shit out of me as one would expect. At least, now I knew what I was in store for when they advised us "to buckle up!"

Forty-five minutes later, we set down on the helipad at Cat Lo. Quickly I noticed it wasn't a small village, but a makeshift military base, accommodating small boats at a wooden pier that jutted out into the bay. The ACVs were parked in the shade at the end of a concrete ramp leading down to the water's edge.

A few semicircular Quonset huts glistened under the noonday sun, reflecting the sunlight as if they were sending signals to the moon. These buildings were nothing to write home about. Two long rows of cots, a ping-pong table, and an ice chest filled with you-know-what and frequently replenished. At the end of the room, there was a six-by-four-foot map of the Delta, which I immediately started to commit to memory.

I loved maps since my civil engineering days at school as maps literally talked to me, and this one had a lot to say. Little did I know, this was the beginning of a love story with this region of Vietnam that would go on for some time.

It was bright, and it was hot, and the PACV boys quickly got me situated in the shade inside one of the nondescript aluminum huts with a Ba Muoi Ba—33 beer. It didn't occur to me that it was only about eleven in the morning, but if it had, I wouldn't have mentioned it. (When in Rome . . .)

Clearly everyone had been expecting me, not that I was so important, but it served as an event to break up the boredom of the day as most missions were run at night.

Kip and I started to put together my wishes with their capabilities. This was no longer a laboratory exercise or a walk in the park along the Potomac out at the Naval Research Development Center (NRDC), then called the David Taylor Model Basin. While taking test data, we would have to keep an eye out for the VC, but that could be easily solved, I assumed, by first conducting our tests in broad daylight and secondly finding a test site close to home in case of trouble.

Kip immediately said he would refer this aspect of the program to Jack, the PACV CO, kicking it upstairs to a higher authority so as to transfer the responsibility as is so often done by bureaucrats and the military.

After a lunch, which consisted mostly of 33 beer and some luncheon meat sandwiches that married a slab of American cheese that resembled a piece of plastic to some slices of bologna or salami, on straight Tip-Top white bread. A good idea would have been to leave the open-faced sandwich outside the hut in the late morning sun and presto . . . a grilled cheese sandwich! We tried to stay as cool as possible and entered into a bull session among most of the men in the PACV squadron.

I was more interested in the who these men were—more than what they had to say, as most of the details relating to the tests had been covered with Kip and Jack. The toughest "nut to crack" was how we were going to measure the boat's speed. Aircraft have what is known as pitot tubes attached to the leading edge of their wings, which converted the flow of incoming air pressure into a speed displayed on the pilot's instrument panel in knots.

The PACVs had no such animal, and a reasonable measurement of speed was paramount to conducting any test. To successfully requisition some pitot tubes, which measured these pressure differences, from fly boys at Tan Son Nhut was a long shot, but Jack Fleming handed out that assignment to someone who was clearly due some punishment.

Finally we decided to do it the old-fashioned way, by calibrating the craft's speed over a measured course right outside the base. Somehow these guys knew how far a "click" was (1,000 meters), probably from an earlier radar reading. All that remained was to secure a stopwatch and time how long it took us, both from a zero starting speed and at full speed to traverse this distance at a given throttle setting. The rest was math!

So much for pitot tubes, but we didn't relieve the poor guy who had the assignment. We outlined a few speed-related tests for the next day and settled down to an afternoon of drinking, playing cards, with some guys reading magazines and writing home. The usual stuff!

That night, I was left behind as the PACVs went out on patrol to a nearby Mekong tributary called the My Tho. Reading one of the paperbacks that were plentiful on base, I stayed up late awaiting their return. After all, I didn't have to awaken at a certain time the next morning for a commute into the city to my desk job!

The three craft had left about thirty minutes before sundown, obviously timing their arrival at the My Tho at dark. I estimated an hour to get to the start of the patrol area, two to three hours on patrol traversing about fifty to seventy-five miles of river and stopping a few sampans. Speeds at times were fifty knots (about fifty-seven miles per hour), which enabled the craft to cover a lot of water.

Returning in about four and one-half hours, I was glad to see them all arriving for a nightcap, just after midnight. Now, after one day, my thoughts were leading me in the direction of going out on patrol. I decided to let it wait until tomorrow after we had gotten some of the tests completed.

After all, wouldn't Dr. Bothwell back at CNA love this, one of his pencil pushers writing a report while patrolling in search of the enemy? It would sound dangerous and could be used as currency for some undertaking I'm sure they always had in mind. I didn't foresee the downside of this decision, which was establishing a precedent that could be dangerous at another time and place.

Complete with binoculars, a pith helmet, sunglasses, a writing pad, and data sheets that I had composed as if I were undertaking a Cornell lab report (no easy task) and without my calculator, which in those days was a slide rule, I proceeded out into the bay north of Vung Tau! Most importantly, we didn't forget the ice chest. *See map 1, page 19.*

My overall objective was to test the ACV's ability to patrol at an optimum range and average speed, while carrying an "efficient payload" for the designed mission. Once again, it sounds easy, but much iteration had to be made, trading off one capability for another. Aircraft designers are faced with the same considerations and manipulation of "the L/D ratio" (lift-to-drag) of the craft under design, in order to optimize the craft's characteristics for a given mission and therefore operating range. Trade-offs of fuel capacity versus payload for the "design range" (payload is comprised of ordinance, cargo, and personnel), and this is what this type of design ultimately comes down to. For this reason, both ships and planes are designed both to operate over well-defined mission routes, and for ships, anticipated sea states on those routes. My apology to marine architects.

The mission Fleming had chosen was apparently "a piece of cake," although one never knows when it's going to hit the fan in a war zone. My apprehensiveness quickly eroded to a point that I took to standing on the outside of the craft, hat in my pocket, and letting the wind blow in what was left of my hair, and holding on for dear life! As we approached fifty knots over the calm and what appeared to be relatively safe My Tho River, my "baby-sitters allowed" this leeway.

Led by LTJG Bill McCollum, tall and skinny from the Midwest and desperately trying to grow a mustache (to make his baby face look older), we inspected a few sampans, drank a few beers, and I wrote down all the data I could muster onto my ill-conceived data sheets, before heading for home a few hours later.

Upon our return from Cat Lo, I took a lot of kidding from everyone on how did I felt "now having been in combat." An afternoon of sailing off Long Island Sound, or the Southampton beach scene, could easily have been more combative. For the time being, I breathed a sigh of relief as this part of the task didn't appear dangerous at all, but then again, it was just the beginning of things.

LTJG Jeff Sampson, a southern footballer from Alabama and an Auburn graduate, was the executive officer of the PACV group. He had a build to match, with a shock of blond hair hiding part of his forehead. He was the point of contact for "materials and acquisitions," and the poor bastard was assigned the job to "come by" some pitot tubes from the Air Force detailed at Tan Son Nhut. He was amiable enough, but didn't appear to know how to deal or shortcut the system, an absolute necessity in the war zone.

One of the prerequisites for this job should have been to come from Brooklyn or the south side of Chicago. Despite this obvious shortcoming, we made good partners playing "hearts," beating Kip and one of the Vietnamese cooks, who was nicknamed Sam as his Vietnamese name was too difficult to pronounce (the locals loved playing cards and gambling for any stakes). In this case, it was for beers and helped pass the time away while the sun beat down on our hut as if we were in a frying pan. Without the fan system, we would have been cooked to a frazzle.

After giving Jeff some assignments that had more likelihood of success than commandeering the now-infamous pitot tubes, I settled down over the next few days to prepare test outlines for the guys to follow and made one more "sojourn into combat."

It was generally another uneventful evening, this time a little farther away from the base, going a shorter distance up the Co Chien River (the lower Mekong), as our transit time to get there was about thirty minutes longer than that of going to the My Tho. We went about five miles short of the naval base at Vinh Long and turned back. We rarely patrolled too close to any of our bases in the Delta. This was clearly a busier river and led to our intercepting more sampan traffic than we had on my previous time out. It was about an hour into the mission, and most of us were on our second beers, when I tried to appear savvy—by concluding we were being observed from the shore about a quarter of a mile away—I made my first not-so-big goof! I shouted to Kip over the din of engine roar and the props whining, much like the noise that one would hear from one of our choppers, "They're signaling our approach . . . Look at those flashing lights all along the shoreline!" To which Kip and someone else trying to control the humor about it all replied, "Keep your head down, sir, those are gun flashes, not flashlights!"

Talk about feeling stupid, I was more embarrassed than concerned about the gunfire, for at fifty knots, none of the bullets were finding their mark, not by a long shot, no pun intended.

It was on the return trip to base, cruising at about twenty-five knots over calm waters, when we heard a thump, and the craft lifted off the surface of the water for a split second. The consensus was we had hit one of the fish traps—poles, netting, and perhaps some of their catch for the day.

It wasn't until our return to the ramp at Cat Lo that we found a fifteen-foot section of the craft's "neoprene skirt" blown away, by what we surmised had been a mine that we had detonated! Apparently, the cushion of air trapped beneath the vehicle had cushioned the blow. Something like a car hitting a small hole in the road at high speed—not good for the tire, but then again, not catastrophic.

Author stands next to underside of PACV 2 under repair at Cat Lo

The key, which became instant "op data" of significance, the PACV had experienced little or no degradation of performance after we had hit the mine! This time, upon my return to base, I prepared a report for the bureaucrats back in Washington "designed to stir up their dander a bit" and establish in no uncertain terms that one of their employees had seen combat . . . something like Senator Kerry perhaps, without the medals.

As work continued reasonably smoothly at the Compound, I started to receive some interesting "feedback" from not only CNA, but the brass at Pearl. Apparently, the early reports were making interesting reading or someone uncomfortable. One guess the staff at our office made, since they were more familiar than I with "the system," was why hadn't someone back in Hawaii thought of this type of analysis, not so much in regard to ACV technology, but in general as to "what the hell the Navy was doing in the Mekong Delta."

After a few mission reports and news of how relatively useless the Game Warden operation was as now conducted, CDR Bronson advised me that we had been invited to have lunch with the good admiral, and this time, not over cocktails. He concluded this was going to be very good or very bad for us, no in between. Fortunately, I wasn't in the Navy, so I could give a shit less.

Navy HQ was in downtown Saigon in what appeared to be like any small multistory office building. It was a little different in that two machine-gun emplacements, well sandbagged with concrete pylons protecting the front entrance, should anyone take to thinking they were at Indianapolis Speedway and come crashing through the front door. After dutifully identifying ourselves, although my round eyes served as better ID than that stupid noncombatant card, we proceeded upstairs accompanied by an armed guard to Admiral Veth's office.

I thought I detected a bead or beads of sweat gently traversing Bronson's forehead as we approached the admiral's office. ADM Veth looked the part—tall, stately, gray hair, navy-blue eyes, confident, and not in a hurry. Born to lead, educated at the academy and having taught at the Navy PG School (this school offered postgraduate degrees) in Monterrey, California, he quickly set about to allay any of our fears that we were being called out on the carpet for past deeds, real or imagined—and using his age and experience, proceeded to put us at ease. Sensing that he had accomplished this, he quickly got to the point. "Wilens, do you think you can figure out what the VC is up to down there [in the Delta], and how we can put a stop to it?" "Well, sir, I have some ideas that have come to mind since I arrived here . . . They might work." Bronson squirmed in his chair, clearly uncomfortable, as if I were about to cost him his career in the USN. He was probably thinking, *If this doesn't work, I'm going down in flames and have to return to civilian life.* Taking a deep breath, I offered that the Mekong rivers were too extensive to patrol effectively as was presently being done. Our assets were limited, especially the lack of helicopters to vector our patrols to suspicious activity along the river. But much more importantly, the rivers were too narrow, and the relative speed of the outboard engine-driven sampans too great for us to successfully do more than intercept a token amount of enemy traffic!

I watched the expression on his face as I was basically telling him—that the Navy was wasting their time patrolling the way they were presently. His expression was not one of surprise or annoyance. He seemed to have already sensed what I had just told him.

"Admiral, this is how you could possibly improve our ability to intercept VC traffic in the Delta."

He replied, "Just what do you propose, Wilens?" As if to say, "You think-tank boys better have a good approach this time!"

"By widening the rivers, Admiral," I responded.

To which the big boss said, "There aren't enough steam shovels in the world to accomplish that."

"Admiral," I chided, "not with steam shovels, but with intelligence."

"Be in my office first thing in the morning," he said. "Let's have breakfast." Now, I could have said I was busy, but I didn't think I knew him well enough, and I figured he wanted to bring in a few members of his staff, the so-called big guns! "I'll be there, sir," I said.

Nonetheless, it was clear he was buying it! To be sure he wanted to "run it up the flagpole and see how it was received," under the premise that three or four heads were better than one. Bronson seemed both relieved on the one hand that we had made it over the first hurdle, but like a steeplechase race, was apprehensive as there were only more of them to be seen ahead. After a silent ride back to the Compound, I was getting the vibes from Bruce Bronson—*You're on your own on this one!* I wanted to think a bit, so I ate quickly at a local place down the street that offered Vietnamese food, McDonald's style, and returned to my room.

I fell asleep making notes to make sure my ideas were straight in my own head, not that I had any idea that they would work. All that I knew for sure was that the way the Navy was patrolling the Delta with Swift Boats, PBRs, and even ACVs, wasn't going to hack it.

The PBRs were small (31 ft.) diesel-powered, water-jet propelled planing boats and were capable of achieving very high speeds up to twenty-five knots and drew little water. Their problems centered around their being fiberglass hulled and lightly armored and as a result were "down" as much as they were "up" due to high maintenance problems, including river debris clogging the jets.

One didn't want to experience the phenomena of the jets clogging at the wrong time, and so the PBRs were limited in the type of action they saw, almost always patrolling in pairs.

The slower Swift Boats as I've said "were not too swift" and as a result vulnerable to enemy small arms fire, but had their place under certain patrol conditions off the coast in Operation Market Time (CTF-115).

Joining about fifty Swift Boats in Market Time were seventeen eighty-two-foot Coast Guard cutters borrowed by the Navy in mid-1965 to fortify the "shallow draft" capability of the coastal patrol force operating in the South China Sea.

By mid-1966, the "brown-water sailors" of Game Warden consisted of eighty PBRs and a few Swift Boats, augmented by about a half-a-dozen UH-1(B) Seawolf helicopters. This was a sparse force for a patrol area, as extensive and diverse as the Mekong and its tributaries.

Moreover, there were an estimated 70,000 VC operating in the Delta. According to Ref. (C), "Allied strength (forces) were 150,000 and this was still not sufficient strength when applied against dedicated guerrillas familiar with the area." Accepted wisdom, under these circumstances, has required an advantage of at least eight-to-one ratio in troop strength to achieve success.

This ratio was insufficient to contest an insurgent force fighting on their home ground . . . sound familiar?

Game Warden bases located throughout the Delta and the RSSZ were 1-Nha Be (Saigon River), 2-Cat Lo (on Vung Tau peninsula at the southern end of the Rung Sat), 3-My Tho (My Tho River), 4-Vinh Long (at the intersection of the My Tho and the Mekong), 5-Can Tho (halfway to the Cambodian border on the Mekong), 6-Sa Dec (halfway to the Cambodian border on the Mekong)[(*)], and 7-Long Xuyen (on the Bassac and the base closest to Cambodia), 8-Battle of Cai Be, 9-Battle of Ap Bac, 10-Plain of Reeds. *See Map 3 on next page.*

[(**)] Sa Dec was located on the southwestern shore of the Song Tien Giang (upper Mekong), about twenty miles northwest of the Game Warden base at Vinh Long.

MAP 3. Mekong Delta—IV Corps Zone—VC strong points (shaded areas)

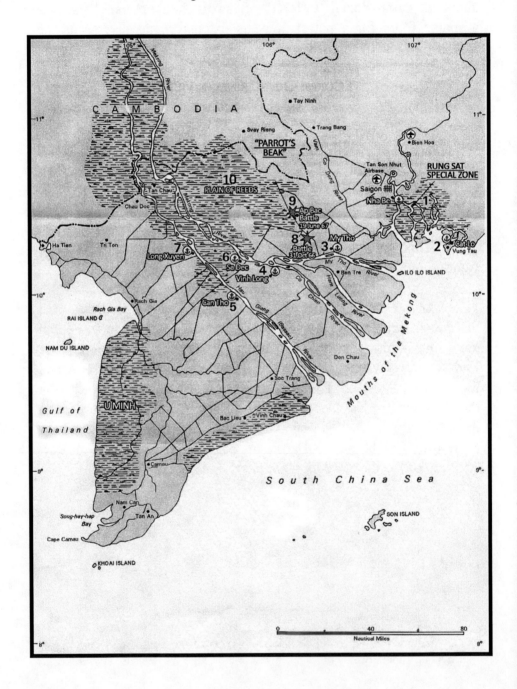

Morning came around quickly, and Bronson and I repeated the same drill from the day before and were escorted into the admiral's dining area. Introductions all around, Ken Veth had brought in his big guns to take aim at this kid from Washington. For all he knew, I might have something, for the way he was proceeding, he had nothing but a "hatful of cosmetics."

After dutifully suffering through the normal amenities of a private audience with the commander of naval forces in Vietnam just the day before and ordering a hearty serving of ham 'n' eggs, as the Navy knew where the chickens were, I launched into an explanation of how to solve this problem.

First, we would establish a mathematical algorithm mimicking the VC network in the Delta. This could be accomplished by gathering intelligence data of enemy movements along the canal system leading to the impending river crossing points. Connecting the source of supply (the origin of which I had some preliminary ideas about) and its destination points, we would create the shape and parameters of the network. Through a simple linear program, we'll establish the shortest and most effective route through the network.

Once established, we would overlay the geography of the Mekong and its tributaries on the network. We will then be able to establish, with a high degree of probability, the most logical river crossing points. There we will be waiting for them!

The parameters of sampan speed versus ours and the river width had been minimized, if not eliminated. I would advise the Navy what complement of forces we needed to accomplish the mission . . . then gather intelligence, and the source and destination data. We would then send this information to my contact back at CNA, George Carson, who would build the network in the computer, which at the time was an impressively large machine, and now is a PC with some memory, microprocessor speed, and hard-drive capacity. He also would write and solve the linear program, which at the time was not yet a packaged program!

For the CNA'ers, it was piece of cake once given the data and the concept. To the Navy brass, they thought we were *geniuses*! Especially if it worked, which they hadn't a clue about, yet!

The admiral looked around the table for reaction from his staff. They were dumbfounded. Finally, one of them spoke. "How long do you think it would take to gather the information to build the network?" Without much thought, because I didn't want it to appear that I had no idea, I offered, "It depends on how quickly and effectively you can gather the intelligence. I'll need some observers to go into Cambodia!" With that, all eyes flashed over to the admiral. As if to gamble for some time, Veth asked why. I responded, "Admiral, after much thought and studying the maps of this region, I think the enemy's supply lines are originating from the opposite direction that you've been patrolling! Instead of looking north and east, I believe it's originating from the Cambodian seaport of Sihanoukville[*] about 220 miles west, southwest of here. I'll need some observers [spies] to go into the hills overlooking the port and monitor the traffic off-loading the Russian freighters in the harbor."

I thought the admiral was going to have baby, and some of his staff were going to faint! Bronson turned white as a sheet!

They had asked for it, and now they had it, like it or not! To a man, they were "out to lunch" or in this case . . . breakfast!

Almost parenthetically I interjected, "Admiral, I've got to run a few operation evaluation type tests on those three ACVs patrolling the coast in Operation Market Time. I wonder if you

---

[*]   Sihanoukville was located in Cambodia west-southwest of Saigon on the Gulf of Thailand, only about 25-50 miles from the South Vietnamese border and the Delta's canal system. It was here, I convinced Admiral Veth to place a few "observers" in the hills overlooking Route 4, leading from this port and connecting with the Delta's canals. This was the origin of the VC supply network! *See map 2 on page 35.*

could arrange for the PACVs to knock off that part of their ops for the time being and have the executive officer come into town and see me?"

He replied he would, as if I were asking him for the time of day. Obviously, I had ulterior motives about getting those ACVs out of deep water, along the coastline. My plan was on course as I just saved myself two weeks of bureaucratic jousting and a lot of paperwork.

Talk about opening a can of worms! Both Fleming and Sampson showed up at our Compound in Saigon the next day. When Smith Barney talks, the Street listens. They knew if Navy HQ told them go see that new kid from Washington, ASAP . . . they had better do it sooner, rather than later!

Dispensing with the usual amenities and military bureaucratic bullshit, I told them for the foreseeable future to "stand down" on any further patrols under Operation Market Time (coastal patrol). Bruce Bronson would visit HQ and provide for an official directive saying so. In addition, don't undertake any patrols under Game Warden (riverine patrol), which in any way risked losing or damaging the ACVs.

We had bigger "fish to fry," and they would be notified as to exactly what that was in due course. Meanwhile, other than completing our tests over the next week or so, I instructed them to, to the best of their ability, to "cum shaw" any shielding or armor they could get their hands on, plus any armament they thought they could add to the craft without seriously compromising weight considerations. LTCDR Fleming tried to show his superior knowledge by indicating to me, "This could be done, but only by sacrificing range."

I didn't want to spill the beans that long-range patrols were going to be a thing of the past, as the nature of our patrolling was about to change drastically. So I just said, "I knew that, but do the best you can anyway."

There were two reasons for this: (1) I still wasn't sure how the new patrolling configuration was going to come down, as a result of trying to predict where the VC was going to attempt river crossings and (2) the less anyone knew about our plans, the better I felt about it.

Besides, I had no idea what our Vietnamese cook at Cat Lo was doing after hours, nor did I want a lot of internal prejudging of the Plan . . . which I nicknamed Operation Steam Shovel (widening the rivers).

For the guys in the PACV group, it was clear this was "the calm before the storm." But since the calm was coming first, they didn't fight it, and I'm sure were looking forward to the respite of collecting test data and downing a few afternoon tonics and beers, while the possibility of getting shot abated.

VC Prisoners—Independence day parade in Saigon,
complete with black pajamas

With this part of the metamorphosis completed, thanks to HQ brass, it was time to set in motion the rest of the Plan or Op Steam Shovel.

First, and most important I had to do was contact George Carson back at CNA and get him started on clearing the deck on his end to secure the assets he would need, not the least of which would be the relief from whatever study he was presently assigned to.

There was no question in my mind, once given "the source and destination data" for the network, he could build this information into his computer. Then, using state-of-the-art software known as linear programming, configure the most likely and efficient routes taken by the VC to pass through it. He could then superimpose these results on an overlay of the Delta's main rivers and tributary system. This latter aspect of the undertaking could get started on immediately by installing the Delta's map coordinates in the computer.

Secondly was the major task of gathering the data, which consisted of the following:

a. Getting "the observers" assigned and on their way into Cambodia. Situated on the southern Cambodian coast, the port of Sihanoukville was Cambodia's only major outlet to the Gulf of Thailand and the open ocean. It was about two hundred and twenty miles from Saigon . . . depending upon the route traveled—about half of which was in VC control. This part of the plan made everyone nervous.

b. Asking the Navy SEAL teams to organize forays into the Delta's canal system, which led from the Cambodian border, both south and east across the main rivers, especially the Mekong and the Bassac, which flowed in a southerly direction into the South China Sea and bisected the Delta.

    c. Obtain some helicopter resources to combine with the SEAL teams to search and identify the location and movement of NVN [*] and VC units, no matter how small, even down to ten—to fifteen-man squads.

Clearly, getting the foregoing set in motion would require a directive(s) from the ole man and HQ in general. I made points with CDR Bronson right away by saying I would run my requests through him, like a good militarist, up the chain of command. I didn't tell him at the time, if my requests weren't heeded, or getting results dragged, I intended to go around him and up the chain myself. After all, I was a captain, wasn't I? For the time being I could afford this way as it might yield the results I was hoping for, and who knew Bronson wore the uniform and I didn't? Maybe that would get more results.

Of course, I immediately set out with my own plan B as I didn't want to make a career out of this, especially from the war zone. How the hell we could get this plan, full of nascent ideas, set in motion, and running to the point where I could return to the boredom of Arlington, Virginia, in six to eight weeks, began to worry me.

Within a matter of days, it became apparent even to me (and literally everyone else engaged in Game Warden), that I had stirred up a hornet's nest. The pace of official communications, first between CINCPACFLT in Hawaii and Saigon, picked up markedly. Then, I started hearing it from OP-93, CNA's benefactors back at "the Puzzle Palace," which the Pentagon was affectionately known as in those days. But then again, it had its salutary effect, nobody was bored anymore, and I might add the days flew by with less drinking.

---

[*]   North Vietnamese Army, sometimes known as Viet Minh Army

As things began hopping around the Compound, CDR Bronson and some of the guys invited me "to tag along for a night out on Tu Do Street," which had to mean trouble. A mini celebration, I deduced.

It was also the night I was introduced to an old Navy retiree, Harry Conners, who made a living out of following the USN around the world. Harry was fiftyish, with a forty-two-inch waist, balding, a red-faced Irishman. Quickly, I surmised, this guy could hold his liquor. No more distinctive than that, he had mustered out of the Navy after serving thirty years, but like athletes who graduate from college, who only a few years later, not being able "to make it on the outside," return to coach at their alma mater.

Harry was extremely useful as he knew all the shortcuts and angles that related to our stay in Saigon. Having been forewarned about Harry's activities, which intrigued me rather than made me apprehensive, we proceeded out for a night on the town in his chauffeur-driven Mercedes. Being a poor kid from Brooklyn and Queens, I had not overlooked the extra-added advantage of being able to drink with relative impunity as long as your driver was close by, which he was.

We headed for the bars and strip shows on Tu Do, which intersected with Le Loi Street, right in the center of town. There stood the most ridiculous looking thirty-foot statue of a Vietnamese soldier, and there it probably stood until the day "Ho came to town" and renamed the city after himself! The statue, erected on a small circular island, which formed a plaza now named Lam Son Square, rather than a "right-angled intersection." If I recall, there was an all-night movie situated just off this plaza, which no "round eye" in his right mind would attend without a gun.

On opposite sides of the plaza were the best hotels in town, where the high-paid visitors from the world's media stayed, also handling the overflow from the embassies. They were the Continental and Caravelle Hotels[*], the latter of which catered to those French that still remained, and major TV network personnel. On any day at lunchtime or cocktail hour before dinner or cocktail hour after dinner, the bars and lobby were humming with the latest scuttlebutt being passed around town and the current version on the conduct of the war.

Very little of it was worthwhile, and most of it was what the public was fed by the media. A number of war correspondents reported the conduct of the war from their vantage point at these facilities. There were exceptions, of course.

First stop, the Continental Bar, it was designed to ease into the evening. Later, I was to find out this was Harry's favorite "watering hole" as one could meet up with friends, real or imagined, on a given evening before deciding upon dinner. The bar didn't have any windows and was open to the street so as to allow one to observe the crowd mingling outside.

Air-conditioning amounted to a few ceiling fans, which prominently dotted the ceiling along with an occasional lizard. Oversized rattan furniture was the motif of the day, and I thought, if you looked hard enough, you could see Sydney Greenstreet sitting at a corner table in one of those high-backed rattan chairs conjuring the merits of some deal with Peter Lorre.[**]

Harry pointed out the big names in attendance, and everything was going along swimmingly when the crowd's humming came to a sudden halt momentarily. Off in the distance,

---

[*]   Now known as the 181 room, Park Hyatt Saigon, directly across from the Opera House; and the 355 room, 24-story Caravelle Hotel at 2 and 19 Lam Son Square, respectively. *See Map 5, page 102.*

[*]   Famous for their roles in the movies—*The Maltese Falcon* and *Casablanca,* circa 1941-'43.

about five or six blocks away, was a puff of smoke rising into the fading daylight slate blue-orange sky, without even a ceremonial boom.

Before I could ask the question, *What was that?* the conversations around the bar and lobby resumed, hardly skipping a beat. I was soon to learn the answer to my question: "Just a mortar." "Oh," I responded, trying to look blasé about it as seemed to be the custom . . . and the chatter continued. Harry caught it though and said to me, "You haven't been here long, have you?" I readily confessed.

After two or three rounds, Harry proclaimed he knew a place where there was some action and good food that he had checked out down on Tu Do Street. There was no other street in Saigon, or for that matter in Vietnam, like this street. I was instructed to move my wallet to my front pocket and not go wandering off alone.

The action overflowed out onto the street as an array of peddlers, money sharks, and hookers brought their business right to you. There were cyclos parked in every which place and direction and rickshaws doing a land office business, mostly occupied by a GI and his *cho'aum*.

There was a fair smattering of drunks zigzagging their way up the street as Harry ushered us into an establishment of unknown repute. After one look around the joint, I kept one hand in my pocket firmly securing my wallet. Clearly, some GIs had figured out how to put this war behind them.

I was beginning to form an opinion about our South Vietnamese hosts, and it wasn't too flattering. I didn't want to jump to conclusions, so early in my exposure to the people in this area of the world, but I saw no evidence of hostility to our occupation, temporary as it may be. Quite to the contrary, it appeared as if "our ally never had it so good."

Certainly, as we've experienced in other limited actions far away from home as in Korea, Mogadishu, Lebanon, and Iraq, there were very few signs of animosity toward the American presence in the country. There were isolated bombings, such as one of the floating restaurants experienced in the eastern part of the city on the Saigon River. There, a number of Americans, along with some locals, were killed and severely injured one dinnertime when a cyclo (motorized bicycle) loaded with "plastic explosives" was left in front of the restaurant and the driver walked away. This had also been known to take place, once in a great while, at military bus stops. Ergo, yours truly, never but never took the bus.

When the "white mice" (Saigon's finest police), named for their impeccably white, well-laundered shirts entered our establishment in the middle of dinner, whistles blowing, it didn't require any conversation among us "to bail"!

Our asses were out in that street, running to our conveniently waiting chauffeured car before you could say, "Sin loi," which the owner attempted to convey to Harry's back. Once safely inside the car, Harry didn't have to give any orders to the driver, as I was to later learn the "white mice" were known for their indiscriminate shooting sprees, using their newly acquired M-16 automatic rifles among civilian crowds. Once a few blocks away, someone said to Harry, "Any other ideas?"

He responded laughingly, "Yeah, the peace and quiet of the Caravelle Hotel," where it was well-known that payment of VC taxes were current.

We settled down to a quiet evening of listening to some outdated French music and something fishy with a French sauce masking its identity, and another round.

Not exactly your typical night out in the States, for dinner and a movie, but we settled for it. On the way home, Harry maneuvered the driver to dropping me off at my hotel last. He asked if I was busy for breakfast. I said "No," and he replied, "Pick you up at nine o'clock." Nodding my head affirmatively, I disappeared into the lobby of the Embassy Hotel wondering what was next with Harry.

At breakfast the next morning, Harry eased into the subject matter for the day by advising me of two areas of interest close to my heart. One being that, "I was a prime candidate for kidnapping by *Saigon's cowboys,* and two, "there was a lot of money to be made in town, if you had the time and money to pursue it!"

My initial response was, "Who in the hell are the cowboys?" I thought Dallas was a long way from here.

He proceeded to open my eyes about the commerce of Saigon, not the least of which was the abduction of very "ransomable civilians" by the city's outlaws. They roamed the streets at night robbing and kidnapping those who left themselves open to such an activity by letting their guard down and/or carrying out the VC's wishes for either "strategic or payback" reasons.

Apparently the Viet Cong were hard up for "hard currency" to prosecute the war, and what better way to get it from unarmed American civilians in Saigon, like me!

"So what do you suggest other than watching my step?" I said to Harry, to which he quickly responded, "I'll get you a gun!" "Whoa . . . and a holster and maybe a horse?" He said, "Don't be funny, I can arrange it."

I had a fleeting thought that there was another shoe to drop, so I said, "And what else?"

The next morning, the "what else" were the opportunities in the wholesale liquor business throughout the Pacific rim and the black market in money exchange. Clearly, Harry knew everyone in town that was important. Some would say—well connected. Turns out that Harry had his hands in the importation of liquor to the Navy PXs from Seoul to Singapore. No wonder he had a chauffeur!

He offered if I was interested in partnering in a few ventures or if I could get my hands on some capital to expend across his territory after the war was over, the business opportunities were limitless.

From my vantage point, which albeit was limited, I could see his point. I did have some Wall Street money connection and who were "money people."

Since my head was already spinning from my meeting with the Navy brass, I offered a "to be continued" response to Harry, not wanting to blow his offer off, and the more I thought about it, the more I liked his idea of carrying a gun.

We agreed to have lunch or dinner in a few days mano a mano in furtherance of this discussion, and in the meantime, Harry would "round up the piece!"

At CNA, George Carson had finally seen his "dream come true." George was an excellent mathematician in a vacuum. As soon as he had to apply the math to real-life situations, sometimes known as a "legacy application," he was dead. But was he? Not if he had this unsuspecting—he thought—"wet behind the ears" kid digging out the data and furnishing him the theory that would work on the ground. He would then be in a position to apply the math, the approach having been handed to him on a platter.

Ergo, George worked feverishly to get the network built into the computer . . . while not advising anyone of the extent of his progress. To no one's surprise, "he had something up his sleeve!"

At the Compound, on "nondescript street" Saigon, things were hopping as almost daily message traffic originating from OP-93, which easily could be originating from CNO's office, was inundating our office through Pearl Harbor.

At least in the south, which by definition meant "south of Saigon," the USN had found a mission, just like events were to follow that the marines inquired if there was a mission for them in the Delta as they were getting tired, and I don't blame them of getting chewed up in the fighting in and around the DMZ (I-Corps).

Slowly but surely, over the next two weeks, while I finished up running tests with the PACV boys at Cat Lo, I was able to spare a couple of days per week making sure the movement of "Charlie's forces" (military jargon for the VC) were being monitored down to squad-like size.

Our main source of information was coming from province chiefs and often district chiefs, while patrol missions were fanning out from Game Warden HQ at Can Tho, and another smaller base at My Tho, both centrally located in the Delta. At first, I feared the enemies' movements throughout the Delta might form illogical patterns, with VC units moving at amazing speed throughout the network, when in fact the information being furnished was in error. But we had very little of that. In fact, aside from this little undertaking we were engaged in for the admiral, I don't know why they weren't engaged in this type of monitoring independent of us. The answer probably could be found in the fact that the responsible entities for controlling the Delta were the ARVN forces, which you will pardon the expression, was the South Vietnamese Navy. They were, in a word, useless!

It was also thought by some that ambushes of our forces, at least early in the war, could be traced to the fact that our plans and force movements were known to the ARVN. Nobody on the ground, at the lower-officer level, wanted to risk their careers and go down that road. I certainly wasn't. I would just make sure we "kept them in the dark" as much as possible as I had a plan to trap some of those guys, but for the time being, the subject was clearly off topic.

CDR Benson was lovin' it! Not only was this undertaking putting him and his office on the map, and that could lead to promotions for him and his staff, but now a sense of purpose pervaded among a number of his men, that made time fly and people happy. That's always good when you're nine thousand miles from home, and you've got the South Vietnamese for an ally.

It was about this time that I needed a break! It occurred to me that Nadine just might be hangin' out at La Baccara tonight, and it was getting close to a month and a half since I left home. When it came "cocktail hour time," I begged off with some lame excuse about being tired and needed a good night's sleep . . . and returned to my hotel for the day's second shower.

I arrived at my favorite barstool, where I was afforded a good vantage point from which to see both the front door and the dance floor. Something like what I was hoping "my observers" were doing in the hills overlooking Sihanoukville, Cambodia . . . if in fact they had made it through the border without detection and were "taking good notes."

It wasn't until around eleven o'clock, after three drinks and a like amount of dances with some locals trying to look like they were at a Paris disco, I spotted Nadine walk in as if she were looking for someone. After being unsuccessful at this, she headed for the door with me right behind her in pursuit.

She hardly remembered me at first, and I could understand that given her line of work. Nevertheless, we returned to my vantage point at the bar, to talk things over . . . After all, the night was young . . . It wasn't even midnight yet! After a few drinks of colored water known around town as Saigon tea, and a dance or two, she asked where I lived . . . and after I told her, asked if I were interested in a villa in the Cholon District. Since I like Chinese food, and attractive women about equally, I bit.

She asked if we could go out and see the place tonight, which I should have said no to, but my testosterone said yes, and off we went, arm in arm, in one of those miserable midget Renault cabs and drove away into the night to Cholon!

Stupid . . . but you've got it! At this point, Nadine was beginning to look better and better to me . . . not a new phenomena.

Nadine

"The villa" turned out to be a three-story house, with front and back balconies running the length of each floor. It was surrounded by a brick wall with about a three-foot wrought iron fence on top of it, with pointed spikes every couple of feet along its length. The house itself, complete with a plentiful supply of lizards, and a gravity system for a water supply originating from a water tower on its roof, was an indescribable example of absurd French engineering. However, it had a nice air-conditioned master bedroom surrounded on three sides by french doors. What else? It had five other bedrooms, which I suspect is the only reason it was called a villa. I immediately recalled about a dozen of the SEALs visiting the office that week, and they were looking for a place to stay when they came to town for R&R.

When Nadine told me the rental, which of course unbeknownst to her, was one-third of what I was paying at the Embassy Hotel . . . a deal was struck. It was finalized behind those french doors, and based upon the real estate agent's performance, it convinced me that I had made a good decision as there was no lease, no more than one month in advance, no lawyers . . . nothing, but promised bedroom tours in furtherance of the rent, of course as Nadine's schedule would permit. If I could convince the SEALs, who were universally feared by the populace, to call this place home, I would have the safest, hottest place in town, perhaps lacking hot and cold running water, but including hot and cold running women!

We parted with a promise to meet the next night at the same barstools, and after dropping her off back in town, I instructed the driver to *nhanh len* me to the Embassy Hotel. What he didn't know and couldn't possibly have known is that after spending one quiet evening in my room having studied a map of Saigon, I probably knew the layout of the town, including some prominent alleys, almost as well as he did.

It was about 3:30 a.m., and being mindful of Harry's warnings about the kidnapping of US civilians, I began to feel uneasy about the route we were taking. After a few *trai lai*'s, *trai bat*'s, *do*'s, and a final *quay lai* (turn around), which apparently were falling upon deaf ears, I made up my mind I was in trouble. I waited for the cab to make a turn onto a well-lit street where I had a chance of hailing another cab, for I hadn't the foggiest where we were, except not on the way to the hotel.

Put in this situation, one doesn't think too many moves ahead, and exiting this car without getting hurt was number one, while number two was not to leave myself in worse shape than I was already in. I hadn't yet thought about number three. My chance was coming up as we approached a well-lit wide boulevard, and protecting my head with both my arms and forearms like a boxer, I rolled out onto the dusty street at about five miles per hour.

Save a few scuff marks on my elbow and knee, which I could now see through the tear in my pant leg, I ran like hell down this boulevard toward what appeared to be some people walking in the street . . . when I remembered the street-roaming Cowboys!

That was number three . . . I was slipping. I slowed to a stroll as I breathed a little better to see that no one was following me. The last thing I wanted to do was ask these guys approaching me . . . for directions!

As the group of "the yet to be identified" approached me at a distance of about twenty yards, clearly sizing me up for some reason, a cab, perhaps another abductor, approached from a long block away. My calculation immediately told me that the cab would not reach me before they did! So being from the city, I employed the old adage, "If you can't beat them, join 'em," and walked directly toward the group as if I was after them. I gained the twenty seconds I needed by asking them some inane question, the substance of which they were still trying to figure out when I spun around and darted out into the path of the cab waving a green bill in my hand! I could barely make out that he had a passenger in the backseat, but he would have had to run me over if he didn't stop. Reluctantly, he did stop!

I jumped into the front seat and told him the bill in my hand was his if he stepped on it, like one of those George Raft gangster movies of the 1930s and '40s where he exits the bank with the law in hot pursuit. He *didi*'ed the hell out of there, which was local jargon "to hurry," into the pitch-black night.

After apologizing to the person in the backseat, it turned out he was a European correspondent on the way back to the Hotel Caravelle! Perfect! He understood completely . . . and I had learned two lessons for the night . . . one of which was "no late-night cabs," especially outside the downtown area, and especially not from Cholon, and preferably with a SEAL or two in my company, complete with M-16s in tow.

So much for my quiet evening at home to catch up on some sleep!

V

Sihanoukville, Cambodia – Behind Enemy Lines

Route 4 ran parallel for most of the South Vietnamese-Cambodian border, tracing out a path along the shimmering rice paddies of the Delta in a general southeasterly direction toward the Gulf of Thailand. Driving along this road in their beaten-up, dirty yellow pickup truck were Haiching and Wang Hsiang—observing the usual daily traffic heading to the markets in the port of Sihanoukville.

Haiching and Wang Hsiang were Chinese and part Lao, and so they blended in perfectly with the peasants transporting their wares to market. The peasants had come by sampan over a latticework of canals from their farms and villages in the rice paddies behind them to the north and east. Once reaching Route 4, they were met by an assortment of pickup trucks and motorized carts for the rest of their journey.

They obtained better prices in Cambodia and had no interest in the age-old conflict between the nations, dating from the fifteenth century, when the Cambodians were expelled from what is now South Vietnam (SVN).

Cambodia was formed by a "forced exodus" from South Vietnam. SVN was originally smaller and known as Cochin—China. The Vietnamese were descendants of nomadic Mongols from China, migrants from the Malay Peninsula and immigrants from what is now known as Indonesia . . .

Reported to be founded in 2878 BC, China ruled the nation from 111 BC until the fifteenth century, and was known as Nam Viet.

Haiching and Wang Hsiang were also headed for the same marketplace and were members of a group of mercenaries known as the CIDG (see description, *"The CIDG Program Begins to Mature", page 283*) which stood for Civilian Irregular Defense Group. Knowledge of their mere existence was classified top secret, and access to their operations was on a strict need-to-know basis. I was prohibited from citing their reports as a source of information in our work. Clearly, exposure of their activities could have catastrophic consequences. Pure and simple, although useful as interpreters, scouts, and intelligence gatherers, our CIDG friends were paid killers. *See references 5 and 6.*

Before long, after breaking around noon as the heat and humidity were overwhelming, they approached the city.

It was not long before they were able to observe two Russian freighters off-loading their wares at the end of two long piers that jutted out about one thousand feet into the harbor. This was to accommodate deep-water ships' draft requirements, especially in the dry season, from October through April.

It is then the monsoon winds blowing from a northeasterly direction had the effect of blowing water out of the harbor, making access to anything but the end of the piers possible at low tide.

After going through the motions of selling their wares in the market, they spotted a monastic-looking temple high above the city in the hills to the north. Having finished conducting business and stopping for an afternoon snack of prawns and rice, they drove up into those hills.

Before long, as the sun began to lower in the late afternoon sky, they observed a convoy of light trucks beginning to form a queue that fishtailed out of the city to the northeast, back in the direction of the South Vietnamese border and the Mekong Delta.

All that remained for our "CIDG friends" to discover was the nature of their stores and where they were to be off-loaded without being detected. Since only about an hour of daylight remained, Haiching and Wang Hsiang decided to follow the caravan of trucks from a respectable distance, as it was clear they would be stopping for the night at some point soon. Clearly, it was assumed they would not signal with their headlights to any observers from the air as to where they were headed.

At one point in time, their truck was passed by an escort of police in two cars, who after glancing at our friends, continued on their way toward the convoy. Lucky for them, for the CIDG carried no identification, and if cornered by unfriendly forces, they were instructed not to be taken alive. This usually meant the others guys taken by surprise didn't fare too well.

The CIDG'ers knew their fate if captured and were highly trained mercenary assassins. When province or district chiefs, village elders, mayors, etc., were caught in exposing our forces to the enemy, which usually resulted in savage ambushes and high casualties, they were summarily dealt with by the CIDG, thereby eliminating any chance of a repeat performance on their part.

Hidden off-road, parked on a small feeder road, "our observers" slept in their truck, not needing to have one of them stay awake alternatively, as it was impossible to sneak up on a CIDG person.

At sunup, alerted by the starting of engines a few hundred meters away, the convoy and our friends continued their trip along Route 4 and, as expected, approached the Vietnamese border before long, near Kien Giang province.

The Delta's main rivers were connected by a series of navigable canals, which made their way through the marshlands in an elaborate, interconnecting labyrinth of passageways, navigable to shallow-draft barges and motorized sampans. Lost in this maze were the Viet Cong, using it as a sanctuary.

Driving right up to the edge of one of the canals, the trucks unloaded their contraband to sampans lined up for several hundred meters. Now, Haiching and Wang Hsiang were faced with a major decision, which fortunately had been considered in the planning of their assignment.

Abandoning their truck on a side road, they approached the sampans on foot, walking aimlessly, as if they were going to work in the area.

In good old-fashioned Vietnamese style, spotting an unattended sampan, they made like Hertz-rent-a-sampan without the paperwork. If I were the offended party I would suspect that "discretion being the better part of valor," they would be better off forgetting about the incident.

Trailing the long line of sampans down the network of canals took over forty-eight hours and led smack-dab right toward the Mekong River!

How surprising! Some sampans did break off from the main group and headed off in the direction of the South China Sea toward An Xuyen province in the southern tip of the Delta. Its capital, Quan Long, 140 miles southwest of Saigon, and its neighboring province of Ba Xuyen, were considered VC bastions! *See map 3, page 54.*

Rach Gia, located in An Xuyen province, was the home of the only usable outlet to the Gulf of Thailand situated in the Delta at ten degrees north latitude, and 105 degrees east longitude, which we suspected the VC used for shallower draft vessels. This would be reported, but our boys stuck with the main convoy as they wound their way through the Delta's network of canals.

With minor exceptions, the convoy continued until a series of major off-loadings of everything from guns to butter[*] only a few miles from the Mekong, in what appeared to be staging areas. Stores included an arsenal, ranging from 90 mm rocket launchers, 40 mm mortars, and 75 mm recoilless Chinese rifles to medical supplies and uniforms—theirs, I hoped.

In order to determine the nature of the convoy's stores, our "CIDG employees" waited for a sampan to straggle behind the rest of the queued line of boats. Haiching pulled his sampan alongside "the straggler" apparently to inquire if help was needed, and in luck for our side and not theirs, they did.

Once on board and speaking the language passably as there were many dialects that existed, Wang Hsiang asked one of the two peasants above deck for a light, while Haiching drifted silently behind the other. Their throats were silently cut and bodies thrown overboard as quickly as it took to tell about it.

---

[*]   Contraband (guns to butter)—USN records have found that included in the Viet Cong shipments were Chinese recoilless rifles 57 and 90 mm, 7.9 mm machine guns, 45 caliber machine guns, carbines, grenades, ammo, penicillin tablets, bags of Aureomycin, packets of hypodermic needles. On December 10, 1966, a Game Warden PBR confiscated off one junk: 80 gallons of kerosene, 27 bottles of glucose, 28 bottles of penicillin, and 500 feet of copper wire!

Below the deck, sitting among the contraband were two other locals smoking away on their opium pipes. Wherever the trip "the dope" was to take them, they were well on their way in a matter of thirty seconds. Haiching inspected the weaponry carefully to see if any of it could be conveniently borrowed, and taking a few of the Chinese rifles and ammo, returned from whence they came.

Now, all that remained of their assignment was to determine where the hell the convoy was headed. Since the visit they just made would probably not be discovered until morning, and by that time the convoy would be miles away, Haiching and Wang Hsiang continued to track from a respectable distance of about "three clicks." Being CIDG'ers, they kept their guard up, but were happy to know that the easiest part of the job— surveillance of the convoy's destination—was all that remained for the completion of "another day at the office!"

The next day, the convoy split, one group heading in the direction of Can Tho, and the other toward Vinh Long, both on the southeasterly shores of the Bassac and the Mekong rivers. They decided to follow the larger of the two groups and were not surprisingly relieved that one "missing sampan" had not yet been discovered. Its eventual disappearance would initially not be traced to the possibility of their presence anyway. They had considered stealing another sampan and splitting up, but they were too close to the completion of their mission to add this unnecessary danger.

After the convoy reached about eight kilometers north of Can Tho, the sampans were off-loaded in a village on a canal leading to the river. There, the supplies were staged awaiting the next directive as to when to attempt to cross the Bassac and their ultimate destination. Our friends considered their mission completed after duly noting the details of their discoveries.

They separated from their prey and headed for Muc Hoa. Once on the eastern side of the Bassac, they headed in the direction just west of the naval base at Sa Dec and into Kien Tuong province, about eighty miles due west of Saigon. Using their "captured sampan" carefully, they made their way across the river the next morning, since now discovery by our forces patrolling the river would cause many questions to be asked, especially regarding the Chinese rifles.

Once safely across, they headed in a northeasterly direction across the Plain of Reeds back toward the Cambodian border, with their story of vital interest to ADM Veth and all the way back through Hawaii to the chief of naval operations, in Washington.

I had only been "in country" one month when I began to get an inkling that the war "was unwinnable," principally for two reasons:

1. We had no ally or one that was grossly ineffectual, and in the course of this undertaking, we had chosen the wrong one.

2. Our principle tenet of fighting the war was to maintain a defensive posture, limiting our operations to within South Vietnam's border.

It was not until the summer of 1970, some three to four years late, did we commence bombing enemy targets in Cambodia.

To every question I asked myself about the conduct of this war, with one exception, the answer kept coming up: Cambodia.

The exception was the need to physically interdict the Ho Trail in southern North Vietnam, in the vicinity of the city of Vinh, which had been ruled out by the powers that be, long before I thought of it.

George Carson and I could now begin to put meat on to the bones of this skeleton. It would not be a surprise to anyone that with this information and a few more similar examples of distribution such as the one our CIDG friends had uncovered, we would begin to form a pattern of "logical river crossing points" in this network.

The only variations in river crossing points occurring as the convoy's destination would change as the NVA and Viet Cong units circulated about the Delta. Keeping up with their movements was equally challenging, but the Navy and "the boys from Langley" had their sources on the ground. In fact, if the same, or close to the same crossing points were continually used, say more than twice, there would be no reason for us to await their attempts to cross the river. Ground units, supported by the Navy's A-37 Skywolves were active in the Delta with their phosphorous ordinance and could pay the off-loading or staging sites on the canals approaching the Mekong a visit . . . thereby having the effect of "widening the river!"

ADM Veth, "Hello!"

It was only a matter of forty-eight hours before our contact at Navy HQ contacted CDR Bronson, and again we were summoned to a meeting, this time with the admiral's staff. Apparently, our CIDG guys had a report to file, and somehow they weren't going to tell us about it over the telephone.

A LTJG, a commander, and two captains greeted us in the HQ's operations center. It hummed with both incoming and outgoing communications, mostly I suspect, from activities of the Seventh Fleet on Yankee Station in the Gulf of Tonkin.

Dating back in history . . .

Primarily the USN's mission in 'Nam emanated from the Seventh Fleet's presence in the north, in a body of water known as The Gulf of Tonkin, lying due east of North Vietnam's main harbor of Haiphong. The fly boys were keeping things moving both with bombing missions to the Hanoi area and blockading and bombing missions against the North's main seaport, Haiphong. Daily ops were being monitored both in Saigon and aboard one of our carriers, the USS Ticonderoga. There aboard, in the ship's command and control Room (CIC), the North's radar, electronic capability, and intelligence gathering activities were monitored.

North and South Vietnam, Laos, and Cambodia, in 1940, taking over certain military bases in the region, while simultaneously being ruled by Vichy-France[(*)] *until 1945.*

French military forces were sent to Vietnam in 1946 to unseat Ho Chi Minh who had seized Hanoi and proposed a unified government for all of Vietnam, under an Annam emperor, Bao Dai. He was declared emperor of all of Vietnam in 1949.

Ho Chi Minh, opposed unification, and as leader of the opposing Communist regime, backed by the Viet Minh government[(**)], *was at first aided by Communist China, and*

[(*)] The Nazi collaborative regime, ruled by the notorious Pierre Laval.

[(**)] This was North Vietnam's government and was independently Communist in nature, sometimes known as the Popular Liberation Front (PLF).

later the United States, fearing Communist expansion in Southeast Asia.

Ho's Viet Minh Army battled both French and Vietnamese military forces. GEN Vo Nguyen Giap, NVN, commander of Viet Minh forces planned the Tet Offensive of '68, was better known for the siege at Dien Bien Phu, commanded by French GEN Jacques Leclerc.

Located in the northwest part of North Vietnam, Dien Bien Phu was besieged by the NVN (Viet Minh Army), surrounded, and through a maze of tunnels tightened the nose around the fortress until its collapse and surrender on May 5, 1954. This culminated the long-standing (1863) French involvement in the region and led to the division of North and South Vietnam.

In 1951, Viet Minh forces joined Communist-led Pathet Lao forces in central Laos, and civil war ensued. The war continued until an agreement reached in Geneva in '54 and followed by an armistice in '55, partitioning Laos and granting two northern provinces to the Pathet Lao.

In 1955, Bao Dai, acting as monarch in the South, was deposed by his premier, Ngo Dinh Diem, and declared himself president.

In 1961, in neighboring Laos in which three warring princes agreed to a settlement with a coalition government headed by Soviet-backed royal premier Souvanna Phouma. However, North Vietnam had expansionist ideas in the South.

From page 812 of the TIME Almanac 2004:
But North Vietnam, the U.S. (in the form of CIA personnel), and China remained active in Laos after the settlement. North Vietnam used a supply line (Ho Chi Minh Trail) running down the

mountain valleys of eastern Laos into Cambodia and South Vietnam, particularly after the U.S.—So. Vietnamese incursion into Cambodia in 1970 stopped supplies via Cambodian seaports[*].

North Vietnam torpedo boats reportedly attacked two US destroyers in the Gulf of Tonkin, in what was considered NVN waters, just west of Hainan Island, on August 2, 1964. Congress voted for a Gulf of Tonkin resolution a few days later, which authorized President Johnson, "to take all necessary measures" to win the war. Johnson retaliates with air strikes in the North.

On August 2, 1964, USN F-8E's fighters were launched from the Ticonderoga, responding to an SOS-type call from one of our destroyers, the USS *Maddox*. They had indicated that at least three NVN torpedo boats had fired a series of torpedoes against them and another destroyer . . . the USS *C. Turner Joy*, twenty-eight miles off the North Vietnamese coast.

It was reported that one of the NVN torpedo boats had been sunk by our aircraft. This "un-wonton attack" by the North was known as the Gulf of Tonkin Incident and led President Johnson to ask Congress for a state of war to be declared against North Vietnam and its Viet Minh regime.

After the war, despite much clamoring from anti-war dissidents that the incident had never occurred, the North admitted to conducting such an attack. In the few weeks preceding this incident, elements of a cadre of South Vietnamese commandos conducted raids against several of the Viet Minh's coastal installations in the North, which had met with some success.

---

[*]   As far as I was concerned, four years too late.

Some media sources conjectured that the North's attack was in retaliation for these raids. Whatever its justification, it was "just what the doctor ordered" for the hawks in Congress and the Pentagon, who supported an expansion of the war in Vietnam.

Against this backdrop and history, Bronson and I met with these USN operatives in the war room at USN HQ in Saigon to discuss the latest development in Operation Steam Shovel.

Specifically it was Haiching and Wang Hsiang's report that was an undeniable link between the convoys originating in Sihanoukville and the cross-river traffic on the Mekong. After covering the mechanics of transmitting this coded information through CinPacFleet in Hawaii to the CNO in Washington, I gave them George Carson's identifying data and dropped a request on them that they clearly were not expecting.

I offered these first early reports—that large amounts of traffic were originating from across the border with Cambodia and from the direction of the port facilities on the Gulf of Thailand. I would like to interview the CIDG boys and go to Muc Hoa, with an interpreter if necessary, "to hear it for myself." Speaking parenthetically, I told them that there was no sense proceeding with this elaborate construction of a computerized network by starting with a weak or false foundation!

They responded, "How soon do you want to go?" After looking at Bronson square in the eye, for he certainly wasn't planning on going into the heart of the Plain of Reeds anytime soon, I said, "Tomorrow."

That is, after they would be so kind as to allow me to study these huge wall maps of the Delta. My theory was, I was sure my "shot in the dark" about Sihanoukville being the major origin of the traffic had proven to be correct. Now, I wanted to see if the checkerboard latticework of the canal system, throughout the Delta could speak to me! I had a reason for this, but knowing I was now going deep into the heart of the region and would be able to interview "our CIDG friends" on the ground, I was starting "to think for myself" . . . again.

But this time, it was running in "geopolitical" directions.

By the end of the day at Navy HQ, I was talking myself into losing my job or my senses! Since nobody could have issued this assignment except the admiral, I concluded, I would have to run it by him. It was so hot that I decided to wait to unleash my bombshell as ADM Veth may have been weak of heart . . . And for certain, running this one up the chain of command was bound to encounter someone who was. More about this later . . .

PACVs maneuver across Plain of Reeds

VI

The Plain of Reeds – Thanksgiving '66, Muc Hoa and Cambodia

Outfitted with a mini tape recorder, a notebook, and pencils (didn't think there would be either in Muc Hoa), sunglasses, two hats, and dressed in jungle fatigues, I flew out from Tan Son Nhut the next morning at 7:00 a.m., as it got hot quickly in the Reeds.

The chopper was a little fancier than before, probably compliments of the HQ guys, and the trip over the Plain of Reeds to Muc Hoa took only thirty minutes, but what a thirty minutes it was . . . !

The Navy chopper whisked through the thick humid air with the slate-blue morning sky serving as a backdrop. Despite being colored brown on the maps I had seen only the day before, the entire trip from Saigon was over "ever-lovin" blue water!

As we flew over the area, we observed that its topography was both vast and uncomplicated. Flat as a pancake, this was clearly a swamp, but protruding through the water surface were these three- to six-foot reeds resembling bull pups, like the ones I encountered as a kid off the south shore of Long Island. But that wasn't all. Interlacing the water surface, which averaged about one click in spacing, were these tree rows forming a checkerboard pattern that ran at right angles to each other. These trees formed thick underbrush that could have served as cover for anyone in or behind them.

It was a great big flat swamp that resembled a blond GI flat top or crew cut with the bristles of hair shooting upward like the Plain's reeds. As we approached Muc Hoa, I observed the installation with incredulity. Not a city or town which I was expecting, nor a village or a base, but instead a large round mound of dirt, a couple of hundred yards in diameter, rising a few feet out of the swamp! It was nothing more . . . but my mind mused in the direction of the PACVs vectoring across this terrain by a couple of helicopters.

Muc Hoa—Plain of Reeds, Thanksgiving, 1966

Muc Hoa—Towncenter with ACV off-cushion
about 20 km. from Cambodia

Two rows of makeshift two-story wooden buildings formed rows on either side of the mound at the highest point in the bases' center. Several water buffalo drove the wheel, which rotated an entire century-old mechanism to pump fresh water from a nearby sunken well, feeding the thirst of this outpost. All electricity was battery-powered or by lantern. There weren't any paved streets, and when it rained, which was often, this base became a sea of mud. The buildings were laid out barracks-style, with one row of buildings forming a tee with a two-story building at the end of the line. There was absolutely nothing attractive about this site, except its location.

It was strategically located between Saigon and the southern Cambodian boundary of the promontory that jutted out like a beak pointing directly at the Tan Son Nhut airbase and Bien Hoa airport complex near Saigon.[*] Not surprisingly, this promontory was known to the world as the Parrot's Beak area of the south. Its beak pointed directly at the Saigon area!

I tried to overlook where I was as it resembled an outpost in Central Africa. Disembarking from the copter, I was met by the base commander, a slim Vietnamese, with officer insignia on his not-too-crisp or clean ARVN shirt. He was a man in his early thirties, clearly happy to see someone paying attention to him and a force of about thirty-five men, eight of whom were CIDG in origin.

Two of the eight CIDG personnel, Haiching and Wang Hsiang, were our friends. I was there to debrief them, but I was also there to "take a look around."

After my tour of the base, which fortunately was dry, we returned to listen to the base commander, partially because he had mistakenly considered me as someone important. Well, as Senator Tip O'Neill once said, "All politics is local." I must say it was a pleasure listening to him as he spoke English better than I spoke Vietnamese.

---

[*]   Muc Hoa was only twelve miles (about 20 km.) from the Cambodian border.

From what he told me about the patrols that were running between the base and the nearby border, he felt the movement of enemy traffic and supplies into the Plain was a foregone conclusion. He related in a very animated and refreshingly interesting way, that some of the night sorties across the border had sited everything from arms factories and hospitals to first-aid stations and rest areas within ten kilometers of the border, the exact location of which nobody knew.

There were no roads, no installations, landmarks or bases. Truly, the middle of nowhere!

The commander liked to be known as Chip, which fit right in with his Americanized looks and mannerisms. Chip and I exchanged some uniform metal insignia, which I had remembered to bring with me for barter purposes, and after getting to know each other a little better through this process, we sat down to lunch. I had asked Chip to invite our CIDG friends, which on the one hand would have been a massive oversight on my part if I hadn't and on the other hand served to restrict some of my planned discussion with Chip, as one didn't know who our guests might be working for tomorrow.

Lunch was truly forgettable as the cuisine and the ambiance was Plain of Reeds-style . . . as it was not Tavern on the Green-style (Central Park, New York)! It was not long before I convinced Chip that I could get help—thinking of the PACV group and a couple of helos wreaking havoc in this very unforgettable and highly neglected part of the war zone, strategic as it may be.

After having a relatively sleepless night in a makeshift army bunk bed, which I think was saved for visitors, especially un-uniformed guests with rank.

I said my good-byes after a few photo ops for my picture album and *didi*'ed back to Saigon the same way I came.

I couldn't wait to tell those Navy experts at HQ that the "brown area" immediately to the west of Saigon and all the way to the Cambodian border was as blue as blue could be! . . . Another screwup!

Bypassing going into the Compound and briefing Bronson, I took a chance and went directly to Navy HQ to see the admiral's staff with my trip report. Besides, I didn't want him around if I was able to get in to see the admiral. What I had to say to Mr. Veth was going to be for his ears only. (I told you I would get to it.)

The shock to the staff that the Plain of Reeds was most likely acting like a funnel for contraband emanating from Cambodia and feeding itself into the Delta was not accepted at first. They offered that the ARVN were patrolling that area, but it wasn't said convincingly, as if to say the Navy doesn't want any part of the Plain of Reeds. Besides, it was impenetrable to both sides supposedly. I was torn between the choices of either awakening them or saving it for the PACVs. I chose the latter. I thought, hopefully so, that this terrain would be perfect for the ACVs, and we would have the element of surprise on our side! After all, I was an "acting captain, USN," a rank just below a rear admiral, and I was capable of making decisions, but I still wanted to see the admiral about something else! Clearly, this newly found power was going to my head. But does Macy's tell Gimbels? Or in secular terms, does Home Depot tell Lowe's?

Sure enough, when I was running out of ideas and nerve on how to approach this problem, of seeing the ole man alone when he came walking by . . . on the way to the john, of all places . . . so I had to pee too, right at the same time. Nobody said our meeting place had to be too fancy . . . after all, I had just returned from Muc Hoa, and anything looked palatial to me at this point.

It is strange that perhaps the outcome of naval operations in the Mekong Delta hinged on my timing to "wash my hands" at the exact same time he was, but then again, I didn't have to pee at all. Suffice to say, I said, "Good morning, Admiral." Starting slowly . . . then picking up speed . . . "I wonder if I could have a word with you about my trip, sir, as I think I've uncovered something that may be of interest to you." Acceding to my request, he very cordially invited me to join him in his office. Sometimes understatement can be "disarmingly powerful."

"Admiral, you can wait for the Russian and Chinese furnished supplies to be distributed throughout the Delta and play war games Navy-style along the Mekong rivers, and maybe intercept some of the cache, or there's a much easier and more efficient way to accomplish this . . . even better than what we at CNA are working on for you now."

"What's that, Marty?" which I appreciated, as now the admiral and I were becoming friends. "Blockade Sihanoukville Harbor, and Charlie is going to have a fit maintaining his force level in IV Corps!" Once again, the admiral was stunned.

"Marty, have you approached anyone else with this proposal?" he asked in a fatherly tone. "No, sir," I responded . . . to which he said, "Good! I'll get back to you on this in a few days. In the meantime, keep working on Project Steam Shovel."

I didn't have the guts to say, "Is that a no, sir?" Or better yet, either you want to "play to win" or continue what you are doing . . . That is, "playing not to lose!" The latter being a tactic employed by many a loser in the "game of life!" Maybe what I had up my sleeve for my next act would pale in comparison, and I was just setting him up.

VII

Vung Tau Peninsula – Home of the ACVs

MAP 4. III & IV Corps Zones, SVN – Insert map of Vung Tau

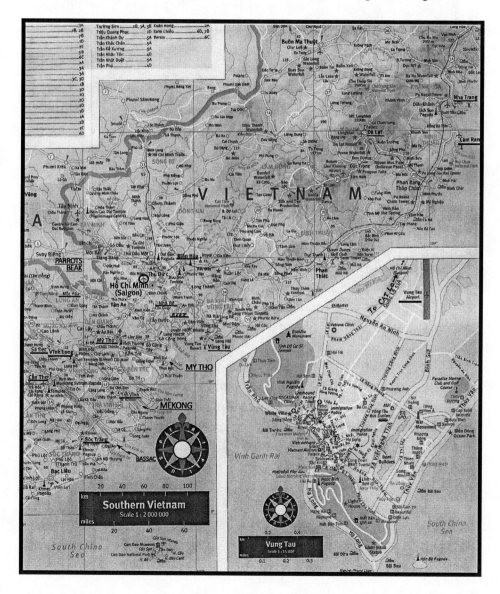

It was late September, and my two-month tour was up. As a result, I thought I had better finish up the testing phase of my assignment and start making noises about returning to the States.

The next day, after "bumping into the admiral," I made plans to make a run for Cat Lo and so informed Bronson I'd be gone for a few days. It was at this point I thought I would first broach the idea with him that "it was time for me to go home."

Not only did he not take the idea too well, but looked at me as if I were crazy. He offered that he would run my request upstairs despite his body English sending me a signal that there was a great deal of work to be done before HQ would look upon my request seriously.

Now that I had "broken the ice," a sudden realization had overcome me . . . There was no way I was getting out of Saigon soon!

The following day, equipped with the usual paraphernalia, I set out for what I hoped would be my last visit to see the PACV boys, at least at this location, and performing tests of the ACV's capabilities.

For now, the plot had thickened to a point where this phase of my trip "was done and gone." While the bigger picture of utilizing the craft in a real live operation, which if successful, would obviate any future study or evaluation as to their utility in action. Live action that would override any model we could develop in Washington.

As usual, the men were glad to see me as the boredom, although safe, was getting to the group. Perhaps they were thinking out loud I would have something interesting for them to do. Little did they know, I certainly did!

After a night of watching some outdated movie, with some of the guys opting for "hearts and beer," we performed the remaining tests I had planned for the next day and asked for a meeting with the top three men—Fleming, Kumler, and Sampson.

At first, I covered the history of the tests we had run and asked if there was anything else that I had not called upon them to do that they thought might be a useful exercise. Getting a quick "we don't think so," I approached them on my plan for the use of the vehicles in combat. I made it clear that what I was about to propose was not to be discussed with the men and that I would have to obtain HQ approval before undertaking this mission. I received their assurances.

I described my trip to Muc Hoa, particularly the terrain, and that I had a strong suspicion that the Plain of Reeds was a "VC funnel" for contraband coming in from Cambodia. There was no need to tell them about the "intel" we had obtained from our CIDG friends.

In my estimation, they had no need to know. I asked them to sleep on it, particularly what other assets we might need to "go a hunting Charlie," which could involve our encroachment of the Cambodian border.

Not only didn't they flinch at this aspect of the plan, but Kip quickly added before we broke up that we would need at least two choppers to vector us around this terrain, so as not to run into a force that either outmanned or outgunned us as we circumvented those tree lines!

Tree lines checker board across Plain of Reeds

Plain of Reeds, West of Saigon—Cambodia in background

I replied, "So noted—we will not undertake this operation without helo coverage." Fleming added, "And I wouldn't say anything about crossing the border to the brass," to which I readily agreed. As if we all had the same thought simultaneously, we agreed to go to town tonight and celebrate. This meant possibly bumping into the VC incognito in Vung Tau proper, but the odds were against it.

After telling the rest of the men that we might be going north and possibly undertaking a more dangerous patrol scheme, a "whoop of celebration" erupted. I was relieved! After all, they could have prevented proceeding with this mission no matter how well thought out by offering an opinion that they thought the ACVs would be vulnerable in this sort of terrain.

The next night, after an easy day spent running my inane testing program, a convoy of four jeeps and a light truck made its way down the flat dark road toward the beach which led to town. Vung Tau resembled many resort towns in the States without the discount malls, kiddie parks, and fast-food joints so aptly described in a book written by a famous Cornellian, a Russian literature professor, Vladimir Nabokov. Nevertheless, it didn't look like most villages or towns in country, as there was a marked absence of any signs of the military, save an occasional MP patrol.

Its main attraction by far were the ocean beaches located along a main road, which extended for about one mile along the eastern border of the village, called Thuy Van. *See map 4, page 93.*

Even we were dressed in summer civies (no insignia). We headed straight for the first bar making the most noise, located in what today is the main business district along Quang Trung Boulevard. The guys were definitely in a celebratory mood. Once there, we met up with a group of Aussies, who were not only great fighters, but good partiers. They could down their Fosters!

I quickly "downed a piss," which the Aussies dubbed, "having a beer," a Foster's at that! There was an ample supply of *chi' mot*'s or *doc than*'s,—single ladies, and the party was rocking.

Somehow, somewhere, a scuffle ensued, not surprising with all those Australians drinking (which is somewhat redundant). When I heard the sound of MP whistles, everyone headed for their vehicles parked in a dark alley next to the bar. In the ensuing confusion, either I took a wrong turn, or the guys left without me. Either way, I was stranded! Hoping the guys would return "to the scene of the crime" looking for me, if in fact they had realized I was missing, I did the next best thing and "hooked up" with my newly made Aussie friends.

At least I would be safe with them, I thought. While I was waiting for them, I made the acquaintance of a pretty *doc than*, who weighed about one hundred pounds . . . tops, and no Saigon tea either.

It turned out that at this point I wasn't missed as the crew was getting loaded, and if anyone wondered where I was . . . they weren't wondering very hard.

As the night wore on, the Aussies began to filter out to places unknown, and my *doc than* acquaintance progressed to a point where I stopped hoping the guys would show up. So I spent the night with her, not realizing how dangerous it was to do so. Her one-room place, in the back of some house close by to the bar, was not too inviting, particularly when I realized we were going to sleep on a flat set of boards covered by a smooth veneer. No mattress or anything resembling one!

Being fairly well-juiced and knowing what I was in for the rest of the evening, I rationalized that "sticking it out" or "sticking it in," as the case may be, was my best course of action given where I was now. I certainly wasn't going to wander around town looking for the guys, but recognized that a safer play would have been to stick with the Aussies. R&R spot or not, the town was crawling with VC! It was later pointed out to me that my acquaintance for the night could have been one.

At first light, I carefully made my way out of my hotel for the night and alertly made my way toward the place I had last seen any of the PACV guys. The scorecard for my stay with the *doc than* was not a shutout, but as the word had quickly gotten around Saigon, "Hey, I had a *doc than* last night, and you know what . . . she moved!" Better off with a *Trung Quo'c Ba*—a Chinese lady!

Talk about luck. As I approached the area I had last seen any American, only a block from the police station, it turned out a couple of the guys were frantically looking all over the town. There in plain view was one of our jeeps with Kip sitting behind the wheel. Was he glad to see me! As we drove around town rounding up the PACV posse, I on the one hand got a little chewing out from my Cornell buddy, and on the other hand, everyone was relieved . . . not the least of which was me!

Before returning to Saigon, I assured both Fleming and Kumler that I, or more likely someone from HQ, would be in touch with them as to the next move. Getting the three ACVs up to the Plain of Reeds, about 125 miles away and not being absolutely sure the boats could make it through the six to eight feet of reeds was still a question that remained to be answered, although the PACV boys didn't think it would be a problem.

How well armed would any of Charlie's convoy of sampans be, and were we going to get chopper coverage to vector us around were questions that worried them more!

PACV hovers on full cushion—dreaded treelines in background

Outside the PACV huts, the maintenance crew excitedly indicated that they had something to show me. There, parked out on the ramp, the crew were busily painting "Tiger teeth," à la the World War II Flying Tiger fighter squadrons, stationed in what was then Burma (renamed Myanmar since 1989). LT GEN Claire Chennault's Curtiss Wright P-40 fighter planes were adorned with painted tiger teeth on the fuselage directly under the nose and prop of their planes to scare the Japanese and the locals. They played an important role in keeping open the Burma Road, a major supply line from Rangoon in Burma, north to southern China.

GEN Chennault was married to the daughter of China's then infamous premier, Chiang Kai-shek, and that could have had something to do with the genesis of this concept.

After helping Fleming compose a message request to Game Warden HQ for the need of various assets needed to traverse from Cat Lo some 150 km. north to the Plain of Reeds, not the least of which would be a "cleared route" as the AAA had no coverage in this area of the world.

A principal worry was the terrain along the eastern shore of the Mekong River, which had to be reconnoitered, in order to gain access to the Plain. Later, Game Warden HQ advised they would make a "helo run" along that portion of the river so as to facilitate easy access for a run across the Plains to Muc Hoa. That was, if providing the density and height of the reeds didn't impede their progress, which the PACV boys doubted.

I returned to Saigon the next day somewhat relieved that the testing had been completed and we could get on with "bigger and better things." I also had a copy of Fleming's request for clearance from Game Warden HQ in Can Tho to undertake the mission. That was the front-door approach, and I was about to see the admiral providing the back door.

I didn't expect any resistance, and I was to find out very quickly and agreeably, there was none. Just the opposite, Navy HQ staff greeted our proposal enthusiastically, as they didn't often receive requests to initiate never-before-tried missions into unknown and possibly hostile territory.

MAP 5. Detailed map of Saigon—(Ho Chi Minh City)

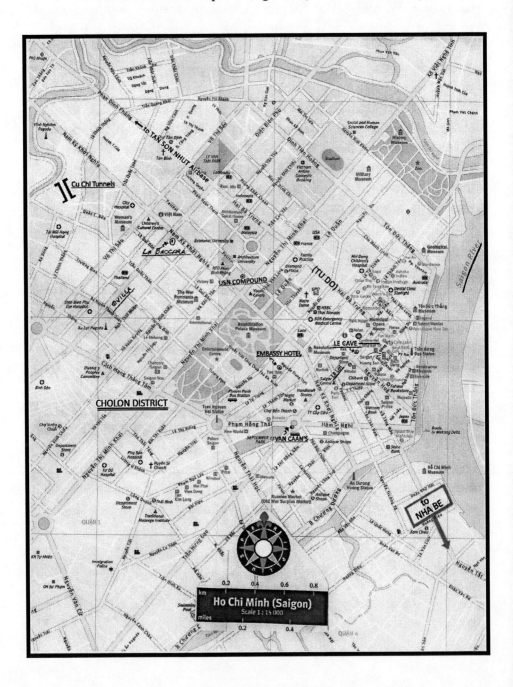

That night, my first in many days back in Saigon, I received a call from Harry Conners wanting to get together as he had something for me and suggested dinner. I immediately accepted, and he advised he would pick me up at the villa in Cholon at 5:00 p.m. Little did we both realize, we had surprises for each other.

Harry received his surprise immediately upon having his driver pull up to the villa's back entrance. There, high atop the wall sat a sandbagged machine gun emplacement, completely surrounded along the length of the wall by rolls of razor-sharp barbed wire. I greeted Harry with, "Welcome to USN SEAL Team HQ—Cholon style!"

He was shocked initially, but loved it! Harry liked anything that both showed initiative and was out of the ordinary. His training, I guessed.

Once inside the barricade, I handed Harry a cold Ba Muoi Ba beer, and he handed me a captured sawed-off shotgun, compliments of the People's Republic of the Chinese Army! It killed him when I didn't do the expected and ask him where in the hell did he "cum shaw" this. After a three-minute lesson on its use, I placed it under my pillow in my "off limits" bedroom.

He said, "Just point it in the right direction," assuming incorrectly that I couldn't aim it, "and it will kill or disable up to six men at a distance of fifteen to twenty feet." Sounded good to me, and we laughingly made our way downtown in his air-conditioned black Mercedes for yet another of Harry's surprises.

On the way, Harry indicated he wanted to stop off at the bookstore to pick up the newspaper and a few magazines. Innocently enough, he said I should join him, so I did. Once inside, I noticed Harry acting very peculiarly. He introduced me to the proprietor, a very tall Indian. Not the kind that killed GEN Custer.

After we left, Harry closed the sliding window between the driver and us and explained how he had just exchanged some crisp, new US greenbacks ($100 bills) for an approximate 50 percent markup to the "official piastre rate." Harry indicated if I wished to make a little spending money on the side and kept the exchanges under $1,000 at a time, this could work for me!

A few days later, at first intrigued by the novelty of the transaction and now having been properly introduced, I decided to try it out.

The bookstore, run by an Indian named Rashid, was nestled inconspicuously on a leafy side street off the beaten path from downtown Saigon, but appropriately on the way to the machine gun-guarded, barricaded Navy officers' club. It was a convenient place to buy *Time* magazine, the *Paris Tribune*, and things such as this only to remind one of home . . . as the articles were somewhat outdated, not that anyone cared.

The store couldn't have been more than fifteen feet wide on the curbside, and about twenty feet deep, crammed with magazines and newspapers from floor to ceiling. Its Indian proprietor, Rashid, stood six feet, four inches tall, with the ubiquitous turban and red-dotted forehead, and sporting a trim mustache and beard against his dark skin, which afforded him an appearance something less reliable than Ben Franklin. I say this hoping not to offend Uncle Ben in that the similarities were more than incidental in that Rashid was a very sophisticated foreign exchange dealer, who basically knew the conversion rates between all major currencies, and particularly the US dollar (USD) and the South Vietnamese piastre.

Whether Rashid ever sold any publications or just gave them away as cover for his burgeoning money exchange racket will forever remain a mystery.

Once a week, after receiving about five one-hundred green dollars from the missus, mailed through the old reliable APO in San Fran, I would pay a visit to Rashid's. After picking out a magazine or two and a large newspaper, I would slide the merchandise across the counter, which now included an extra magazine that I had entered the store filled with five $100 green dollars from the USA.

Without so much as a "good morning," Rashid slid the papers off and below the counter level to bag the merchandise. Amazingly fast, he surfaced with a bag of magazines and newspapers minus the magazine I had walked into the store with. I dutifully paid Rashid an arbitrary sum for the magazines and newspapers, and quickly but nonchalantly, I left the store without looking around or suspiciously casting an eye about as if I were looking for someone.

Inside the innocent-looking paper bag was approximately 10,000 piastres in exchange for the 500 green. The official exchange rate, published daily in the *Saigon News* alongside the list of "Missing Persons—in other than enemy action," was the official piastre rate of about 117-118 to the USD. Rashid paid anywhere from 187 to 200 piastres to the USD for large bills, representing a 60 percent markup from the official rate. This practice was against the rules and perhaps someone's law. I never found out whose law.

In between paydays, various Navy personnel in my compound would pay me a visit looking for Marty the Bank. After comparing their dog tag IDs with the information printed on their check drawn on a US bank, I would exchange 117 piastres for each multiple of $100 checks, duly endorsed with their military IDs, including the dog tag info. Wrapping the check in a sweet "I miss you and the kids letter," I mailed the check home, whereupon the missus deposited the checks. For most of the time I was in Saigon, I exchanged about US $20,000 in this manner, making about a 50-plus percent profit. On the way home, I stopped off at the China Fleet Club in Hong Kong to which I had ready access, being an "acting captain, USN," and bought the place out of Seiko watches, Yamaha skis, Mikimoto pearls, a Nikon SLR camera with telephoto and wide-angle lenses, an ivory chess set, gold and jade jewelry, Akai tape recorder, Pioneer stereo receiver, Kenwood speakers, and the like.

You should have seen the rickshaw man running through the streets of HK balancing my speakers on a bamboo pole across his shoulders on the way to the Hilton. All thanks to Rashid . . . and Harry!

Only the Akai reel-to-reel tape recorder was damaged as the US Postal carrier dropped the recorder on our front steps of our home in Bethesda, Maryland! It had traveled nine thousand miles without a mishap, except for the last five feet. Figures . . . .

Back in Rosslyn, Virginia, at CNA headquarters, George Carson was summoned "upstairs" to Dr. Bothwell's office. George had to have a notion as to what our chief was calling him about from some of the reports I had already sent back home. He, being my partner on a previous study, was copied on all of them. Besides, George was one of the mathematical geniuses who gamed everything, including who had the greatest probability of success at any number of endeavors. He was brilliant to the point of general incoherence relating to everyday matters—and a prick besides.

Bothwell knew this and broke the news to George that the work I was doing in the Delta was meeting with general acceptance both in Saigon and Honolulu. After securing George's opinion that what I was proposing to the Navy's bigwigs had a reasonable chance of success, he elicited from George as to how long it would take us to construct the network and ultimately show results.

106

George could see immediately, if not sooner, his response was going to assign me to 'am, possibly for the duration of the war. He asked our boss, if he could give him an answer in a few days after undertaking some investigation—a request which was granted.

If you knew George as I did, you would know that he had to mull over the various permutations and combinations by which his answer to Bothwell's inquiry would benefit him the most. In my direct communications with George, he had praised the undertaking of creating a supply network out of the Viet Cong's activities in the Delta. Additionally, it occurred to him that this project could be successful to the point that "fame and fortune" could accrue to its benefactors.

Like all pricks, George being no exception, his mind was running in the direction of taking credit for this enterprise. At least with Marty stuck in 'am, he could initially take credit for its successes, and if per chance this venture should bomb, there would be plenty of time to have Marty return to the States to take the fall. Perfect gaming!

After allowing twenty-four hours to pass, as if he were researching this problem like a good analyst, George returned to Dr. Bothwell's office to tell him, about six to nine months ought to be sufficient time to know if things were working! I could have killed him, especially if I knew!

To make matters worse, CNA was constantly in a position justifying to CNO, through OP-93, that we were worth the money being spent on us, as CNA was not cheap. They were always in competition with the Rand Corp. and its overly publicized accomplishments for the Air Force, and Bothwell had, as one of his major "crosses to bear," to advise the Navy how well we were doing their thinking for them!

This project in the Delta fit the bill to a tee and was directly related to war operations. George had sunk me, and it was just what Bothwell wanted to hear!

All of this was unknown to me as I was thoroughly occupied with pulling off this Plain of Reeds caper. I proceeded to Navy HQ, this time with CDR Bronson in tow as his career was at stake, even though he didn't quite get it . . . yet.

The staff greeted us enthusiastically, as if we were brightening up their lives somehow, and I handed them the plan that the PACV boys and I had developed a few days before at Cat Lo, along with Fleming's letter to Game Warden HQ, requesting both clearance for the mission and transit approval, plus helo coverage. To make a long story short, they loved it and called for one of the admiral's adjutants, asking for an immediate meeting with the boss!

While we waited, I got a cup of the always superb Navy coffee, even though I didn't drink coffee . . . when in Rome. We were granted an audience with the Navy's equivalent of the pope in fifteen minutes. Apparently we were getting important, I thought.

The meeting lasted almost an hour. About halfway through, it indicated to me that, with a "certain amount of tweaking," we were going to obtain the old man's blessing. Hanging over the entire discussion was the obvious question as to why any of us hadn't thought of paying the Plain of Reeds a visit before this, but I wasn't going there, at least not now. As you will recall, that Navy brass was ignoring this area of the world as the map had it colored brown! Not only did we get approval, but two choppers, and standby assistance at Tan Son Nhut airbase should the need arise. There were only "two buts."

"One, don't lose those ACVs to the VC under any circumstances, and two, stay the hell out of Cambodia."

And then there was number three, as if it was an afterthought: "If circumstances do arise that you stray into Cambodia . . . don't get caught!"

I flew out of HQ wanting to get the word to the boys at Cat Lo, but we couldn't afford to take a chance sending the news over the wires. Bronson was able to find out that HQ sent some JG down by helo the next day playing secured messenger. All that remained now was a communiqué from the PACVs that they had made it safely to Muc Hoa and all the supporting assets were in place—especially the "gunship choppers," complete with their 7.62 mm, M-60 machine guns, capable of firing 550 rounds per minute, and an "effective range" of 1,100 meters (a little more than a click).

It was time for some personal R&R for yours truly while I waited for everything to fall in place, and my thoughts ran in the direction of Nadine. I called Harry, and we went to dinner at the Caravelle, now that I decided I could afford it, as all the media moguls on expense account ran up the prices at that hotel, but the food and especially the wines were superb.

There would be time enough for the La Baccara and Nadine later, as the evening was young and the club didn't start to hop until around ten. Harry and I had a most delightful dinner of veal medallions and coq au vin, topped off with an absolutely robust burgundy—Pommard '57, and a Chassagne Montrachet '59—a robust red and a dry white. Apparently, the chef at the most expensive hotel in Saigon knew where to find at least one chicken.

We exchanged small talk until Harry blurted out, in a rather hushed and discreet manner, that he had heard I was shaking up the boys at Navy HQ with some new mission. I shouldn't have been shocked, but I was.

He actually knew the PACVs were headed up to Muc Hoa, and I was afraid to ask him what else he knew . . . so I didn't ask. Harry agreed to join me "for one" at the club which was great as there was no assurance Nadine would be there . . . and so we proceeded uptown in the Mercedes.

I was getting to enjoy this whole thing! Tough duty, this Vietnam! So far it was probably more dangerous in the back streets of Washington, DC.

Soon after Harry left, I saw Nadine enter the club appearing to be looking for someone. Eventually, her eyes gravitated over to our favorite spot in the far corner of the bar. She openly smiled in recognition and came over and sat down. She said, "I've been looking for you out at the villa, and you haven't been around." I explained I had been down in the Delta for a few days doing some work for the Navy.

Nadine ordered a wine spritzer (with soda), not a Saigon tea, and I had my usual vodka tonic. After a little small talk about the house and what was happening in town, she asked about the ACVs and the work I was doing. It appeared innocent enough to me, but I kept the explanation general enough so that no specifics were divulged. Besides, it didn't appear to me that she knew what the hell I was talking about half the time. A few dances later in what was a torrid night even for this area of the world, Nadine, whose smile and eyes were such a beautiful mixture of a sophisticated European look and Asian eyes and cheekbones, grabbed my hand and said, "Let's get out of here."

Once in the cab, her warm body only added to the heat of the night, and when she gave the driver directions to my place, my heart started beating at a noticeably faster pace. Not that we hadn't "made it" before, but there's nothing like a beautiful woman in heat and—you, yourself are as horny as a church mouse—and you've both got all the time in the world to put the two together!

As we walked down the dark back alley leading to the villa, we observed the usual drunken cookout, almost always going full bore at this time of night, by my Aussie neighbors and the ever-present "Barbie."

We turned down their invitation to stay, after some boisterous introductions all around, as I had always looked upon the Aussies' presence in that alley as an element of safety in a not-so-safe neighborhood.

When we arrived at the villa, there were a few SEALs sitting around the kitchen table drinking beer, smoking weed, and listening to the music broadcast from Armed Forces Radio, while cleaning their M-16s. After introductions, I asked if they could turn down the music to an acceptable level, and Nadine and I retired to the sanctuary of my private bedroom, now outfitted with a Chinese shotgun under the pillow.

Before I could ask her to be careful of the shotgun and to forget who she had just met, she had undressed and lay stark naked on top of the sheets. Within a matter of seconds, I decided the questions could wait 'il later! Nadine's only words were to turn on the air-conditioner so the guys couldn't hear us making love. I immediately complied with her request.

After a night filled with various forms of erotic behavior on both our parts, we slept late and wandered through the streets of Cholon hand in hand. I guess it was a good sign that I could feel my prostrate (*cu'i lay*) throbbing.

After an "eggless breakfast" at one of the little shops on a side street filled with children playing and the *cho' ba*'s doing their laundry by a nearby water hydrant, pounding their clothes into the curb to get them clean, Nadine asked if we could picnic this afternoon. Who was to say no at this point, as it was Sunday and this beat the NFL anytime!

I kissed Nadine and gave her a hug in front of the married women (*da'n ba'*s) and an isolated single lady (*doc' tha'n*) busily performing their chores, washing clothes at the curbside next to a hydrant, in the bright noonday sun. The oppressive sticky heat was gradually bringing activities to a halt until things would cool off later in the day.

She went to visit her mother (*me'* or *ma'*), and I was off to Tu Do Street to rent a car. We agreed to meet back at the villa in two hours optimistically. I was already carrying American Express checks and my ID cards as there was no place to safely leave them other than in your front pants pocket. Never the back pockets—not on Tu Do Street!

I was not looking forward to becoming involved in the commercial noonday hustle and bustle of Tu Do Street, but Nadine wanted to picnic . . . and as in the Broadway play *Damn Yankees* . . . whatever Lola wants, Lola gets!

Haranguing with a "Hertz Rent-a-Car agent—Vietnamese style" portended to be a hassle in the making, but I was to have no idea how frustrating it was to become. Two very attractive *doc than'*s dressed in a very proper businesslike dresses (*va'i da'i*) adorned the "no name rent-a-car" desk as I hopelessly searched the building for a recognizable name—at least Avis—as an alternative. I met with no success.

I don't know if the problem was that I was a "round eye" or they were a little confused by my passport coupled with my Navy noncombatant card (the latter ID they had never before encountered), or they just plain had taken a dislike to me, but things were not going swimmingly.

After the most ridiculous series of unexplainable delays, requests for three different credit cards, which I finally circumvented with a $100 Amex check, and a great deal of paper shuffling, I was the proud lessee of an underpowered Citroën!

It was France's answer to the Ford Edsel—maybe worse. But transportation for the day was just that, nothing more.

Trying to make heads or tails out of the French dashboard and its control panel readings would have required at least two years at the Sorbonne. I attempted this as I made my way through the God-awful midday Tu Do Street traffic . . . or mayhem.

Out of the corner of my eye, I saw a sign, which I interpreted as a good place to ease the hunger anxiety that had suddenly come over me, causing me to stop for a quick lo mein and shrimp roll. A big mistake!

Not that lunch didn't hit the spot, but from the corner of the alley immediately adjacent to the food shop (*cua' ha'ng*) I had just left, I overheard a "Psst . . . hey Yankee call." I responded, as my curiosity got the better of me. "Green dollars—you have?" I was about to say, "No," and head for my Citroën (if it was still there), when I remembered the American Express checks in my pocket. I already had considered myself an experienced money changer—which I was not but didn't know it—when I replied affirmatively. Another mistake!

Speaking in broken English, these three Tu Do Street Cowboys and I knew this from the outset, "quoted 220 P's to the USD". My greed couldn't be controlled, and I showed them the unsigned American Express checks. All their faces—all three of them—lit up like a Buddhist tree!

After a few minutes of negotiations, which was a scream given we didn't know each other's language but could both count—the exchange proceeded. We were now much farther off the street, about 100 feet into the alleyway.

Sensing I had them where I wanted them as I could walk away at anytime, I blurted out: "250 P!" "OK, OK," came the retort from what appeared to be the ringleader. "1,000 green," he said.

Quickly, being a Cornell engineer, I realized that amount would come to 25,000 piastres! In 50s and 100s, that's a lot of bills.

"No," I responded. "500 dollar." They reluctantly settled.

Now it was time for the counting fiasco. Holding down a massive amount of piastres (P's) in the palm of <u>his</u> hand, "Mr. Tu Do Street" proceeded to count out 2,500 P's for each $100 "Amex check" I was signing. What he didn't fathom was that the signature I was executing in the lower right-hand corner of the checks didn't come close to matching the identifying signature in the upper left-hand corner of the check! What I didn't fathom was that one of the oldest carnie tricks in the book was under way.

The bills held in the palm of his hand were folded in half, with only the unfolded portion sitting in the palm of hand—not actually being counted. After the first half of the bill was counted, then he counted second half . . . quickly . . . very quickly! In this manner, he was counting the same bill twice! I should have known given the speed at which he was counting . . . Another mistake!

That's how a rate of 250 piastres to the dollar instantaneously becomes 125 P's to the dollar! It was about two-thirds of the way through this process that I woke up to this fact, but no matter, I was busily forging my own American Express checks!

Then the unexpected occurred just when the transaction was nearing completion as "the Cowboys" had my five $100 checks, and I was about to fall over from the sheer weight of all the piastres stuffed in my shirt and pants pockets—when the three of them had me surrounded! Uh-oh!

I was about six foot one inch tall and weighed 185 pounds, with a strong shouldered athletic build. My newly found friends weighed 110 pounds tops, and about two of their physiques equaled one of mine. In addition, what they couldn't possibly have known was that as a high schooler, I fought my way out of many a Brooklyn and Queens (NYC) school yard or party.

Stuffing the remaining P's further into my shirt, I picked up the two cowboys nearest me by their shirts just below the collar and "clanged them together," making sure their heads met. Having disposed of them for the moment, I whirled around to see Number 3 staring at me apprehensively.

The look changed to pain quickly as I kicked him in the balls, and as he doubled over, I hit him with my much stronger left arm with an uppercut to the jaw! He went flying (without a ticket) up against the wall and slumped to the ground . . . all 105 pounds of him!

By now, the first two of my friends were beginning to stir and appeared to be considering coming up for a rematch!

In a flash I decided this was not Madison Square Garden Friday fight night! I had their piastres—how many ever there were—and they had my "forged Amex checks." Next . . .

It was time to check out. I had won the Queens (Borough of New York City) 440-yard dash in fifty seconds as an eighteen-year-old and anchored the Cornell mile relay team as a freshman—albeit some twelve to fourteen years before. I easily got the hell out of there . . . losing a few P's flying out of my shirt as I made for the street, now about forty yards away, and was gone before they knew what had happened.

Safely back in France's finest auto and shocked to see over two hours had elapsed since I left Nadine—even on "Nam time," I was going to be very late. I stopped an MP as there were plenty of them on Tu Do Street. He directed me to the nearest American Express office only a few minutes away.

Once there, naturally they couldn't help me except to give me the Amex TWX address in Paris. It was SPAGAMEX—PARIS! I had to go to the Saigon PO—a fate worse than death—to cable them that $500 worth of my checks "had been stolen."

That was only half of it, as my shirt was bulging with an unknown number of piastres, and it wouldn't have taken a rocket scientist to figure out what I had been up to. And all I did was stop for a "quick lunch," and Nadine was waiting! If only there were cell phones in those days! To make a long story short, after a lot of bullshit at the Saigon PO—although I had plenty of piastres to pay for the wire—I sent the cable to Paris giving them the check numbers and amounts whose carbon copies conveniently remained in my "Amex check folder."

Many months later, back in the States, I received an affidavit from American Express asking me to execute it attesting to the alleged "theft and forgery," and of course furnishing me with copies of the checks in question. I executed and notarized the affidavits and noticed on the back of each check read the rubber-stamped, red ink of course, endorsement: Communist Bank of China—HK! American Express credited my account with $500 a few weeks later. And I had an extraspecial good time spending the Communist's money as well as the last laugh!

I sped through the streets of Saigon headed for the villa in Cholon and hoped Nadine would still be there and my mistakes for the day would be over.

Unfortunately, my mistakes were not over for the day!

Nadine was sitting at the kitchen table with some of the SEALs, as this was Sunday, an R&R weekend for some of them. The men were engaged in their usual activities of drinking, smoking, and cleaning their weapons. It had completely escaped me—given the events of the day—that allowing Nadine to be exposed to the SEAL teams, considering their youth and general naive exuberance, was not a good idea.

One couldn't count on their judgment when it came to security . . . not in this context anyway. And who was Nadine . . . and where did she come from?

Fortunately, there was no reason for any of the SEALs to know of our plans in the Plain of Reeds. It did bring home the age-old maxim used in security matters. As the SEALs weren't involved in the mission, they "didn't have a need to know!"

Nadine didn't press me for an explanation as to where I had been—she had packed a picnic Saigon style—and off we went "to God knows where!" All I know is that we crossed a bridge from the northeastern part of the city spanning the Saigon River, and I became a little concerned. East of the river was spotted with VC here and there. It was definitely off-limits for civilians.

My second concern arose about ten minutes later when the gas gauge started approaching a level—given the accuracy and adequacy of French automotive engineering—to a point where we didn't have enough gas to make it back to the city.

"No problem," Nadine offered. "I know of a gas station just down this road that will be open on Sunday."

As we pulled into the station, it appeared to be like "old home week." She knew the people at this station! She clearly had been here before. My heart started beating faster . . . again!

We filled the tank halfway as "Hertz Saigon," to no one's surprise, had rented the car to me with about one-third of a tank of gas—or I was driving a tank! Probably both were true!

I really don't remember what happened at our picnic on the grass under a shady tree, after Nadine informed me that the gas station crew were VC at night—and "petrol pushers" in the daytime!

The rest of the day—both at the remainder of the picnic and the trip back to Cholon—after dropping off Nadine at her mother's place and returning this ridiculous excuse for a car . . . was simply unnerving!

And I had said before, who in the hell was Nadine, and what was she up to? Or was I overreacting . . . perhaps!

From this point on, my mental guard became elevated, but still I couldn't conjure up a set of circumstances other than those that indicated Nadine was a poor girl, hustling her way over from the wrong side of the tracks.

It was the usual slow Monday morning again at the Compound, but CDR Bronson was busy as hell. As soon as he saw me, he blurted out, "You're cleared to join the PACVs on their trip to Muc Hoa or meet them there." Bronson's head was spinning over the rapid pace of events, and to me, it appeared that he was "opting out of this one"! After a few minutes of thought, I advised him I would make one more trip to Cat Lo—to oversee for myself that the crew down there were adequately prepared for this mission—and return the next day.

Another mistake!

Once the PACVs made it to Muc Hoa, I would meet them there as there was no need for me to waste my time on the transit from Cat Lo to Muc Hoa, some 100 km. away traveling in a straight line, due north, which the PACVs would not be able to do, obviously requiring river transit for as much of the trip as possible.

Secretly, although the reasons given for my return to Saigon before going to Muc Hoa were valid, I wanted to visit HQ and make damn sure those requests from both Fleming and the Game Warden commander at Can Tho, CDR Walt Weldon, for the helos to vector the PACVs around the Plain were going to actually be assigned.

Those crafts could be sitting ducks for VC ambushes or mortar/rocket attacks without those helos. To improve the probability of success, I wanted to ask HQ if I could hitch a ride to Muc Hoa with the choppers, as Bien Hoa airport was located only twenty miles northeast of Saigon. I would have to "table this for later"!

I made my way by the usual route and method to Cat Lo—having Bronson arrange for a Huey ride for a supposed VIP. It would be a quick trip as my intention was to make a fast inspection of the ACVs and huddle with management over first- and last-minute plans. It didn't take a lot of intel to figure how something could go wrong—and in war, as our old friend Bob McNamara has recently pointed out, "there is a fog of war," which prevails over operations such as this.

Passing over the Rung Sat, my thoughts were on the one-hand reflective of Nadine's recent activities—or you might say machinations—and on the other hand looking down at this impenetrable swamp wondering subconsciously about what we were going to encounter in the Plain of Reeds.

If those reeds, purported to be "willowy and easily brushed aside," if either they were not as advertised or were ingested into the horizontally mounted centrifugal fan, whose airflow formed the jet-air seal, trapping the cushion of air under the craft, we were duck's soup—VC style!

It was about the time I started to think of what to do if that occurred. As one always (and particularly me) has to have a plan B, we sighted the base at Cat Lo. Other than running into a well-armed convoy, or still worse encountering a well-hidden, camouflaged VC base, I didn't have a worry in the world.

I received a surprising hero's welcome, I think more than half a put-on, as I disembarked keeping my head as low as my physical ability would allow. People were literally known to "lose their heads" this way. Jack Fleming and Kip Kumler were there at the helo pad to greet me, and I could see the visible excitement both in their faces and body language.

We quickly got down to business as the weather was hot 'n' sticky, more than usual, if that were possible. As soon as I entered the main Quonset building, I noticed some of the drinking and all the card playing and junk reading were gone! The place was abuzz with activity as it seemed everyone was doing something!

Anxiously, I joined in as we met a few more men who were detailed to this particular part of the mission and proceeded out to the ramp leading to the water's edge. Here the ACVs were parked, miraculously and mercifully out of the sun, awaiting final inspection. Really, it was my inspection, but I underplayed this aspect of the undertaking as best I could. These kids knew by this time just as well, if not better than I in some cases, what they were going to need.

I didn't act like a "captain, USN," or even importantly, as the men knew my role and that was good enough for me.

I was particularly encouraged by the presence of extra fuel tanks, thereby extending our range by about 20 percent plus, and the improved communications gear that had been added for this mission. It was clearly their plan to maintain almost constant contact with the helos directing, or in military jargon, vectoring them around the terrain below.

Emergency- or Mayday-type calls for our Navy F-8 fighter planes standing by at Bien Hoa Air Base could be left up to the helos. Once scrambled by prearranged signal, Navy Central Command could have the aircraft to us in a matter of a few minutes.

That is, if the enemy were where they could be found. The VC were not always cooperating brethren. Insidiously set traps, ambush, and deceptive military tactics were clearly their preferred methods of engagement.

The NVN had been known to fire SA-2 rockets with 2,000 lb. warheads at our bombers operating in the North. These rockets possessed speeds approaching 3.5 MACH or 2,450 miles per hour.

As this was obviously overkill when operating against our choppers, our pilots had been trained in the conduct of elusive maneuvers if attacked in this manner with smaller rockets. In this case, an understanding had been reached to gain altitude and attempt to hide behind an available tree line where heights attained of as much as thirty feet. Otherwise, the pilot's plan was "get the hell out of there," unless the source of the rocket launch was identified.

We spent about an hour to an hour and a half rechecking Fleming's list. About half of the time was spent talking with each member of the crew whose area we were inspecting. I thought we had plenty of 40 mm mortar rounds, but Fleming and his "ordinance man" didn't, so I dropped it!

One new item was the addition of a "chicken screen"! Apparently the crew was encountering "fowls fouling" up our centrifugal fan, being ingested by the vacuum created as air passed through the horizontally mounted fan into the skirt system, which formed the air-jet seal around the perimeter of the craft. It was duly noted.

I asked the crews about our optimum range given the trade-offs that could be made, now that our payload weight had increased about 15 percent due to the extra fuel, ordinance systems, and ammunition. We figured that despite adding about 15 percent to the original 7.5-ton gross weight, principally through the addition of extra fuel, we gained more than that in greater range capability and armament effectiveness.

Kip responded they had just changed the filters in the gas turbines and washed the salt and dirt off the turbine blades thereby improving operability. If we didn't experience over 100 degrees Fahrenheit in the environment we were about to operate, as our turbines' power degraded under severe temperatures, we might get another 5-10 percent extension onto our range.

If engaged in a firefight, which necessitated evasive tactics, this could prove to be of paramount importance. Every mile could prove to be important!

I was satisfied. We were prepared and so were the "PACV crews." If we were to engage the enemy in all-out firefight, so be it. We had tried to think of all possible circumstances that we could encounter, and the boys seemed ready!

Cocktail hour was fast approaching, and with the PACVs scheduled for an early morning departure the day after tomorrow, we retired for the day with a feeling of having done all we could do in the way of preparation for the unexpected . . . for surely in war . . . it was coming.

All that remained now was receiving the final approval from Game Warden HQ as to the shortest and safest route up the My Tho River en route to the Mekong and into the unknown awaiting them in the Plain of Reeds.

There was a Game Warden base for the vehicles to stop at, in case of trouble, at the intersection of the My Tho and the Mekong, well known to all our naval operations personnel engaged in the Delta—Vinh Long.

This base was strategically located in that it was about midway to their destination. Recommendations from Can Tho suggested proceeding to Ilo-Ilo Island at the mouth of the My Tho and proceed past the bases at My Tho and Vinh Long. At around ten miles, or a little over sixteen kilometers past Sa Dec, on the Mekong, the PACVs were to enter the Reeds.

Part of this proposal had been made by CDR Fleming, suggesting they were to cut off the corner so to speak, by transiting the My Tho to the Mekong River and entering the Plains from the much wider, and therefore safer, Mekong.

Approval of this plan and the recommended entry point into the Plains from the Bassac awaited HQ approval. It was surely true that members of Game Warden's staff at HQ were not in favor of this mission for at least two reasons.

One, "it was not invented here," the NIH syndrome had to prevail.

Two, the Plain of Reeds had long been considered impenetrable for both sides and therefore downgraded in importance. Jurisdiction for the area was assigned a lower grade of priority and as a result assigned to the ARVN[*].

Nevertheless, CDR Weldon knew enough not to throw himself in front of a freight train and rendered to us his and his staff's fullest cooperation.

---

[*] South Vietnamese Army.

His job wasn't to plan the efficiency and strategy of the missions, but rather to carry out orders, and in this case, he obviously had clear-cut instructions. *See map 4, page 93.*

He had not notified the commander at Nha Be, a base on the nearby Saigon River, and had "the recon boys" checking out several possible entry points off the Mekong. Their main concerns which were elevation and vegetation, sometimes ten feet high, would pose the least problems for the vehicles upon initial entry to the Plain.

It was thought that once entry to the Plains themselves had been achieved, with "choppers vectoring" the ACVs from about 500 to 1,500 feet above the craft, the men could maneuver their way through the maze of reeds and tree lines that the craft were about to encounter.

HQ at Can Tho had promised the PACV boys an answer by tomorrow.

The PACV men on patrol

CIDG mercenaries go for a ride

Satisfied, I settled down after what I considered "a day well spent," and it was time to party as was customary in Cat Lo. This meant some serious drinking, eating, and a few guys smoking with their feet up, jabbering away about sports and women . . . neither of which they had experienced in quite a while!

It was an hour after dinner, which consisted of baked ham, potato salad, USN-issued baked beans, overcooked corn on the cob and plenty of beer and soft drinks, not exciting but filling. Once again, my heart rate once again experienced another fibrillation.

It had just grown dark to the point where we had to turn on the overhead lights and began using flashlights outside when a commotion appeared to be taking place.

Word had spread through one of the contractors serving the base and had just completed a trip, coming into the base from the northeast, in the opposite direction of Vung Tau at the end of the peninsula, that larger than usual VC units were "active in the area." And were headed straight for Cat Lo!

Oh shit . . . Here we go again! What can go wrong will go wrong! "The Fog of War." Couldn't Charlie have waited a few more days? At least until I left! What luck!

Someone, I can't remember who, in the ensuing excitement, said, "How long will it take for us to get geared up to leave for the mission now?"

If it wasn't pitch-black out by this time, one hour was the almost instantaneous response. Seeing it was as dark as Hades and the CO of the base had just ordered, "All lights out," it would be two hours or more. This alternative was quickly dispensed with.

We were still mulling over the alternatives when a South Vietnamese security officer came in to alert us to grab some guns and ammo. The VC appeared to be maneuvering to surround the base!

Oh shit . . . again!

Fleming conferred with Kip Kumler and Jeff Sampson and gave the order to leave the base in twenty minutes—get ready to go! Upon a few seconds' reflection, I was able to gather my thoughts enough to think clearly and wholeheartedly agreed.

This raid could have something to do with the VC getting a hold of the ACVs, and getting them the hell out of there would serve two purposes. The other was getting our bodies the hell out of there!

The downside, which was quickly dismissed, was returning to the base before starting out for the Plain of Reeds.

However, the overriding consideration, which I concurred in was, we couldn't take the risk of allowing these three craft to fall into enemy hands!

Besides, remember what the admiral had said about the mission, "Don't let the ACVs fall into enemy hands"? Well, I assumed that went for anywhere . . . any time.

I had an additional thought that supplemented this consideration—which I kept to myself—which Fleming and the PACV crew weren't voicing . . . They couldn't take the chance of "yours truly" falling into enemy hands. Oh, the forms!

MAP 6. Mekong Tributaries and key outposts—Insert of Saigon areas

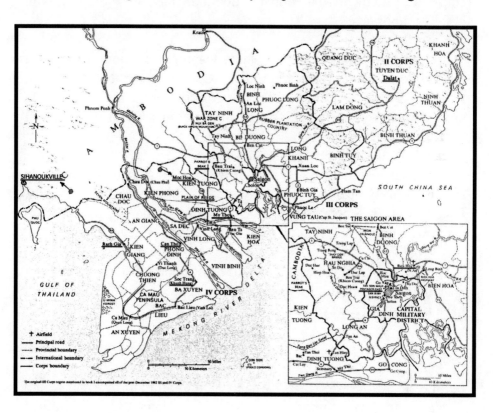

Either way, the next order of business was for me to arm myself and get my behind down to the ramp where the ACVs were already cranking up their engines. I literally, for once in my life, did *not* want to "miss this boat"!

To my initial disappointment, rank set aside for the moment, Fleming denied my request for a gun. In quick explanation, as this was no time for an argument and remembering my rank, he said, "There's too much danger in this pitch-black darkness that you might shoot one of us!"

I saw his point and quickly agreed.

It does prove one thing: when you are under attack and the chips are down, all that bullshit about being "an acting captain, USN," evaporates!

At this point, everyone began leaving the Quonset huts and headed down to the ramp where the ACVs were parked. Somehow, I took a wrong turn and in the pitch dark found myself running around, unarmed, unable to find anyone of our crew or the ACVs. I was not a happy camper!

That would be great if they left without me, as remote as this possibility had seemed only a few minutes before. Finally, I saw what I thought was Sam the cook who we had played cards with and began following him . . . wherever he was going.

I asked him if he had an extra gun, but no dice . . . but like a seeing-eye dog, told me to follow him. I said to myself, "I should have known, it's always good to know the cook!"

It was about this time as visions danced in my head of being stranded in this camp as Charlie breaks through the perimeter of our defenses, whatever they might be, and I am engaged in hand-to-hand combat with some highly trained guerrilla fighter dressed in black pajamas . . . when God answered my prayers. The sky lit up as if it were the Fourth of July at an Iowan fairground!

Only it wasn't God . . . or at least it was his personal emissary in the form of two Navy helicopter gunships, Seawolves, from a nearby base, dropping flares suspended by parachutes. Charlie was being illuminated around the base perimeter, turning this area into a shooting gallery, like one I worked at as a teenager during my summer vacation, on the boardwalk in Atlantic City, New Jersey.

Almost immediately, I was being serenaded by the all-too-familiar *rat-a-tat-tat* as the gunships M-60s strafed the illuminated perimeter areas ringing the base. It was if to say to the VC, in USN fashion, "This is our house . . . Stay away!"

The night sky, brightened from the eerie glow emanating from the phosphorous flares burning the night darkness away, improved my vision to the point where I was able to make some order out of the chaos that was unfolding.

Sure enough, I spotted a very welcome sight to say the least . . . the ACVs with their turbines whining in the night air off on a distant ramp leading down to the water's edge. It didn't take me long to get over there.

I was standing alongside one of the craft that Kip had instructed me to stand by . . . you might say closer than I had laid beside Nadine a week ago . . . as this was one flight you couldn't afford to miss.

Kip arrived, and I inquired, "How long could the helos keep it up?" He responded to my absolute delight and relief, "All night if necessary!"

Upon hearing this, my heart started to return to its arrhythmic normalcy, when the word was passed that we would be leaving in five minutes!

Not only for the first time in my life did I *not care where in the hell I was going*, and at that, it was none too soon for me!

It turned out that the PACV communications officer, no, not Sparks, but a ragin' Cajun named Randy from one of those parishes outside New Orleans, who communicated in another language only Fleming seemed to understand, had made contact with a small helo base located just on the other side of the bay.

The base turned out to be only twenty kilometers away, and once under way, we could be there in fifteen to twenty minutes depending on the wind, and therefore the wave action.

They could accommodate us for up to forty-eight hours based upon the supplies on hand, even though we had only asked for twenty-four. They had a ramp of sorts that would allow the three craft easy access to the base grounds.

By the time I had put all this together, Fleming had given the order to "shove off" as incoming mortar rounds and sporadic gunfire continued. It was none too soon for me as once again I was armed with pad and pencil!

As we proceeded north into what was known as Vung Tau Bay, we turned around to witness the sky around the base aglow with the light being given off from what seemed to be about thirty or more flares floating slowly in the night air casting bluish glowing light toward the ground. Gun flashes could be seen on three sides of the base.

Kip worried about Sammy the cook, who we had to leave behind. Regulations! I had once called him Charlie the cook, which he didn't particularly favor. It was my not too subtle way of telling him, "I don't care who your nighttime employer is." In case he thought he was pulling a fast one over on us.

My Cornell buddy—LTJG Kip Kumler

Kip obviously thought I had figured Charlie wrong and worried about his safety. At this point, I was more worried about my safety. In what had seemed longer than twenty minutes, we arrived at our new temporary base, which the locals had named Truong Doc, but I couldn't locate on our maps . . . not that it mattered, except perhaps for this book!

By noon the next day, paratroop elements of the US Army's 173rd Airborne Division, better known by most "in country people" as the Air Cavalry, had moved into the peninsula—some by chopper landing in the immediate area of Cat Lo—and formed a "protective ring" around the base. They and the 101st AirCav paratrooper divisions were some of our best!

There was the initial nasty business of cleaning up the area where the fighting had occurred the night before, making sure that those elements of the VC that were "left behind" were in fact left behind for good, before darkness set in again.

Upon our return to Cat Lo forty-eight hours later, the men put on the finishing touches for the transit to the Plain of Reeds. Game Warden HQ in Can Tho had reported two different entry points from the Bassac River and had offered helo coverage for the trip—which was sweet of them.

Fleming and I weren't worried as much about the VC during the transit to Muc Hoa as we were about those tall reeds the craft were to encounter once having entered the Plain itself. Vectoring, or direction from the air, with the helo's superior vantage point at least 500 feet or more in altitude above the plain, should prove to be a great help. Several radio frequencies had been arranged in advance so that continuous contact could be maintained between air and the ground units.

I wasn't going to chance it another night at Cat Lo, 173rd AirCav Division[*] or not, and after some last-minute double-checking, got my ass the hell out of there. Besides, I was beginning to think egotistically that my ass was worth more to my country at this stage of the game than losing it at Cat Lo.

---

[*]   The 173rd, along with the 101st and 82nd, Airborne Divisions were some of our best, if not the best, US Army combat divisions operating in 'Nam.

PACV 3 stops to inspect junk on the My Tho River.

Upon my return to Saigon, I once again bypassed CDR Bronson as he had made it clear by his lack of enthusiasm for this exercise in the Plain of Reeds, that it was at best "a needless diversion" from the main task at hand. I did not.

I didn't agree with Bronson as I felt we could "kill two birds" with this operation. One, it would reinforce my premonition that the enemy's major supply routes were originating from inside and along the Cambodian border—just like our "CIDG friends" had reported.

Secondly, we had unearthed, quite by accident, a new type of mission for the ACVs: shallow draft swamp patrol through and over seemingly impenetrable terrain, which was considered off-limits to other naval patrol craft and therefore overlooked by the USN.

The morning following my return, I slipped over to Navy HQ where I intended to check on our requests for helo coverage. The admiral learned of my presence and called me into his office.

Seemingly not the least bit disturbed, the "old man" looked as if he had some fatherly advice to extend to me. I was "all ears" as he related how he had initiated an interim summary report on Game Warden Ops and its future plans through CINCPACFLT in Hawaii to CAPT Savadkin in OP-93 at the Pentagon. Savadkin was the officer who granted my "preposterous requests" way back in the early days of my accepting this assignment in the first place. The admiral went on to explain that apparently word had reached as far as Arlington, Virginian, that commencement of the Plain of Reeds mission was imminent.

What couldn't have gotten back to CNA was that I intended to accompany the first patrol out of Muc Hoa. The reason for their not knowing was clear . . . I hadn't asked permission. I knew better than to do that . . . It would have been denied!

ADM Veth didn't have to add since word about the impending mission was getting to be common knowledge around the halls of both my shop and the "puzzle palace," which he thought he had better extend the courtesy to Dr. Bothwell at CNA. He added that the report endorsed my plan for setting up a network of enemy supply routes in the Delta in an attempt to predict likely river crossing points for our riverine assets to preferentially patrol. Just today, he had sent out a supplementary advisory to both CNO and OP-93 (this meant the big cheeses) notice of our planned operations in the Plain of Reeds.

I could only surmise that my world, and for that matter anyone and everyone that mattered to my boss and CNA and had the usual "need to know," were tuned into developments as they occurred.

My first response was to thank him profusely while carefully maintaining my composure as I didn't want him to read any lack of confidence or resolve in my demeanor. Inside, I must admit, my stomach was churning a bit.

I also detected a "little push back" on this to me, placing the origin of this whole mess squarely at my doorstep, although at his level there wasn't really anywhere for him to go!

I figured if he was trying to pass the buck on this, there wasn't really anyone for him to pass to!

At this juncture in the meeting, I thought it was time to both advise him of the critical nature of having the helo coverage to vector the ACVs around those tree lines. After he matter-of-factly assured me those assets and backup plans were in place, plus all our other requests were being met, I went for the big enchilada!

"Admiral, as a personal favor to me, seeing as it's only a few days more until Thanksgiving, could you arrange for me to fly to Muc Hoa on one of those choppers you're arranging for?"

I saw an affirmative smile break out across his face as he knew I was, in a not too subtle way, assuring their "on-time delivery." I added, "With a load of turkey dinners for the men!"

I didn't have to tell him that this was a big request as we were talking over fifty dinners. That's a lot of turkeys to be flown in from Manila or Tokyo plus all the fixings, although I imagine this was a drop in the bucket to what his overall requirements must have been.

Holiday time in the war zone or anywhere away from home and the family is a very tough time for the sailor or soldier and is treated very attentively by the commanding officers in charge. *It was a close second to mail!*

135

His response, with a broad friendly grin was, "You've done a good job so far. We're depending a great deal on your plan and the entire USN command, up to CNO, and probably the joint chiefs are watching this project."

Don't let us down! I answered quickly, "Yes, sir . . . of course, sir! What about the turkeys?" "Of course, . . . *you've got em!*"

Just two days before Thanksgiving, I received word to get ready to report to Bien Hoa Air Base on eight hours' notice. This base was just about ten miles farther from Saigon than Tan Son Nhut, directly north of the city. A phone call to my newly found friends on the admiral's staff commandeered a Navy jeep to ferry me to Bien Hoa the next day.

On this same day, Navy HQ informed Bronson that they had received a message from the PACV command.

It read, "ARRIVED PLANNED DESTINATION 1500 hrs. Nov. 21—WITHOUT INCIDENT. TERRAIN POSES NO PROBLEM. ADVISE WHEN TO EXPECT OTHER SUPPORT UNITS. WE ARE READY!" CDR Fleming

Phew! . . . . Round one over . . . what a relief!

Equipped with the usual two legal pads, a tape recorder, two pairs of sunglasses, and a soft camouflaged jungle cap that neatly folded into my pants pocket, my trip into "the last century and Muc Hoa" began. I felt ready too!

Aussie paratroopers at Bien Hoa Airbase

Bien Hoa Air Base was as chaotic as I had found Tan Son Nhut several months earlier. Clearly, a military buildup of significant proportions was under way. CH-47 Chinooks and Cobra attack copters were lined up carrying men and supplies heading out to the north and east. This was the Navy's main airbase in the entire south and home for the helicopter squadrons known as HAL-3 (helicopter attack light).

Lined up on the tarmac, in a separate queue, were two Navy Huey gunships, mounted with automatic firing systems capable of discharging up to 550 rounds per minute. That's a lot of firepower! The sailors code-named them Seawolves. It seemed that other than the crew, a load of 40 mm mortar shells, and a generous supply of turkey dinners in freezer packs, I was the only passenger, except for CAPT Stephen Lewis. I hadn't met Lewis before in all my meetings at HQ, but upon some reflection figured that he was assigned as a briefing officer by ADM Veth to report directly back to HQ on the conduct of this mission. It wouldn't have surprised me that he had "an intel background" and was brought in for an "up close and personal" fresh look at things.

Under the heading that two heads are better than one, given the fact that all our requests had been filled, plus the turkeys, I had "no *squawk* coming!"

It wasn't more than thirty minutes after liftoff that we arrived at Muc Hoa. We flew across the early-morning moisture-laden sky, over the Plain of Reeds "a mite slower than usual" due to the payload we were carrying and arrived to what once again appeared to be a well-anticipated luminary's welcome.

Aerial view of Plain of Reeds and Muc Hoa

The welcome erupted into a genuine handclapping, high-fiving, uproarious affair, when the turkey dinners were off-loaded. I received many a slap on the back for it. Besides, I was looking forward to that white meat and stuffing, with cranberry sauce as much as anyone. It was my first T-Day away from home since college days some ten to twelve years earlier when we usually were on a trip to some early season basketball tournament or stuck at school practicing for the season that was just getting under way.

The next day, after a night spent exchanging an update on how well the ACVs had handled the terrain crossing the Plain and some serious beer-drinking Turkey Day at Muc Hoa was enjoyed by all—Spartan as it might have been and homesick as we were.

That night, after listening to an NFL football game rebroadcast over Armed Forces Radio from Dallas, which at this point—the game had been played the day before—we settled down to some serious planning of our first patrol scheduled for early the next day!

I was assigned a lower bunk berth for my overnight stay at the "Muc Hoa Hilton." At 6:00 a.m. I was startled by the sound of a bugle blaring in the pitch dark of a humid equatorial morning. Thinking we were under attack, I awoke with a start and banged my head on the underside of the bunk above me, cutting my forehead slightly.

I became the only sailor in 'am slightly wounded during reveille!

The next morning we were presented with a dilemma. One big proviso had presented itself: had the second Navy gunship arrived from Bien Hoa? We weren't going to chance it with one helo, just in case. The pilots that flew CAPT Lewis and myself to Muc Hoa assured us they had been in contact with the other crew and they would be arriving late in the morning. It figured they had wanted to celebrate T-Day at Bien Hoa. I couldn't blame them! No one, in their right mind, would want to spend more time in Muc Hoa than was necessary.

We waited as long as we could for the second chopper, and after being informed it was leaving Bien Hoa in the next few minutes, we decided to get the show on the road!

CAPT Lewis stayed behind in Muc Hoa awaiting the arrival of the second chopper. That was fine with me as it served as insurance that the helo would show!

Naturally, without CAPT Lewis in tow . . . we headed straight for the *Cambodian border!*

Last-minute checklists were checked, including the skies to the southeast of us for incoming traffic, and we got the show on the road. All three of the craft and the helo above us established radio contact and decided upon an alternate frequency for Mayday and other emergency use. The helo flew about 400 to 500 yards ahead of us as we proceeded across the well-anticipated checkered treelined plain. *See pictures on page 96.*

As we approached the dreaded tree lines of the Plain of Reeds, with not only their enormous height cutting off our visibility for more than 1,000 yards but also density, I was reminded of the hedgerows of Normandy, France.

In that campaign, after D-day in June 1944, as Allied forces advanced inland from the beaches of Normandy, they encountered rows of heavy underbrush, not as tall as these tree lines but similarly laid out in checkerboard fashion, which served as a haven for Nazi gun emplacements from which they conducted both lines of defense and ambushes.

In our case, the open flat expanse of water between the lines of trees, albeit spotted with patches of the Plain's reeds, neither served as protection nor camouflage to assist us from being detected. This placed the ACVs out in open, creating dangerous fields of fire for any ambush.

And so it was, some three miles from what we thought might be the Cambodian border, we encountered our first problem. I was in the command boat with Fleming and Kip Kumler, flanked on both sides for a few hundred yards by the other two crafts as we emerged from a small opening in one tree line and started across the open expanse of reeds and swamp water, to the next tree line. The second helicopter had not yet arrived, but through communication with Zebra Romeo, the handle on the helo hovering above us, there was no indication of any problem ahead of us. The first indication of which was when small arms fire started splattering around us, about halfway across the open area between the tree lines.

Jonesy was our .50 caliber machine gunner, who we had nicknamed Jones of Chicago, sitting about twenty feet above the personnel cabin in the gun turret located atop the craft. He opened up with return fire while we notified the chopper of the approximate location of the source of the automatic gunfire. It appeared to be coming from Russian AK-47s, which was the enemy's answer to our M-16s.

We immediately picked up speed and headed straight for that point, thus affording Charlie as small a silhouette as possible for a target.

Fleming had Randy on the radio directing Alpha and Tango (our other craft) around the tree line from opposite directions, outflanking any force that might be held up in these trees.

Not knowing what to expect, Tim, who was manning the grenade launcher, was told by Fleming to load and prepare to fire on command. Tim, who was from a small town in Wisconsin, was our

141

youngest at twenty-one and our most accurate gunner, winning most of the contests back at Cat Lo for cases of beer when things were slow, which had been most of the time.

Tim fired for effect and created an amazingly close hit on the area we had spotted as the source of the gunfire as Jones of Chicago placed another burst of machine-gun fire into the same area. Those .50 caliber bullets could cut down a tree four to six feet in diameter at a distance of 1,000 meters! In this case, it was clearly better "to give rather than receive."

Zebra Romeo cackled that there appeared to be no other sign of enemy activity behind this line of trees and was going down for "a closer look," for us to cover them with some strafing fire.

Our chopper swooped down over the tops of the thirty-foot high trees, guns blazing, "did a one eighty" and returned from a different angle this time with their guns silent.

Helos accompany ACVs around the Plain of Reeds

Cackle . . . cackle . . . came the interference over Zebra Romeo's ADF Radio to PACV Command. "We see no signs of life in target area . . . suggest you confirm your intention to investigate . . . Over."

PACV Command . . . *cackle* . . . to Zebra Romeo . . . "We're going in for a look-see . . . cover our backs" . . . cackle . . . "Roger and out."

After nearly putting the craft within one hundred feet of the tree line, Fleming radioed Alpha and Tango to each send in our CIDG friends, Haiching and Wang Hsiang, who were aboard the other two craft, to investigate.

While we were awaiting their findings, the sound of familiar chopper engines were heard in the distance—the second helo was in the process of joining us, and for some reason, perhaps strength in numbers, everyone seemed to breathe a little easier. *In combat, it's never good to have "one of anything!"*

With their combined firepower in the air above us, coupled with what we added from the surface and our relative speed of reaction to any unfriendly incident, we presented a *formidable force.*

"Zebra Romeo reporting to PACV Command . . . Two VC dead at single gun emplacement . . . no other enemy present or sighted . . . no radios . . . apparently sentries for something ahead . . . Advise . . . Over."

Fleming and Kip conferred and answered, "PACV Command suggests you proceed . . . one to two clicks ahead of us . . . to reconnoiter the area on heading of zero to twenty degrees . . . We will fan out separated by five hundred meters or about 300 yards, with command ship 180 degrees from your intended flight path and follow you . . . . Out."

The premise, helos vectoring ground units with our speed and firepower, was about to be put to the test. Certainly we had one of the most important provisions of battle in our favor . . . *surprise*!

The pilots of the two Navy Huey's apparently agreed with Jack Fleming's plan and within a few minutes cackled back over the radio, "Unidentified motorized sampan convoy of significant numbers, on a heading of 180 degrees, directly for us, at a speed of approximately ten knots . . . Advise . . . Over."

Immediately Fleming replied, "Break contact until size of convoy and possible armed escorts present . . . Out."

"Affirmative, Roger," came the reply. "Advise us disposition of your craft . . . Over."

As amazing as it may seem to you now, my reaction to all this was simple. Not only was this fun *so far*, but it looked as if we may have *hit the jackpot*!

Fleming was in touch with the two other craft, Alpha and Tango, indicating the position and heading of the sampan convoy and assigning Alpha the task of taking on the lead sampans from the end of a given tree line. Similarly, Tango was to attack the last third of the convoy and any stragglers, while maintaining no more than a 500-meter separation between themselves and the command craft. Aboard the command craft, we would attack the middle of the convoy, keeping ourselves the same distance from the Alpha boat. I was concerned that Fleming might have thought he was GEN Robert E. Lee at Gettysburg, attacking the center of the Union's defenses, assuming it was "weak in the middle." And we all know how that worked out. Since we were all on the same radio frequency, our fly boys upstairs were "on board" and indicated they understood the plan of attack.

We waited . . . with our engines at as low an RPM as possible . . . while still maintaining our cushion beneath us. When the convoy spotted the helos, they would think the engine noise was emanating from them and not have "an inkling" what awaited them.

The five minutes it took for the first elements of the VC convoy to appear in our vantage point through an opening in the tree line *seemed like an eternity*.

Most of us had been waiting for this moment for a long time!

Zebra Romeo to PACV Command cackled to the radio: "Estimate enemy strength at 100 to 120 sampans, none appear heavily armed, *however, two escort sampans . . . armed!* One armed escort just ahead, on far side of convoy. The other on near side at the rear."

"Suggest we take out lead escort . . . PACVs, the other . . . Roger."

Jack Fleming concurred ASAP as he did not want any part of sending one of our vehicles on the far side of the convoy, directly into our field of fire.

This long-awaited firefight got off to a rousing start as both ACV—Alpha and one of the gunships—opened up with automatic fire on the leading sampans in the convoy, and one of the choppers fired a rocket at the more heavily armed escort on the far side of the convoy.

By the looks of the evasive action, the helos were receiving return fire. It didn't appear Alpha had been detected as Charlie was predictably looking skyward. Confirmed by our ADF radio, Fleming ordered ACV Alpha to head straight for the convoy as the resistance being offered by the sampans was that of ineffective small arms fire.

Less than thirty seconds later, we spotted the main elements of the convoy breaking ranks so to speak and scattering, heading to a distant tree line. With that, Fleming radioed Zebra Romeo to take pursuit of this "splinter element" with the second gunship as we were going in to make contact with the main elements of the convoy before they became too dispersed. At this point, ACV Tango contacted us, informing us that the rear section of the convoy "was hightailing back toward the border." Fleming immediately gave the order to "pursue and destroy wherever that would take them and that we would join them ASAP.

Did you ever play pickup sticks? To begin the game, one empties an oblong cylindrical canister of long sharply pointed splintery sticks on to the floor in a randomly formed heap. Each player, using one of these sticks, tries to pick any stick out of this heap, without disturbing any of the other sticks. The player that recovers the most sticks in this manner wins!

That heap of sticks is what this VC convoy was rapidly turning into!

The enemy's return fire was quickly becoming more sporadic and dwindling to occasional sniping, and little, if any, mortar incoming.

By this time, radio contact with ACV's Alpha and Tango confirmed that although some small-caliber arms fire was being received, no incoming rockets or mortar rounds were being taken . . . That is, until a huge explosion in the water some twenty yards from our starboard side sent a plume of water some twenty-five feet skyward!

In the middle of Zebra Romeo reporting that the VC escort on the far side of the convoy had been destroyed, Tim, our mortar grenade launcher, informed Kip that Jonesy had been hit.

In all the confusion and rapid-fire action, no one had noticed that our .50 caliber machine gun had not been heard firing in the last minute or so. Sure enough when Tim went up into the gun turret, Jones of Chicago was holding his right shoulder.

Quickly the crew got Jonesy down into the cabin and tore his shirt off to see remnants of mortar shrapnel had entered his upper shoulder area, no bones appeared broken, and our lone medic crew member started the process of stopping the bleeding and bandaging the wound.

Tim quickly took Jonesy's place up in the machine gun turret.

The combined firepower of our force was too much for the enemy, especially when combined with the fact that we had just turned the tables on Charlie—ambushing him. He was finally getting a taste of his own medicine!

The forward two-thirds of this one-hundred-sampan convoy now looked like those pickup sticks. And with that, Fleming ordered ACV Alpha to remain behind to assure themselves that we were in for no surprises from what was left of our end of the convoy. Once satisfied, he was to rejoin us!

He then contacted ACV Tango in pursuit of the remainder of the convoy busily fleeing back into Cambodia. We all looked at each other and had the same thought at once.

"Let's go get 'm!"

"Zebra Romeo, we are leaving ACV Alpha to mop up . . . vector us toward ACV Tango and the remainder of convoy . . . Over."

At full throttle, we took off straight north, on a 360-degree heading toward the Cambodian border, leaving longitude and latitude designations off the radio transmissions between us, with the gunships above, once again in the lead.

The combined effectiveness of our collective speed and ability to react to changing circumstances in the field was creating a new dimension in small-boat naval warfare . . . limited in scope as it might have been.

The scene now began to appear like a grade B cowboy movie, with the good guys in hot pursuit of the bad guys . . . *only no horses*!

In all sports, including this one, if there is a mismatch in speed, the slower player or team is in big trouble. As the two ACVs—the command craft and ACV Tango—sped across the open plain sweeping away the four-foot reeds in their path, they quickly closed in on the exiting motorized sampans.

"Zebra Romeo to PACV Command, main body of convoy on heading due north, out in the open, traveling at ten to fifteen knots, about two clicks away. We will mop up stragglers on a more northeasterly path. We are leaving our radio on . . . Out." PACV Command, "We acknowledge . . . good hunting . . . Out." As we gained on our prey, I noticed Kip furiously taking notes and marking down several coordinates, which turned out to be either VC base camps or staging areas, apparently deserted at this point in time, but we suspected not at other times—*Luckily for us!*

It only took between a few minutes for it to be all over. Tim must have thought he was in a shooting gallery as wood was splintering and swamp water was splattering. Charlie met his untimely demise.

Then someone, and I forgot who made the point, seeing these small installations appearing with more frequency, as we finished off the last of the "exiting VC sampans," that we just might, perhaps, be in Cambodia.

Kip responded with a broad boyish smile, like a kid that had just been caught with his finger in his mother's freshly baked pie, that we crossed the border—if in fact there was one in these swamps—about five minutes ago.

That placed us about ten kilometers inside Cambodia or outside SVN depending upon your frame of reference. Nobody seemed to care, and we proceeded to finish the job at hand.

Author and Kip Kumler take pictures of each other from
UH—1E helo to PACV 2—Plain of Reeds

PACV's hover on full cushion on Muc Hoa airstrip—Plain of Reeds

If we had someone from the JCS (Joint Chiefs of Staff) on board, it might have changed the course of the war. I would have settled for the CNO, but it was not to be. "Mission Accomplished," no matter where you are sounds good to me!

In that instant, it flashed across my mind, what the Israeli tank commanders must have been thinking during the Six-Day War as they chased and routed the Egyptian First Army across the Negev to the eastern shores of the Red Sea. I doubt if they cared precisely where they were!

In one short morning, which by now was fast becoming afternoon, noticing the blazing sun high overhead, we had proven that the VC were using Cambodia as a main sanctuary from which to conduct the war south of Saigon, and for all we knew, upon Saigon itself.

Upon hearing from the choppers that they had met with similar success in cleaning up the remnants of the convoy, Fleming looked at me, and reading my mind simultaneously, broadcasted over the radio, "Let's get the hell out of here . . . a place we've never been . . . Over."

It was just about this time, I began to have thoughts I never thought I would have. A cold beer and the dust and yesterday of Muc Hoa started sounding very good to me!

Besides, there was the small matter of getting Jones of Chicago medevac'd, out of here and back to Bien Hoa ASAP. Although when Jonesy started complaining about the lack of cold beer aboard, we knew he was going to be all right!

I think it was LTJG Sampson who offered the lamebrained idea that maybe we should stop off and investigate one of these staging areas or base camps on the way back to Muc Hoa.

I liked Jeff despite his having a "football player mentality" at times, and after eyeballing Fleming and Kip, we collectively couldn't hold back a big smile, as if to say, "Are you out of your f— mind?"

Aside from probably being heavily booby-trapped, I think the appropriate phrase of the day, and even more so in this instance, "You have to know when to quit when you're ahead!"

Fleming, trying to humor Sampson, said, "Let's talk about it over a cold one—after we get back!"

I reminded Fleming and Kip that there remained a not-so-small matter of coordinating our stories with the helo pilots, as it would allow me to take up the matter of locating the mission site with HQ in Saigon at another time . . . later! For the time being, we were never there, coordinates and all!

Besides, the success of this mission didn't depend upon our actual interdiction of the enemy inside Cambodia. We all knew where they were coming from.

On a broader perspective, there were a few other matters to consider:

Now all that aimless Swift Boat and PBR patrolling was instantly put into perspective. The longer one waited for the enemy to distribute contraband into his network and disperse it—the more difficult it would be to interdict it. Not unless of course, you knew its destination, which with the VC constantly on the move, remained highly problematical.

In this case, other than blockading its source, trail(s) or port(s) of entry, *intercepting and disrupting the supply chain before it entered the distribution network*, i.e., the Delta's canal system and the tributaries of the Mekong, was the preferred course of action.

The notion of blockading Sihanoukville had been left on the admiral's desk, most likely to die a lonely death as it represented an act of widening the war, in direct contravention to the wishes of those directing the conduct of the war.

Remaining in a defensive posture within the borders of SVN was the order of the day! Offensive tactics were limited to long-range bombing missions and "search and destroy" tactics conducted mainly in country.

As far as I was concerned, these tactics didn't have a chance! Did you ever ask yourself the question, knowing the war was being mismanaged, how to change it? Not easy!

Not then and not now!

Be that as it may, my mind reverted to the present, and I asked Fleming to make sure we "huddled with the helo crews" upon our return to base. I wanted to make damn sure we were all on the same page!

That is, to emphasize the success of interdicting such a formidable force, where it was obviously coming from, the totality of their destruction, *and above all, where the combat took place!*

I think it comes under the heading of "staying focused!"

As the helos preceded us back to Muc Hoa, we arrived to "a heroes welcome." It wasn't exactly a ticker tape parade down Broadway, but to us, it was! To a man, we felt that sort of smugness and sense of accomplishment, knowing we had outsmarted the enemy! It was as the saying goes, *"a job well done!"*

We exchanged war stories over a few cold ones awaiting the medevac helo coming in for Jones of Chicago, who was having such a good time embellishing his account of being "wounded in battle," that he reluctantly bid us adieu as he set out for the clean sheets of the military hospital in Saigon. Funny animal . . . war. He was in for some serious R&R and often dreamed about pampering, and he didn't want to leave the guys, especially with all this celebrating going on. Funny animal . . . war!

As leftovers were being prepared from the T-Day celebration the day before, I couldn't help drifting off mentally to the meeting with the admiral and his staff, which was bound to take place tomorrow in Saigon and was the next shoe to drop!

I was sure he was going to ask me to immediately get started on speeding up the process of putting the rest of my plan in motion . . . and that was not going to get me home any time soon!

My six-week spin in the Orient had now become almost five months! I was starting to wonder if I would be able to recognize the kids upon my return . . . It was no joke!

After dinner, with the celebration going strong and our briefing with the helo crews completed, I decided to shake up Jack Fleming and Kip Kumler.

I informed them that they were returning to Saigon with me to see the admiral! You should have seen their faces! I made it clear that there could easily be questions relating to the conduct of the mission, particularly the aspect of the efficiency and effectiveness of the helo vectoring, which they would be far more qualified to answering than me.

Secondly, and most importantly, I was interested in seeing them getting a promotion . . . That's the way it is in combat!

The phone rang at 8:30 a.m. in Dr. Bothwell's office in Arlington, Virginia. It was CAPT Savadkin, OP-93, telling Bothwell's secretary to pull him out of his early morning staff meeting.

As the head of the US Navy's think tank picked up the phone, he sensed this call was not only important, but was related to the mission undertaken in the Plain of Reeds. He decided to skip the pleasantries and asked, "How did it go, Captain?"

The news that the PACVs had hit a home run, intercepting an armed one-hundred-sampan convoy coming into the Plain from Cambodia and had completely destroyed it, without any casualties, except for one wounded . . . poor Jonesy . . . hit CNA like a thunderbolt!

Bothwell asked only two questions of Savadkin.

Is CNO informed of this, and is Wilens OK?

One, CNO is more than pleased and wishes you to know, he has informed the joint chiefs, and they have already ordered him to proceed full bore with the remainder of Operation Steam Shovel!

Secondly, not only is Wilens OK, but he had accompanied the PACVs on the mission and will be filing a report directly to you!

Dr. Bothwell thanked CAPT Savadkin for the update and told him he would get back to him upon receipt of Wilens' report and hung up.

Bothwell returned to his staff meeting to announce the news and asked for recommendations from them, by the end of the day, as to how CNA could exploit this news—as finally "we can point to our usefulness to the war effort," aside from reviewing and analyzing the bombing sorties in the north.

The staff's recommendations were submitted for review before the end of the day. It reflected a divided opinion that centered upon two distinctly different points of view.

One view was to keep Wilens in Vietnam until the completion of the present operation as this could be "just the beginning of something big," and not so incidentally, beneficial to CNA. Secondly, get "Wilens the Cowboy" home and out of harm's way, before we lose him, and the accomplishments we've already attained are lost. This too was analogous to "quit while you're ahead!" Among Bothwell's advisors was Doc Colladay, my best friend at CNA. Doc was called upon for his advice as his relationship to me was well known.

Doc, torn between knowing damn well I wanted to get home by this time and that Bothwell knew his opinion would be affected by his relationship with me, came up with a compromise solution. "Since Wilens' value to the cause" will be maximized best by achieving success of the broader objectives associated with Operation Steam Shovel, we should leave it up to him and Admiral Veth, on the ground, as is often said. They will know best when the operation no longer needs his "on-site presence."

After all, daily message traffic was carrying op. data back to Washington, and analytical results were being returned on almost a real-time interactive basis through CINCPACFLT's office to Navy HQ in Saigon. Once we reach this point in the progression of the operation, "Let's get Wilens back ASAP!"

Dr. Bothwell thanked Doc Colladay for his perspective and wisdom, and Doc could see by the expression on his face that this compromise had struck an affirmative and receptive note with the chief.

And as if to say to Doc, "what else do you think we should do as you know him best of all of us, any other recommendations?"

Doc knowing that I liked to talk as well as travel—not necessarily to war zones—replied, "Show him off at every military installation in the country that you can get clearance for! You can pass him off as one of a kind!"

And so the die was cast . . . Thanks to Doc Colladay.

Plans were immediately set in motion, with Doc's advice as sort of a thank-you for his wisdom, to get me home before the present operations were completed and send me out on to what was then known as "the rubber chicken circuit".

Once again, Colladay had pulled me from the abyss of being lost on assignment in Vietnam and set the wheels in motion to extricate me from the trouble I had gotten myself into. What a guy!

Our helo had just set down at Bien Hoa airport, and as Fleming, Kumler, and I walked across the tarmac to the main control tower building, one of the admiral's adjutants met us with a smart salute and "Follow me, sir!"

There, staring us right in the face was the admiral's car, complete with driver and four-star flag flying from the right front fender. Not bad!

As we entered the admiral's office complex, we were greeted with a few high fives and pats on the back from his staff, some of whom we knew. Once inside his office, we were greeted by the admiral's inner sanctum of top advisors and a broad congratulatory smile on the ole man's face! It was "worth the price of admission," as the saying goes. Introductions all around proceeded, Fleming and Kumler receiving a hero's welcome, which I'm sure they would never forget. I gave the floor over to them, and they proceeded over the next twenty minutes to describe details of the mission and then asked for questions.

A deluge of questions ensued, as if the floodgates of some great dam project had opened, and Fleming and Kip handled them smartly, especially the part about how well the coordination between the ACVs and the helos, vectoring us about this particular type of terrain, had worked out. That is, until someone asked, "Had we encroached the border with Cambodia?"

All eyes turned to me, including the ole man's, and I replied, having known for the past twenty-four hours this question was coming. "I'm not sure, sir, perhaps." As if to say, without coming right out and saying it, who cares!

I quickly followed up with, "As you, gentlemen, know, during the heat of battle, the last thing we were concerned about when encountering the enemy in an ambush situation was what coordinates we had encountered the enemy, and where the combat that ensued was going to take us."

CAPT Lewis must have alerted him to the truth, despite arriving on the scene late. To everyone's amazement and relief, the admiral replied, "Good . . . Let's keep it that way!"

Which meant to me, and I could see Fleming's and Kip's agreeing smiles, the boss without specifically saying it was condoning our "cover-up!" Having gotten over this hurdle and other preliminaries, the meeting's participants got down to the serious business at hand, proceeding with Operation Steam Shovel!

And with this, a new member of the admiral's staff was introduced to us for the first time . . . it being LTCDR Ed Rodriguez from Charlotte, North Carolina. Ed was our intel officer in charge of receiving reports of VC movements in the Delta, from several different sources presently on the ground, whose identity they would rather keep *on a need-to-know basis* for the time being. He had been collating this information and forwarding it through CINCPACFLT, to our coworkers, particularly George Benson at CNA, for incorporation into their model of the Delta's network.

To date, results of the model's output have been "sketchy at best." We're getting some indication of potential hot spots along the Mekong and the Bassac but nothing very definitive, i.e., something we can plan a mission around, employing significant assets as we had hoped for.

At this point, Fleming and Kumler joined in with a great idea, which was in furtherance of something I had advised the admiral a few months before. That is, we need to have more information about the presence of sampan convoys, before they reach these major river crossing points.

This is precisely what our CIDG friends, Haiching and Wang Hsiang, had covered on their little sojourn into Cambodia and apparently had conveyed to Jack and Kip while they were together at Muc Hoa.

Instead of waiting for more precise results from the computer algorithm being compiled back in Arlington, why don't we insert into that model these various staging areas, located off river, as "destination points"?

Then, if George Benson can handle it as new input, treat these locations as "new points of origin" for transshipment of the contraband deeper into the network, basically compressing the network!

I liked this new twist in the modeling for two reasons. On the one hand it had to have the effect of speeding things up and get me home sooner while simultaneously tightening up the analyses, as the route alternatives for the enemy would become shorter and leave less room for error!

The downside, we were going to need more information, meaning intelligence, about these "off-river staging locations." The CIDG boys had come up with one of them . . . There had to be more! The key question of the meeting quickly became, "How can we assemble this info, quickly and reliably?" The answer would have to wait . . . It was lunchtime!

At lunch, in the officer's lunchroom of course, we exchanged war stories with Jack and Kip centerstage, relating how the helos had spotted the convoy from miles away and set Charlie up for the kill by positioning the PACVs for the ambush that ensued.

We also got to know more about Ed Rodriguez's activities, and sure enough, the more we exchanged views about each other's perspective on the problem at hand . . . we came up with a plan . . . just about the time the pie à la mode arrived. Navy-made, vanilla bean ice cream on freshly baked apple pie . . . just in from Pearl!

Everything came to a halt for a few minutes . . . as we all remembered home.

The basic premise of the plan was to combine our SEAL team operations with the CIDG group of operatives into a highly trained, formidable "recon team" to seek out the possible locations of these staging areas.

And where were they going to look? That was easy . . . where George, back at CNA, told us the heaviest and most often used routes the computer model was yielding thus far. This info would tell us where the enemy's staging areas were most apt to be located and the routes the VC were most likely to employ to get to them.

It was a perfect marriage of data gathering on the ground, combined with the technology and disciplined organization of database management. Military tactics and methodology for the future was inexorably evolving.

Author (center of photo) posses with arms around two CIDG mercenaries

Two VC prisoners—their last picture, somewhere in Cambodia

VIII

Preparing for Battle – A New Concept

Upon return to ADM Veth's office, I started off the basic proposition of the plan that had been developed over lunch stating that, if successful, could significantly shorten the time required to yield some results in interdicting the enemy supply routes. Fleming and Rodriguez concurred and asked that the head of the Navy SEAL teams in country be brought in for consultation.

After receiving the green light from the boss, seeing it was going to take at least forty-eight hours or more to set this plan in motion, I suggested Van Caan's on the Circle for Chinese dinner, and it appeared we were going to have a crowd as this was a treat for Jack and Kip, which few wanted to miss.

While bunks were being arranged for them, I opted out, as I had not been home, to the villa in Cholon, in days. I thought it wise to see if it was still there, and of course, find Nadine.

Fleming and Kip were catching a ride with the admiral's driver to the local Navy billet at the officers' club across town. I went that far with them in order to have a few words with them alone.

Over some cold Japanese beer—thick, creamy, and full bodied, which put American beer to shame. Kirin or Asahi I recall, we discussed, that once we received the go-ahead from HQ, what assets we would need to accomplish the task ahead of us.

Aside from everything Game Warden had to give, from PBRs to Swift Boats, the more firepower the better. But most importantly, gunships. The more helos the better, although so many of the Navy helos were in demand in the North, especially for search and rescue missions, pulling our pilots out of the Gulf of Tonkin and even over land. It was going to be a stretch getting the helos we needed.

Rodriguez offered to contact the commander of the HAL-3 helicopter squadron at Bien Hoa to see if he could get some choppers reassigned. This placed even more emphasis on CNA's computer model, pinpointing the most likely river crossing points.

There also remained the question of procuring SEAL team assets, which probably meant the admiral giving the order. So not surprisingly, the full force HQ's cooperation was going to be needed, and with that, Fleming and Kumler looked at me.

I accepted this responsibility with a nod, bringing to a conclusion a very successful day at HQ, and took off for Cholon by taxi. It was still light out—the heat and humidity of the day finally abating—barely.

As I entered the kitchen to see some of the SEALs hangin' out, I asked if anyone had seen Nadine in the past few days.

A smile broke out on the faces of the kids, as if to say, surprise, surprise, why don't you see for yourself? I quickly beat it upstairs to my bedroom to find Nadine sound asleep in one of those slip dresses that was easy to slide off.

Nadine, could not have expected me, so she awoke with a start, but quickly extended her arms in a welcome-home hug. There was the small question of "had she moved in, in my absence," or what . . . but having been away in the Reeds chasing Charlie, that was not what I had in mind, at least not now.

After a very quick shower, a cold one at that as the SEALs must have used up the hot water, and this was no time for a cold shower, I slid under the sheets for some much-needed R&R! Spending the next two hours with Nadine turned out to be more than I bargained for as she insisted, after sapping every ounce of energy I had left in me to resist her accompanying me to Van Caan's tonight and meeting the guys. Surprisingly, she said she had just been there with Harry during the week when I was down in the Delta and loved it. I fluffed it off as incidental information as Harry didn't represent a modicum of competition, nor did I draw anything from this admission, except that Harry needed some company for dinner, and why not a pretty one like Nadine?

This admission did give me the idea, that given who they were and how it might be something of a shock to some of them, I decided to cover up my relationship with Nadine by calling up Harry Conners.

"Harry," I practically pleaded into the half-assed French telephone unit, which could have doubled as a bad Rube Goldberg joke, "pick me up at 8:00 p.m. at my place in Cholon. We're going to Van Caan's with a group of guys from HQ and Nadine." I exhorted him to be on time and told him that Nadine was his date for the evening! "Don't protest, I'll tell you why when you get here."

Harry arrived fifteen minutes late, which wasn't bad for him or the way things went in this town. After I told him who the dozen or so people we were meeting for dinner were and where they were from, he understood—sort of—completely. "Besides, I hear you've been here with Nadine last week, so you've had some practice at it!" We had a good belly laugh over it, and I fluffed it off as just noise.

Nadine, needless to say, was the center of attention. Fleming and Kip went for the story hook, line, and sinker, keeping to aquatic terminology, even though Kip, naive Kip, thought she was pretty young for a man of Harry's age!

We ate and drank ourselves silly, with Nadine dancing with everyone but Harry, which seemed a little odd to everyone, when all of a sudden, three or four of Saigon's finest "white mice" burst into the main dining room chasing some poor bastard. That presented two problems: one, I was catching a little from Nadine under the table as she was sitting between Harry and I, and secondly, bullets were flying everywhere!

They pursued and raced across the dance floor, hopped over a table for four, and dove, literally dove, out the open second floor window! Although none of the pursuers followed suit, the shooting stopped. Then we all heard a resounding thud as the pursued hit the corrugated metal roof of the shop some twenty-five feet below.

As the waiters offered *sin loi*'s to everyone, the band struck up the tune, "East of the Sun and West of the Moon," by "it's Shearing you're hearing," and within seconds, things returned to normal as if nothing had happened!

Without missing a beat, Nadine, after helping us order some of the more nontraditional Chinese dishes, asked me to dance, and it was a slow one. Everyone at the table turned around to watch.

If I didn't know better, which maybe I didn't, Nadine pressed her body to mine as if she hadn't come three times this afternoon and placed her legs on either side of one of mine, proceeding to ride me like an unbroken bronco, to which the guys started whistling and applauding.

Apparently, Nadine wanted to blow her cover and let everyone know who she really was with, which for the time being, I couldn't figure out for the life of me. Either she was on an ego trip or was up to something else.

Dinner was scrumptious as usual, and Harry tried to pick up the tab, but I split it with him, and some of the guys from HQ followed us to the Continental Bar for a nightcap, including Jack and Kip.

As we rode across town half-gassed, I had a premonition that Harry had put her up to that little escapade on the dance floor, but why? Being totally confused by this time, I decided to sleep on it as it certainly could wait 'il morning.

For the life of me, I couldn't figure out Harry's motives. That was, until Harry brought it up at the Continental Bar when Nadine headed for the ladies' room. He said that he had nothing to do with it, but sensed Nadine was embarrassed in front of all those young guys, to be with an old codger like him. For the time being, I accepted his explanation, as Nadine approached us, returning a little more quickly than most women normally do. She didn't have to put all that crap on her face for starters.

God, she was beautiful. That straight long black hair streaming down her back, with shining eyes to match, giving her that sensuous Oriental look—it was just what the doctor ordered.

I couldn't wait to get back to the villa although we had a blast of a time with Harry, the PACV and the HQ guys. Given the fact that the Plain of Reeds and Muc Hoa were in the history books, and I needed some downtime before taking on this next caper. After all, one more success like the one we just pulled off, and someone back at CNA was going to wake up and ask for my return to the "salt mines!"

Hopefully that would be Doc as George would just as soon say I stay in 'am for the duration of the war!

As I left for the Compound the next morning, I didn't have to ask Nadine about whether she was moving in since having to shower and get dressed, it wasn't difficult to notice that I was sharing the bathroom and the closet with someone that wore some of the most provocative dresses imaginable, along with some other little things. And those bright-colored print dresses with a slit up the side clear to her behind. Well, what's a guy going do? If you can't fight 'm, join 'm!

There still remained the matter of last night, but Nadine was sleeping as I left for work, and I rationalized that it could wait!

I arrived at the Compound on a usual slow-starting Monday to find Bruce Bronson in a stew over something. I inquired if I could help. "You sure can," snapped CDR Bronson. "We've been assigned the job by HQ to assemble the joint SEAL-CIDG force to reconnoiter the canal systems off the main tributaries in the Delta." The mission, he announced as if he was making news, was to ferret out other off-river way stations, villages, or bases like the one the CIDG had just uncovered just north of Can Tho. Bruce didn't know where to start, so I pushed him over the cliff so to speak and said, "Have HQ call the commander that heads up the SEALs. Let's allow him to figure it out, and he will be in a position to commandeer the force complement of CIDG'ers and SEALs we are going to need. Contact Ed Rodriguez and tell him we're going to need his help, in contrast to reassigning the job!"

CDR Bruce Bronson thought this was a good idea and got on the horn immediately and asked for LTCDR Rodriguez. I went to get some Navy coffee and read the *Saigon News* to see who had been kidnapped over the weekend. There I saw the notice of the Independence Day parade to be held in downtown Saigon, scheduled for late October, around Halloween time back in the States.

I forgot who I told in the office that I wouldn't miss it for the world, seeing I could borrow Harry's SLR Nikon, with all the lenses, including a telephoto with a 2x converter, making it a 350 mm lens. To my surprise, I was told that civilians were banned from attending it as the VC had announced they were going to bomb it, which meant mortars!

166

I made up my mind right then and there, seeing I wasn't going to be around for the next one, I hoped, and that I was going on the QT!

Bronson got Ed on the phone, and Rodriguez cooperating, contacted CDR Rob Grummond, chief, USN SEAL forces, IV Corps, and had him coming into HQ at 1400 hours. We were to be there. So much for a leisurely Monday lunch, but at least we could eat at HQ's officers' club, which softened the blow of having to start the week so quickly.

Grummond was all business and surprisingly young for his rank. He must have been through some crap in his job as the SEALs were known for an inordinately high rate of casualties—and as a result, had no-nonsense guys. He was no exception and couldn't have been a day over thirty.

What at first appeared to start out as a lengthy meeting came to a screeching halt when it was determined we didn't have enough information to either estimate the size and complement of our search teams or where we would deploy them.

I suggested I contact George Benson at CNA to get a feel for the where, as the algorithm he had built in our computer should be yielding some results by this time. I asked Ed Rodriguez to conference the call with his office as there might be some questions about the intel he was feeding back to Arlington that would need clarification.

We agreed to meet later that night as George would probably not be in the office until 9:00 to 10:00 p.m. our time, at best. In the meantime, the group batted around possible force strength and search and rescue arrangements in case we needed Seawolves to come to the rescue.

After dinner at the officers' club, Ed and I sent everyone home as he and I could handle it from there. Although I was looking forward to getting to the villa at a decent hour, of course!

It wasn't until after midnight Saigon time before we were able to contact George Benson busily sifting through troop deployment data in CNA's computer room. We needed a temperature—and humidity-controlled room in those days to house the computer whose power didn't match that of a modern-day laptop.

George observed that the algorithm was indicating three to four potential high-yielding river crossing points, but asked for forty-eight hours to review what off-river staging areas showed the most promise.

Ed, Rob, and I were satisfied and agreed to meet the day after tomorrow to make our final decision as to where the search teams were most likely to meet with success. In the meantime, Grummond would contact the local CIA office about the availability of CIDG participants, while he would set his staff in motion to consider the question, how many and who the SEALs could spare for this undertaking.

It wasn't a question that this mission was any more dangerous than others currently under way, but rather a question of priorities, something the admiral's staff or the old man himself would have to decide.

George Benson, with Bothwell's OK, replied in quicker than usual time and outlined four possible missions: three along the Bassac and Mekong in Kien Giang and An Giang provinces, the fourth in the southeastern region of the Plain of Reeds, near Ap Bac, and less than ten miles from our base at My Tho!

We thanked George for his assistance and indicated that Ed Rodriguez would continue to feedback to him the results of our reconnoitering in these various off-river sites.

CDR Grummond indicated that his staff had recommended three or four search teams of twenty-five men per team, which would include six to eight CIDG personnel, working in pairs of two per team. Navy HQ would assign one military intelligence operative per team. Each team would be working closely with a Seawolf and in close contact with Navy A-37 fighter plane squadron, based at Bien Hoa.

Inserting these teams entailed a high degree of risk as the likelihood of ambush was great, not that the Navy SEALs and CIDG'ers weren't used to it.

Many of the province or district chiefs and town elders and sometime mayors of small villages were either in the employ of the enemy or were the enemy themselves. Open retaliation by both the SEALs and CIDG were commonly known in country, but not back home.

Furthermore, it was decided to concentrate in one specific area at a time for two reasons. One, we didn't want to alert Charlie that this type of mission was going to be undertaken throughout the Delta.

Secondly, in case of trouble, big trouble, we could send one team in to save another, bringing to bear twice as many men to the scene and most importantly could concentrate our fighter-based assets in one particular flight path or zone, in order to maximize the firepower we could bring to bear, should we encounter a large enemy force.

The German military command or Wehrmacht used their highly mobile Panzer tanks in much the same manner during WWII.

Rodriguez and Grummond were to brief the admiral first thing in the morning and secure the go-ahead! I attended the meeting more as an observer, adding little to Ed and Rob's analysis of the mission as they understood it and, with an approving tilt of my head, kept reaffirming their analysis of the force levels they thought were required.

Once again, we were embarking on a newly tried operational procedure, relatively unfamiliar in the annals of naval warfare history . . . and dangerous.

The PACVs continued to operate out of Muc Hoa, running missions similar to the one ran on T-Day plus one, while they awaited orders from HQ.

The three of us left the admiral's office with his assurance "that everything would be done to fulfill our requirements as presented." In Vegas, they called it "pressing your bet," and why not, he was playing with the house's money at this point.

Having been given the green light by the admiral the next day, two search teams were inserted into the network of canals and villages, in Ba Xuyen province, some ten miles above Can Tho, and the other ten miles below Vinh Long, in An Giang province between the Bassac and the lower Mekong. *See map 4, page 93.*

These locations were in the heart of the Delta, in close proximity to each other, and represented new and fertile ground for our patrol forces, as in some cases, American forces had never appeared in these locations.

Search Team Alpha, commanded by a young LT Halvorsen, was inserted into the area above Can Tho by two Seawolves and was set out to establish a base camp just off one of the main canals. His squad was comprised of twenty-three men, including two CIDG'ers. They had an arsenal of weapons and ammo, enough to take on an enemy force of three to four times their size, but not more than that.

Consequently, from the get-go, arrangements had been made to contact backup forces at Can Tho only ten miles away, and if necessary, units at Vinh Long, some thirty miles away.

Direct contact with the Navy gunship squadron at Bien Hoa and A-37 Skyraiders with their phosphorous rockets was left up to the commanders in charge at those two bases.

Meanwhile, Search Team Bravo was inserted in the An Giang province about twenty miles to the southeast in what was considered by Navy HQ, after reviewing the computer reports from Benson at CNA, an alleyway between the Bassac and the Mekong Rivers, sometimes referred to the Hau Giang and Co Chien Rivers respectively.

This being the case, Team Bravo, commanded by LT Hannigan, was thirty-men strong and equipped with enough firepower to encounter a formidable enemy force. Part of their arsenal included an antitank weapon, a flamethrower and three grenade launchers, and a number of recoilless rifles. In addition, they possessed a generous cache of ammunition and closely resembled the makeup of a weapons company, although smaller in number. Teams Alpha and Bravo together resembled a platoon in size and firepower.

These precautions were necessary for two very good reasons. One, the teams were operating in virgin territory and didn't know what to expect, especially if they were interdicted by a large enemy convoy. Secondly, our intel was predicting that the force would encounter a significant amount of enemy traffic, which probably would not be unsupported.

In other words, we were out looking for trouble and were most likely to find it, *so we had better be prepared.*

Not that we needed any other reason to be prepared for the worst, it was the fact that there were a lot of important eyeballs watching this mission, right up to CNO, and who knew who else. This was no time for a f—up!

I returned to my cubbyhole at the Compound on the nondescript street and waited for some news. At this point, I had done everything I could do or think of. Furthermore, I knew better than to ask permission to accompany one of the search teams. I could figure out it was both unnecessary and too dangerous for HQ to even consider it.

At some point, over the next couple of days, as the teams were being inserted, Rodriguez and Grummond invited Bronson and myself to lunch. I wondered if this was important—a new twist—or just a courtesy visit.

Apparently these two men had been designated by the ole man to be the point men for his office, for this search-and-destroy mission—which had as an important secondary objective, to prove or disprove the theory behind Operation Steam Shovel.

Collectively, CNA and, less importantly, my ass were *sticking out a mile!*

It was the morning of the Independence Day parade, and things had slowed down a bit. I dressed a bit incognito and tried to blend in with the locals, chameleon-like. It was a beautiful, clear, sunny day—just perfect for picture taking, as I stealthily made my way over to the wide boulevard street that ran in an east-west direction and ultimately directly into the east gate of our embassy. Today it is known as Le Dua'n Street.

Independence Day parade. US civilians banned. Presidential palace.

South Vietnamese Navy (SVN), parade in their finest.

South Vietnamese premier kicks off parade.
Nice car. October 30, 1966.

Montagnard commander salutes American Review stand
and Vietnamese premier

Montagnard elephants march toward presidential palace.
South Vietnam's fiercest fighters.

Decorated vets parade. Overseen by Saigon's finest (White Mice).

Independence Day parade—Special Forces

South Vietnamese Marines and Paratroopers parade

South Vietnamese Nurse Corps

*South Vietnamese Cadets with red berets
from Dalat Academy—Vietnam's Westpoint*

Mortar explodes at parade. US naval officer killed.

Only about ten minutes before, I passed through an expansive open courtyard in front of a Catholic church located a few blocks from the site of the parade. As I said, it was a beautiful day, not one that anyone would expect to die on. A USN commander walking innocently through this treelined courtyard, its area equal to that of about three basketball courts, was struck by the ricochet of one these mortars. The VC had inadvertently fired it off the church's steeple. He was killed instantly.

One might ask why the Viet Cong would mortar their own people on a day comparable to our Fourth of July. The answer was that there was a built-in disdain, even an animosity between the people of the North and the South—the North clearly being more the industrialized center of the country, where the South being more agrarian, particularly because of the Delta and the general layout of the terrain.

Industrialized, better educated, and more industrious, the people north of the DMZ, especially in the heavily urbanized Haiphong and Hanoi areas "looked down their noses" upon the people of the South.

Their claim being that the South was mainly an agrarian society, not prone to being industrious in their work habits and looked upon them as second-class citizens.

I had no way to judge as I hadn't any exposure to the people of the North. I can say this, I wasn't crazy about the crowds of men gathered on many a downtown street corner, sitting on their haunches (like a baseball catcher), playing cards in midday, for hours at a time!

Sometimes we don't realize if you've lived until the mid-late seventies, those people who might remember more than you—are dead—and the people who are much younger than you weren't there! This makes you somewhat unique.

The weekend was fast approaching, and it didn't appear there was to be any further news until contact with some VC convoys was made. My thoughts were muddling this unexpected hiatus for *moi'*, when the phone rang, and it was Harry.

"What are you up to this weekend?" he said? "Nada," was my reply.

"I've cum-shaw'd. Two seats on a Navy plane taking some Marines from the Eighty-Seventh Division for some R&R to Bangkok, leaving tomorrow night, returning Sunday—a long weekend!"

After about fifteen seconds of thought, I said, "OK, let's go." Quickly, Harry indicated he had something going in Saigon this weekend and couldn't make it.

"Why don't you take Nadine? I'm sure she would love to see Bangkok."

My first thought was that of elation, but my second thought was one of suspicion. Why was Harry trying to promote this relationship with Nadine, or was I being a bit paranoid? No matter . . . a free trip to Bangkok with a beautiful woman reminded me of an old adage of "not looking a gift horse in the mouth."

Nadine couldn't pack fast enough! I decided to skip the formality of inquiring about her job etc. She was going—a team of horses couldn't.

Despite getting caught in Thursday's late-afternoon rush-hour traffic, we made it out to Tan Son Nhut twenty minutes before our ETD. We were the only civilians on board as the twenty or so passengers were vintage USMC—crew cuts and all.

Nadine just loved the attention she was getting, and so did the Marines! It seemed to work both ways as the leathernecks were anxious to tell us some war stories and ogle Nadine as much as she was ogling them!

Upon arrival at Don Muang, Bangkok's international airport, we separated from our travel companions, and if you believe this, Harry had arranged for accommodations in a small hotel in the Siam Square District that some of his "friends" ran. When I attempted to present my credit card to Gong, the desk clerk, he advised me that it had been taken care of! Harry was playing Cupid . . . sweet of him!

Not wanting to burn ourselves out on the first night in town, the owner's wife, who extended Harry's wishes to enjoy our stay, directed us to a Thai restaurant close by Pratunam Square.

I've never seen a more interesting variety of food in one place in my life. After fresh crispy flounder for two in a hot Thai chili sauce—preceded by an appetizer of Yum Talay (pieces of shrimp, squid, and mussels mixed with spicy lime vinaigrette and cut vegetables) and a bottle of dry white, we made it an early evening despite being directed to a disco place in Nana Plaza.

Romantic as the setting was, there would be plenty of time for that tomorrow night, and we turned in early. Sometimes the best entertainment for the night can be found at home, and this proved to be the case, as Nadine was in a very appreciative mood!

We stopped by the lobby desk to see Gong and get directions and wound up with a map of the city and a list of what to do and see.

Bangkok was situated on the Chao Phraya River, which wound its way through the city in a serpentine fashion basically forming the city's western border. The river housed close to one hundred "floating markets" and some restaurants—being one of the busiest centers of commerce in the city.

Catching a sightseeing long-tail boat, we made our way up river and were able to see the Royal Grand Palace on the west bank and the Temple of the Dawn on the east bank. The architecture was dramatic, statues colorful, and the vistas breathtaking.

The old part of the city built in 1782 and, today encompassing a canal system said by many to outdo Venice's system, is housed by about ten million inhabitants. Its Thai name is Krung Thep and means "City of Angels."

The city had several distinct sectors, and after visiting the floating markets and having lunch, I headed for the Temple of the Emerald Buddha (Wat Phra Kaeo), famous for an emerald Buddha, standing on a thirty-three-foot-high gilded altar and constructed entirely from translucent green jade. Asians claim it is one of the world's greatest architectural and colorful sites.

We finished a long day of sightseeing at Ploenchit Square, where if there was something you wanted to purchase, it was there. You name it! It was known to hold its own in this regard to Hong Kong.

Nadine couldn't make up her mind whether she wanted the light green jade earrings, always "light green" never dark, when she spotted a Thai princess ring. It had a round globular setting, resembling a pin cushion, made of 14-carat white gold and contained about ten multicolored sapphire chips that could knock your eye out. She settled for that! I got nothing. That was OK. I was getting plenty as it was!

We stopped for a late afternoon drink at a local bar as there were more bars and places of entertainment in this city per square foot than New York and rivaled Las Vegas, although in its own ethnic way. There, we were directed to Sukumvit Road in the center of the city, where the cockfights were held, in what today is known as Lumpini Stadium. We had a ball, especially the betting!

By chance, we bumped into some of the leathernecks at the fights that we had hitched a ride with from Saigon. Nadine was in her element rooting for the "cock" we had our money on, while coming onto our not-so-horny Marines at this point, listening intently to their heroics in the street fighting in Hue and Danang.

The Marines insisted on showing Nadine a hot disco, which of course, she played naive to all the intrigue that ensued, sort of a busman's holiday, and after giving a couple of the Marines a surprise on the dance floor, we headed for our hotel. Both of our tanks were running low!

On our last day, having exhausted ourselves seeing the town, we spent a leisurely afternoon by the lake in Lumpini Park picnicking near a grove of palm trees and the surprisingly large lake in its middle. Only this time—no VC!

It being our last day, I finally broke down and bought two jade green and lilac-colored bolts of Thai silk. I hadn't a clue what was to be done with them, but I couldn't afford to wait until I got back to the States to figure it out. Dresses or blouses, I guessed.

The short flight back to Saigon was smooth and uneventful—a weekend to remember—*the costars being Nadine and Bangkok itself!*

LT Hannigan and his men made their way from village to village along the interconnecting navigable canals, as they made their way in checkered fashion through these marshy wetlands. Some of the waterways were dangerous in that they were lined with eight- to ten-foot grasses, affording the enemy a convenient hiding place from which to stage ambushes.

Traveling in the cooler early-morning weather, Hannigan would send out patrols of four men each, including one CIDG scout in order to ferret out any ambush sites such as this. Another part of Team Alpha would stop off at a few of the villages to interrogate a province or district chief or village mayor as the case might be.

Often, using the CIDG personnel as interpreters, as they spoke a number of different dialects, conducted the Q&A sessions. This proved invaluable as it was not necessarily what the chiefs told them, but rather how they told it and what they left out. It took a Philadelphia lawyer to piece together the truth.

Surveillance was shared by sentry duty as it was inadvisable for everyone to sleep at the same time. Monitoring of the canal traffic also took on a similar aspect of scouting in pairs and rotation of duty.

Everyone was under strict orders that if any enemy movement or suspicious activity was sighted, to avoid contact and, most importantly, not be detected while reporting back to base camp of their findings.

The plan was to set the ambush and *attack in force*.

Hannigan maintained a blackout on communicating with the Game Warden base at Vinh Long as long as he could, as there was no sense risking detection when there was nothing of consequence to report.

After almost a week of being unable to detect any significant movement by Charlie, except for some straggling incidental traffic, we gave in and contacted HQ in Vinh Long. He asked for new orders to relocate to a more fertile area.

Twenty-four hours later, he received instruction to proceed further southeast into Vinh Binh province, about twenty kilometers toward the mouth of the Bassac where it emptied into the South China Sea. This redeployment meant moving his team farther away from Alpha Team, but new information of VC units active in the lower reaches of the Delta caused George Benson to uncover the likelihood for a need by the VC to resupply farther to the South. *See map 3, page 54.*

Instructions were relayed through Pearl Harbor to Navy HQ in Saigon that enemy activity, in numbers more sizable than usual, were reported in the vicinity of Route 60 connecting Soc Trang on the southwesterly side of the lower Bassac with Tra Vinh on the opposite side of the river.

Not trusting radio message traffic, HQ secured the coordinates of Team Bravo whereabouts and sent a newly arrived ensign by chopper on his first gofer assignment to deliver Hannigan his new mission details.

The computer was spitting out indications that Charlie was using a large island in the middle of the river as a hiding place for storing contraband shipments, and the island itself was serving to narrow the exposure to any convoy attempting to cross the river in this area.

Jim Hannigan was optimistic as he carefully proceeded down the peninsula toward Tra Vinh and what today is known as Route 60. He observed activity in the canals had picked up noticeably, and he readied the team for action as they neared the road connecting the two villages on opposite sides of the Bassac. An extensive series of interconnecting canals led from the shoreline for over fifteen miles to connect with this road.

As there was only an hour of light remaining upon their arrival, LT Hannigan decided to bivouac for the night and take their first look around at these marshy grasslands at the first break of dawn.

Meanwhile, to the north, in the alley that was linking the canals leading to the upper Bassac and serving as a fertile route to supply VC units operating in the vicinity of Sa Dec, on the upper Mekong, LT Halvorsen wasn't having much luck either. He broke radio silence too, asking for new orders.

Team Alpha was instructed to move in a southwesterly direction to the northeastern bank of the Bassac. Sa Dec had been raided just the week before insertion of Team Alpha, and VC units in the area were lying low after that raid, probably awaiting resupply.

All hell broke loose for both teams within twenty-four kilometers of each other!

LT Hannigan redeployed Bravo Team to the junction of the main canal linking the Bassac with Route 60 and placed his sentries so that both the waterways of the canal and the roadway could be observed undetected. Jim looked for some high ground to gain an advantage over any enemy force looking to transfer supplies from the canal to the road, but there was pitifully little. These wetlands also didn't always furnish the best footing or the safest place in the world for reptiles.

Be that as it may, it was about 9:00 a.m. when one of the sentries posted by Jim reported back over the radio that a convoy of sampans and junks were proceeding up the canal, heading in their direction. He didn't have an indication of their strength yet, but the force appeared formidable.

It was about the time when one of our SEAL sentries had been detected by advance elements guarding the convoy, and gunfire erupted causing Jim to radio Vinh Long on an emergency frequency and called for help. *See 1, page 127.*

After advising the control tower at Vinh Long of the sizable armed convoy and its approximate coordinates, Jim ordered the team to take cover and contain the enemy convoy for fifteen to twenty minutes. This was his estimate of the time for the gunships to arrive under the best circumstances.

The convoy consisted of over eighty shallow draft barges and sampans, accompanied by four heavily armed escort barges. These barges had firepower that posed a problem until help arrived. As in all firefights, if you're in command, they last less time than imagined. As mortar rounds and heavy machine-gun incoming were being experienced, off in the northwesterly sky, there was a lovely sight to behold!

Flying in formation, two A-37 Skyraiders followed by a mile or so by four USN choppers *didi*'ed toward the battle area. Immediately upon arriving on the scene, the enemy was attacked with white phosphorous rockets fired from the A-37 gunships, the rockets slamming into two escort barges.

Seeing the enemy under heavy attack, LT Hannigan ordered his men to close the distance between the convoy leader and our lines. At one point, two SEAL team members entered the water behind one of the escort barges that wasn't hit by rocket fire. They disappeared undetected beneath the water surface for a few minutes wearing their scuba gear.

Having affixed plastic explosives to the hull, the SEALs retreated to the shoreline about one hundred feet away, hunkered down, and waited. The timing device was set to allow time for the demolition team to retreat a safe distance from the escort barge. The explosion was deafening and devastating! Large chunks of the barge together with its crew, guns, and ammo flew skyward in no particular pattern and landed in the canal in a similar manner! In the meantime, havoc reigned throughout the convoy as one after another of the sampans was attacked and destroyed by machine gun fire from the SEALs hidden in the surrounding marshy grasslands and the helos and Skyraiders above. In less than ten minutes, the firefight was over.

Hannigan radioed one of the choppers to land as he had been advised of two wounded, no KIA. Quickly, the two SEALs were loaded into the Huey and medevac'd out to Vinh Long, as neither men were wounded seriously enough to head for Bien Hoa Air Base directly.

After making sure the convoy had been completely destroyed, Hannigan ordered the men to move out on the double as the place would be crawling with members of Charlie's team in no time.

He opted to head north, in the direction of the base at Vinh Long.

He recalled they had gambled on redirecting the mission in the opposite direction from Team Alpha some forty miles to the northwest in the vicinity of Sa Dec. He correctly deduced that reporting back to HQ in Saigon the nature of the interdiction, the quick reaction of the Navy pilots to the unsuspecting contact made with the Viet Cong, and the ultimate destruction of the convoy were all elements of this new operation that the brass would want to know about quickly and accurately.

Farther up the peninsula, Team Alpha was experiencing a different problem as LT Halvorsen's men were experiencing repeated contact with small elements of Viet Cong traffic. Unfortunately, the amount of sampan traffic was not enough to expose the team's presence. He informed Rodriguez at HQ of his dilemma.

On a hunch and with the old man's approval, LTCDR Rodriguez radioed Halvorsen to redirect his force due west across the province to the shore of the upper Bassac, halfway between the Game Warden main base at Can Tho and the base farther up river at Long Xuyen twenty-five miles away.

A message had been received from Pearl earlier in the day indicating CNA had uncovered a high-probability crossing point across from an island located in the middle of the river, about halfway between the two bases.

Rodriguez had obviously gone to school on the interdiction by Team Bravo the day before and, apparently, in sections of the river where the VC could utilize the presence of an island in the middle of the river as a way station had proven to be fruitful areas to patrol.

Team Bravo traveled by night and arrived on the shores of the upper Bassac directly across from the island in question, and it was almost midway between the two naval bases located on the opposite side of the river. There they waited.

But not for very long as scouts sent out by Halvorsen the day after they arrived had sighted a large convoy of sampans and barges, loading at the opposite shore of the island across the way from their camp. Halvorsen quickly set in motion the makings of a plan to ambush this convoy.

First he alerted the base commander at Vinh long, who relayed the message on to both HQ in Saigon and the commander at Bien Hoa.

This time, the ball game had a new twist to it. Not only was the size of the convoy estimated at one hundred and thirty vessels, but elements of the NVN Army, purported to be the 304th Division known to be operating in the area, along with some squad-size VC units, appeared to be protecting it.

LT Halvorsen became the key operative in this ambush as the commander at Bien Hoa asked him to estimate when the convoy would be in the river. The plan was to render the ground units relatively useless, stuck in the middle of the river. In addition, he moved the SEALs up close to the river's edge so as to catch the enemy in the river and not allow them to reach the protection of the road and canals leading down to the shoreline.

Units patrolling in the area near both Can Tho and Long Xuyen were ordered to proceed to the scene of the opposite side of the island, the southwest side, to cut off any retreat for elements of the convoy attempting to retreat to the shoreline they had started from. Essentially, the convoy was being surrounded.

Much the same way Team Bravo had ambushed the VC convoy down the peninsula, the A-37s and Navy gunships appearing out of nowhere, but this time, the force was twice the size of the one used only a few days ago.

As units of the NVN Army and the VC either dove overboard or headed for the shore, they received a rude awakening. Not expecting Team Bravo to be waiting for them in the safety of the nearby shoreline, the carnage was completed. Using everything in their arsenal and opening fire at point-blank range, the slaughter was swift and complete.

To the extent that some of the sampans at the rear of the convoy returned to the island behind them, Game Warden units on the other side of the island opened fire, their fire being vectored by our Hueys circling overhead.

On orders from HQ, given there were two Navy bases within fifteen miles of the ambush, the Hueys that participated in the attack airlifted Team Bravo out to Can Tho where they would be debriefed and would await further orders.

The news of the second successful ambush with its total destruction of the enemy convoys while experiencing four wounded—none seriously—hit Navy HQ like a thunderboLT Damn! This Operation Steam Shovel had become an overnight success! Coupled with the Plain of Reeds Operation, the tide had turned in favor of our side.

There was one piece of negative news from Muc Hoa, which could have been worse. Not since one of our craft had collided with a PBR in early October did we experience damage to an ACV. One of the ACVs during routine patrol had been hit by sniper fire from one of those nasty tree lines, and although no casualties had been taken, the starboard vertical stabilizer had been knocked out, rendering the craft rudderless. Attaching a long line to the starboard tail section and with the crew pulling on the line, the ACV, despite yawing out of control, was manually steered back to base.

PACV-3 steering disabled by gunfire. Crew steers craft back to Muc Hoa.

Note: Rope attached to rear vertical starboard tail assembly being used to steer craft back to base. Later lifted out to Saigon by helicopter

Now the question before the house was, how in the hell do we get the craft out there, or can it be repaired in the field? ADM Veth made the decision after consultation with CDR Fleming by radio. It was determined that a CH-47 Chinook helicopter would lift this 7.5-ton craft out of the Plain of Reeds!

It took the better part of the day, but the Chinook managed to carry ACV 3 back to Tan Son Nhut for making the necessary repairs!

Having solved this problem, HQ celebrated, calling CDR Bronson to come over to join in the festivities, and oh yes, to bring that analyst with him from the States! It was OK with me, I had just taken a one giant step toward getting out of 'am!

I did get some pats on back upon my arrival at HQ and was feeling pretty good until I was called in to see the admiral. Oh! Oh! The good part of the one-on-one meeting was the look of satisfaction on the old man's face. He was clearly pleased, but then again . . . so was I!

After bringing me up-to-date on the successes of both SEAL teams, he reeled off some statistics about the 70,000 VC operating in the Delta and how he estimated that these interdictions had been a significant blow to the enemy. Despite this, the results of the past week had been more than the destruction of two important enemy convoys, but rather a fundamental change or shift in USN strategy to combat the Viet Cong in the Delta! This, plus the fact that he had requested additional assets to begin patrolling the Plain of Reeds—he offered that the job of disrupting the enemy's supply lines was just starting!

Staying in Vietnam for the rest of my life flashed before my eyes! I had to think quickly and be very persuasive . . . *My life depended upon it!*

"Sir, I think after a few more weeks here, I can be more effective for you in Washington securing those assets you just referred to and intend to ask for! After all, I might be able to bring some pressure to bear from a different source and a more independent viewpoint!" Once again, I could see he bought it, despite the smile on his face.

Whew! That was a close one!

I spent the next few days at Navy HQ helping plan further combined SEAL team and Game Warden ops interfacing each other and coordinating a smoother relationship between our forces on the ground and the Navy pilots at Bien Hoa. This had to be coordinated with our plans for stepping up patrols at certain places along the rivers and canals as we were sure the Viet Cong would not repeat their mistakes of last week!

Rodriguez and Grummond put together a task force committee, which included Bronson, an asset management lieutenant; and the commander of naval air forces from Bien Hoa; and myself.

We were given top priority by the admiral and proceeded in a matter of days to put together a plan for expended patrolling using both beefed-up assets combing aerial vectoring with ambush-type tactics by Game Warden vessels of all kinds.

Of course, designating where to patrol was being transmitted from George Benson's group at CNA (he was now assigned two analysts as Dr. Bothwell was beside himself with the results being achieved).

Arrangements were made to send instructions directly to Navy HQ in Saigon, advising CINPACFLT in Pearl by copy. This eliminated an unacceptable delay in advising forces in the field of any significant shifts in the location of enemy force elements, thereby changing the output of the network analysis.

In addition, there was the unavoidable problem of a difference in time, being halfway around the world from each other.

For those of us who are not Einsteins, add eleven hours to EST in Washington, DC, to arrive at local Saigon time, or change a.m. to p.m. and subtract one hour. As a result, there was no good time to call Washington as their workday of 7:00 a.m.-6:00 p.m. corresponded to 6:00 p.m.-5:00 a.m. the next day in Saigon. The best time to call DC was late in the evening Saigon time, when everyone was either too tired, drunk, or getting laid! War is so inefficient.

We concluded, in order to utilize the assets at our disposal most efficiently, that we would utilize aerial surveillance and vectoring to direct our forces, both on the rivers and those inserted into the canal network.

Since the effort to interdict a supply system supporting a force of this magnitude presented such a formidable task, it was decided that random patrolling aimed at interdicting "onesees and twosees" (individual units) could no longer be afforded.

Rather, Game Warden would now concentrate on the interdiction of larger convoy-like traffic. Operation Steam Shovel would emphasize planned ambush-type tactics, both on and off river, in conjunction with naval surveillance and utilization of helicopter and fighter aircraft when necessary. In order to compress the reaction time for aerial support to respond to calls for help, it was decided to have at least one, and ideally two, gunships, if available, in the air near the location of the intended mission or stationed at the local naval base.

During lunch one afternoon, Rodriguez managed to get me off to one side and asked if we could have a private talk. There was no question his star was rising, particularly as a result of the redirection of SEAL Team Alpha at the last minute and its unmitigated success.

He had two things on his mind, both of which didn't pose any problem. First he wanted my recommendation for promotion of PACV personnel. That was easy as I already had thought about this some time ago.

I told Ed Rodriguez this and recommended that Jack Fleming and Kip Kumler be rewarded equally, along with battle ribbons for the entire crew, including a Purple Heart for Jones of Chicago.

Secondly, Ed was thinking ahead to the time he might no longer be in the Navy. Essentially, he was feeling me out for a position at CNA. I asked him about his qualification, including his education, as he didn't have the mathematical training they look for in think-tank organizations. I tried not to discourage him and said to furnish a résumé to me, emphasizing the importance of his prior naval positions and experience. You never know—it's just paper!

I told him I would see that it got into the right hands—no guarantees!

Relieved that this meeting was no more than it turned out to be, I called Nadine and asked her to dress tonight as we were going to Le Cave. She was excited as usual, like most women, and said that Harry had called during the day looking to do something with us tonight and if she should invite him."

I innocently replied, "Of course, but tell him to meet us there." I didn't want my time alone with Nadine to be on the clock.

When Nadine dressed continental style—as opposed to Asian style, she exposed the part of her that was French. It was the first time I had been to Le Cave with her, and Mr. Bernard, not surprisingly, was immediately captivated by her looks and charm.

Harry had reserved a quiet table in the corner of the small dining area but was at the bar waiting for us. He kissed Nadine in a long embrace so as to let everyone in the place know that he still had it—something along the lines of—"it pays to advertise." Personally, I could care less.

Harry wanted to know how we had enjoyed Bangkok, and of course, besides raving about the time we had, we thanked him profusely for the arrangements and told him dinner was on us. He readily accepted!

If I blindfolded and parachuted you into Le Cave that night, you would have sworn you were in Paris having dinner in some chic bistro on the Seine.

In a very preliminary way, after dispensing with the scuttlebutt of how the day went, how Harry's liquor biz was going at the PX's and Nadine's report on how her constituents were talking about the war up country in Nha Trang, Quy Nho'n, and Hue, Harry asked how things were going in my neck of the woods!

Trying to appear frank and open about things, I indicated that actions in the rice paddies and swamps for our search and destroy teams were meeting with unparalleled success. It was what I didn't say that was important!

Nothing about where force compositions or aerial support from Bien Hoa Air Base. There just wasn't a need to know, but I got the carrot-and-the-stick treatment after the second round of drinks.

Nadine probed, "Well, I guess your ideas about ambushing convoys on the canals must be working!" I responded, "Yeah, it is!"

Both Harry and Nadine got the message, and the topic of conversation was switched to who might play in the Super Bowl this year.

If you're wondering, Harry had scallops, and we shared a rack of lamb for two with a mint jelly sauce, topped off with two bottles of wine, a burgundy Château Lascombes Margaux, and a slightly less robust Bordeaux, St. Émilion, both '57.

It might have been my imagination, but the crowd seemed to be more effusive tonight, and war talk dominated the night. I chalked it off to the fact that we were in the throes of a significant military buildup throughout the country.

196

Harry agreed and said he had heard from a reliable source that we were planning on constructing a huge harbor seaport facility near the Twelfth Parallel, about one-third of the way up the coast toward the DMZ, at Cam Ranh Bay.

Harry was certainly well connected!

I paid the bill as promised. Harry once again received a big hug and good-night kiss from Nadine, and to no one's surprise, Mr. Bernard, with a very low continental bow, kissed Nadine's hand and bid us adieu.

Even Harry's chauffeur ogled Nadine in that provocative Western-style dress as he drove us to the villa in Cholon.

It was a beautiful evening, and as we made our way through the downtown traffic along Le Loi Boulevard, heading west toward Cholon, it was inescapable not to notice the stepped-up activity in the streets.

The military presence had clearly increased, and with that, business was booming. If I were a Saigonese businessman, I wouldn't have wanted the war to end soon!

CDR Bruce Bronson finally had an original idea of his own, "Let's go out to Tan Son Nhut and visit the PACV crew. They're in town with ACV-3, and we should go out there and get an update on how things are going."

Making our way out to the airport in the office jeep, a shock to the system after Harry's limo the night before, we ran into the usual traffic associated with MACV HQ, with personnel and supplies coming into the city.

It was like old home week after we found ACV-3 in an out-of-the-way hangar on the outskirts of the airstrip, as Jack Fleming and Kip Kumler were there, and we had a lot of catching up to do on subsequent operations in the Plain of Reeds.

Initially we inspected the damage done to the starboard vertical stabilizer (read right tail) and the events that ensued after the craft lost its steering ability. Technically, after enemy fire had struck the stabilizer, ACV-3 lost yaw control.

Necessity being the mother of invention, someone found a long line on one of the ACVs, and it was tied to a metal loop on the tail.

That being accomplished under fire, led by Fleming and Kumler and other crew members, exposed on the outside starboard bow of the craft, manually pulled and tugged on the starboard stabilizer stirring the craft back to Muc Hoa! This was an occurrence not at all unusual under wartime conditions.

Chart 9. Command Relations for Riverine Operations
(Military Assistance Command organizational chart)

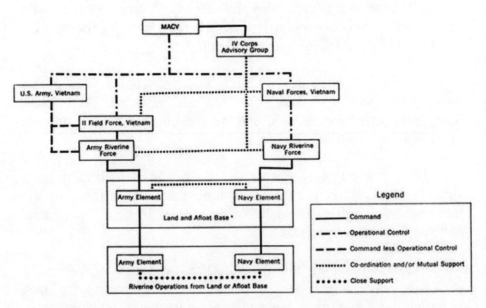

Source: CINCPAC Command History, 7966, Vol. II, p. 620

A word should be said about the Military Assistance Command:

The US Military Assistance Command (MACV)[*], led by GEN Westmoreland, was located within the Tan Son Nhut airbase complex. To my knowledge, I had never heard of or saw any correspondence or message traffic between MACV and COMNAVFORV[*]. I'm sure some message traffic existed, perhaps at the highest levels. As far as I was concerned, they were fighting two different wars. The naval carrier forces stationed in the Gulf of Tonkin in the north, mainly bombing North Vietnam's principal port, Haiphong; and the industrial centers around the capital city of Hanoi were also fighting an entirely separate action.

Commencing in 1967 and continuing after the Tet Offensive by the North in early '68, an additional bombing campaign was undertaken against the Ho Chi Minh Trail. The trail led from deep in the north's industrial area, south through the key junction point of Vinh[**], and continued through the extreme southeastern corner of Laos, and then along the Cambodian side of the border with the South, into the

---

[*]   MACV = Military Assistance Command—Vietnam, famous for, among other things, alleged inflated reports of enemy KIAs and general mission results, which is currently being contested in the civil courts of this country. See epilogue. COMNAVFORV is the designation for Commander Naval Forces Vietnam

[**]   Vinh was located about 15 km. inland from the coast and just below the Nineteenth Parallel in lower NVN. I considered this city the northern terminus of the Ho Trail. A severe blow to the trail's ability to function efficiently could have been struck by eliminating Vinh as a functioning terminal. For reference purposes, the DMZ was located just below the Seventeenth Parallel and represented the demarcation point or area between NVN and SVN. The only effective way to accomplish this would be by the introduction of ground forces into the North. Vinh's location being so close to the coast rendered it open to a commando-like amphibious landing, which in fact I recommended to the powers that be after my return to Washington. In every instance, particularly in my meeting with representatives of the Defense Intelligence Agency (DIA), I was told, in no uncertain terms, to forget and bury this idea.

highlands of South Vietnam, both south and north of Dalat (the West Point of the South Vietnam). See *infiltration routes, map 2, page 35.*

Listening devices, known as MK-5s, the existence of which were classified top secret, were dropped along the trail to alert our monitoring stations of impending shipments. Unfortunately for us, the North ran their shipments at night while the daylight bombings exploded their ordinance in the thick canopy of trees protecting the trail, resulting in little impedance of the trail's traffic. Similarly, when key sections of bridges in the North were bombed out, duplicate or spare sections of the bridge would be floated back in place at night from their hidden locations along the shore. Subsequently, the traffic along the trail would be resumed.

Dalat was a beautiful city of pagodas and the former residence of the Emperor Bao Dai. Located in the highlands, experiencing the coolest temperatures in SVN, with the Dalat Palace Golf Course overlooking a two-mile lake, Lake Ho Xuian Ha'o'ng. It served as a retreat for the establishment and was served by a local commuter air service and later Vietnam Airlines. The military academy of SVN, the University of Dalat, and the home of the former South Vietnam Nuclear Research Center were all located northeast of the city. *See map 6, page 127.*

Note: To convert kilometers to miles, multiply kilometers by 0.6 (100 km. = 60 mi.)

IX

The Battle for the Mekong – December '66

The PACVs continued to run a few more exploratory missions after T-Day plus one, but were not looking for trouble—more on reconnaissance missions designed to probe the area—setting the stage for future operations in much larger force strength.

The incident in which ACV-3 was damaged by enemy fire apparently was little more than accidentally running into a sentry outpost, and having drawn the fire had accomplished their objective and *didi*'ed the hell out of there. This was especially true given the immediate problem of evacuating the disabled craft.

We broke for a cafeteria lunch at the airport, Le Cave it was not, and on the way back from lunch as we walked among the helter-skelter activities on the airstrip, Bronson broke the news to Jack and Kip that they were being recommended for promotion, along with campaign ribbons for the entire PACV crew. In a flash, it became apparent to me that this was the real reason for our visit.

As one can imagine, this news was sufficient to touch off the commencement of a raucous celebration among the men, and the rest of the afternoon was written off as nobody was capable of making any rational decisions after about thirty minutes of partying.

Returning to the compound later that day, Bronson found a message on his desk to call Rodriguez ASAP. Having returned around 7:00 p.m., we decided it could wait until tomorrow and braced ourselves for a new round of mental gymnastics with HQ—whatever it might be.

I was ready to spend a quiet evening at the villa, watching some of the SEALs cleaning their M-16s and drinking beer. Hopefully, Nadine would come home early! She did.

Despite being a little late the next morning, Bronson had not yet returned Rodriguez's phone call. Apparently, Bruce wanted me on the call with him. *See map 3, page 54.*

Call it sixth sense or what have you, Navy HQ had received an alert advisory from CNA advising them of an usual amount of troop movement east and south of the Bassac in the vicinity of Tra Vinh province.

If previous data compiled by CNA's program was any indication of impending enemy activity, this was it! Rodriguez and I concluded the VC might me moving to blockade or somehow impede our patrol forces from entering the Bassac and the Mekong from the South China Sea.

It also could be an attempt on the part of Charlie to control this key province for a myriad of reasons, not the least of which could be payback for the recent ambushes by our SEAL teams.

In either case, it appeared to be *"high noon at the OK corral!"*

Ed Rodriguez asked an ensign to advise the admiral that the task force commander wished to meet with him, at his earliest convenience, and that the matter was urgent. Besides assembling a few key members his staff, including a lieutenant familiar with Tra Vinh province, he called Rob Grummond to come over to HQ on the double.

Since Bronson and I were on the spot, we called out to the repair hangar at Tan Son Nhut to advise Fleming not to return to Muc Hoa with the PACVs and stand by for orders to move into the Delta.

Rodriguez raised the commander of the Skyraiders and HAL chopper squadrons at Bien Hoa to assess what assets he had available over the next twenty-four to forty-eight for a specific mission deep into the Delta.

The ensign returned saying the ole man would be available in one hour. With that, we sent the ensign down to the lunchroom for a ton of sandwiches and soft drinks to be brought upstairs to Ed's office.

I called Nadine and told her I'd be home late and not to wait up for me. In twenty minutes from the time we called him, Grummond walked in saying, "What's up, guys?" Grummond was a quick study and in a matter of minutes was throwing out ideas as to what the "intel" we were receiving might mean.

Rach Gia, situated on the Gulf of Thailand approximately seventy nautical miles southeast of Sihanoukville, was a much smaller port than Sihanoukville. It had a shallow draft harbor, which precluded deep ocean-going vessels from docking at its piers.

It was located just inside the Vietnamese-Cambodian border in Kien Giang province and, consequently, was a Viet Cong bastion.

It was somewhat axiomatic that the farther one got from Saigon, the deeper into the Delta one found oneself, and the area became more unfriendly and controlled by the Viet Cong. There were reported to be 70,000 VC in the Delta at the height of the war.

Kien Giang, An Xuyen, and the western half of Ba Xuyen provinces, deep into the southernmost provinces of the Delta, were prime examples of these areas. It did not come as a surprise that an insertion of a large number of NVN troops would be attempted in one of these provinces.

Our reports received from two CIDG operatives in the last twenty-four hours indicated that regiment strength elements of the NVN Army's 325th Division had off-loaded at Rach Gia! There they were joined by a local contingent of Viet Cong to form a force of close to 5,000 men.

They were observed heading south, along what today is Route 60 leading into Can Tho province. This report, coupled with the alert advisory received from CNA, formed an ominous picture that the enemy had initiated a mission of strategic importance and was engaged in forming a force of considerable strength and numbers.

In the hour we had before the task force committee was to meet with the admiral, we poured over a blown—up map of the area south and east of Can Tho, on both sides of the Bassac River.

Grummond was the first to speak and postulated the combined NVN-VC force was headed for Game Warden HQ at Can Tho, and they should be alerted to this possibility immediately. Everyone concurred!

Rodriguez countered there was a series of interconnecting canals, which today parallel Route 60 and intersect with a major north-south canal (today called Route 1-A), just ten miles west of Can Tho, and for his money, they could be headed for Soc Trang, ten miles from the lower Bassac (Hau Giang) River.

This village was at the head of a major junction of the canal system and roads near the mouth of the river (*Cu'a* Hau Giang).

The lieutenant familiar with Tra Vinh province, just across the Bassac from Soc Trang, offered the opinion that at least part of the force could have as its objective, Tra Vinh, the province capital whose location on the lower Mekong (Co Chien) River made it strategic. It was also the midway stopping point for canal traffic linking Soc Trang with Ben Tre and My Tho, on the My Tho River where an important Game Warden base was located. *See map 4, page 93.*

Since there were numerous canals connecting these two possible routes for the enemy to pursue, a series of diversionary actions were at their disposal, opening the possibility that Can Tho might only be a decoy.

The committee arrived at two possible courses of action regardless of the enemy's destination:

1. Alert Can Tho immediately to the possibility of an attack from the west and inform them that the extent of reinforcements and air cover would be decided upon before the end of the day.

2. Send a recon team of squad size (no more than fifteen or twenty men) to a point close to the junction of the major canals, about ten to twelve miles west of Can Tho (in the vicinity of what today is the intersection of Routes 60 and 1-A).

Grummond volunteered his SEALs for the job, emphasizing they could be "choppered in and out" as they had done before on many an occasion.

This being accomplished, we turned our attention to forming the big picture, based upon the reports emanating from CNA and Rach Gia.

Finally I had something to say and offered, "I'd like to take the first crack at this," and received the green light from the committee.

The recent actions by our SEAL teams in this general area had alerted and forewarned the Viet Cong that we were about to carry the fighting and interdiction of their supply lines inland. Without control of the various naval bases throughout the Delta, coupled with our ground forces unpredictably showing up on the canal networks leading to the major tributaries of the Mekong, the enemy needed to take a bold step to counteract that which was clearly a new initiative by the USN to disrupt VC supply lines in the Delta.

1. One way for the enemy to accomplish this would be to cut off our access to the Mekong River and its tributaries from the South China Sea.

2. If we look at the key villages in the provinces at the mouths (*cu'as*) of the Mekong and typically located on major canals, they are the following:
   a. Soc Trang
   b. Tra Vinh
   c. Ben Tre and My Tho

All connected by the same major canal network (on what today is Route 60), the same route the NVN-VC force forming out of Rach Gia was sighted on!

"Gentlemen, my bet is they are headed for Soc Trang!"

Rodriguez, satisfied that there was general agreement with this analysis, was ready for the admiral except for the fact that we compiled a list of assets that would determine the approximate force strength we were recommending to the admiral.

1. Personnel: 5,000 Army (101 and 137th Air Cavalry); 1,000 SEALs and Rangers, the 91st Battalion (airborne) flown in from Dalat, all in the next 24 to 36 hrs.

2. Highlands of III Corps: 2,500 reinforced infantryman from the newly formed Mobile Riverine Force (MRF) of the Ninth Infantry Division [*]

3. Boats: The entire contingent of Game Warden PBRs, 16 Swift Boats (PCFs) from Market Time Boat Divisions 101 and 103 (8 from each division), fifteen armored troop carriers (ATCs), three 82-foot cutters from Coast Guard Divisions 11 and 13 (3 from each Market Time Division), three PACVs, two Monitors (riverine battleships), and two Neptune, twin engine SP-2Hs to conduct offshore patrolling, and two CCBs—command and control boats.

4. Aircraft: Twenty Huey gunships, six F-8 fighters, six Skywolves, and troop carriers for the airdrop to be assessed by the Army.

This was a wish list and by no means was achievable without help from *the ole' man*. He was going to have to pull some strings!

We broke for coffee and awaited an audience with *the man* upon whom the success of the conduct of the war *south of Saigon* would now depend!

While we were waiting, the discussion among our team continued. Rodriguez asked if the enemy force were headed south toward Soc Trang,—did we think that they would attack with their full complement.

---

[*] This division, commanded by MAJ. GEN Eckhardt, did not *formally enter the war in the Delta as a unit until the following year.*

Bronson and I concurred that we didn't think so. If the objective of their mission was what I thought it was, they would divide their force, cross the lower Bassac, not at the same point they tried to against SEAL Team Bravo, and head straight for Tra Vinh. Our group took notes furiously as I went one step further.

"Before this operation of theirs is over, they will attack Ben Tre and My Tho on opposite sides of the My Tho River." These villages, the latter being a Game Warden naval base, form the northern terminus of the canal system in question and guard the lower My Tho River and the naval base at Vinh Long further upriver.

"Based upon the recent interception of a large convoy by the PACVs in the Plain of Reeds, the enemy is attempting to bring significant supplies into the southeastern section of the Plain of Reeds in the vicinity of Cai Lay. They could be accompanied by the force that would attack My Tho and Ben Tre, thereby avoiding the necessity of having the large force coming down from Rach Gia making two river crossings."

MAP 7. Infiltration Routes—including Sihanoukville trail

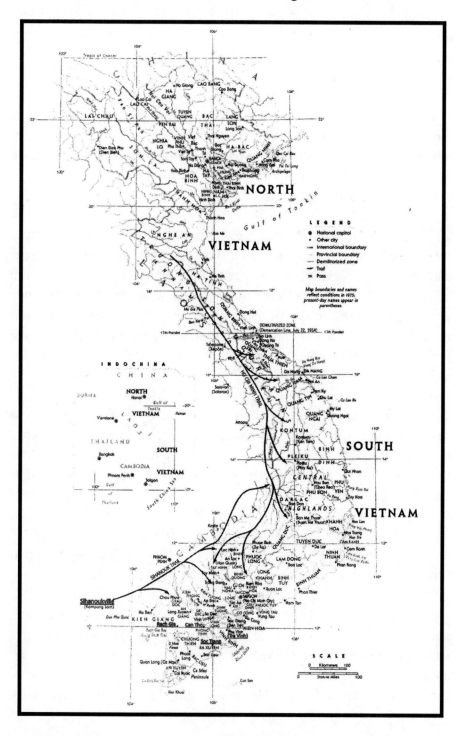

With this possibility out on the table, the team poured over the map and reread the intelligence reports. Nobody had any different ideas, except to say, "OK, if this is what Charlie is up to, when will we know it for sure?"

Grummond once again offered to insert a SEAL team squad or two, reinforced by either special forces or elements of the MRF's Ninth Infantry Division, for if the NVN had in fact turned south toward Soc Trang—a major engagement could ensue roughly here . . . as Grummond pointed to the village of Phung Hiep, about twenty miles northwest of Soc Trang.

He also said it was also possible that this force would splinter off before reaching Soc Trang, cross the lower Bassac, and head for Tra Vinh. A gofer ensign bounced out of the admiral's office and told us ADM Veth was ready to see our group. Rodriguez made the introductions and quickly dispensed with the small talk. He indicated that two reports received since yesterday at HQ had a serious impact on naval activities in the Delta.

After being briefed on the gravity of these recent developments, the admiral asked to be excused for twenty minutes as he wished to make a phone call. Upon our return, we were informed that ADM Veth had talked to GEN Westmoreland at MACV HQ.

MACV had the reputation, to put it mildly, "of being slow on the draw," especially when it came to logistics support and especially when it came to another branch of the service.

In GEN Eckhardt's "Vietnam Studies—Command and Control," *see reference documents,* LTGEN Jean Engler was commissioned by Westmoreland, in his role as deputy commanding general, MACV, to study the logistical advisory functions of the USARV. He found this function performed by the J-4 section of MACV (logistics directorate), had lost control as a military assistance command as US tactical forces greatly increased and expanded.

When the meeting resumed, he indicated that this event, namely drawing the NVN Army out in the open to fight in battalion or greater size, was just what he had been hoping for! As you know, they have, up until this time, adopted the VC's hit-and-run guerrilla tactics, operating in squad—and company-sized strength, avoiding any major contact with our forces.

For one thing, this had the effect to neutralize our air superiority over them. Now, if we had them out in the open in size, "the good general" was ready to commit whatever resources we needed!

ADM Veth confided that he had asked for a regiment of paratroopers from the 101st and 137th Air Cavalry, half held in reserve at Tan Son Nhut, the other half to be inserted into Can Tho within twenty-four hours.

Even if Can Tho turned out to be a decoy, they could be reassigned into Soc Trang or Tra Vinh, within a matter of hours.

The remaining half of the AirCav would be held in reserve for the unexpected! In addition, MACV committed to supplementing any aircraft assets that might be needed, after ADM Veth had contacted the commander of Bien Hoa Air Base to determine how quickly the HAL-3 choppers and F-8s, along with the squadron of Skyhawks, could be assembled.

The commander of the MRF, Maj. GEN George Eckhardt, had been advised of the participation of his men and was on his way over to HQ. Rodriguez was asked to get the captain of the Coast Guard on the phone, and members of his staff scurried about as if the president was coming over for dinner. The rest of us were thanked and dismissed, with the understanding we would reconvene in two hours. There was plenty for us to do in the interim.

This was clearly shaping up as an all-nighter. No Nadine tonight!

For Bronson and myself, our first item of business was to contact Fleming and tell him to ready the three ACVs for transit to the lower Bassac, a long haul for them from where they were now. Their participation would be best used if the NVN choose to attempt to cross the Bassac and head for Tra Vinh. This required a great deal of coordination with the other Game Warden river patrol assets in the area.

CAPT Allison, a strong, tall midwestern farmer from Illinois, arrived at Navy HQ and was introduced all around. He was field commander of the Mobile Riverine Force, and he was in the midst of forming the Ninth Infantry Division when he received the admiral's call.

His first assignment after being briefed by our task force, and recent developments causing this reaction by naval intelligence, was to coordinate deploying his forces in consort with MACV's AirCav contingent.

It was no small problem holding a contingency force back in Saigon, probably assigned to Nha Be, a naval base located just down river, and the closest base to the approach to My Tho from the Plain of Reeds. *See maps 3 and 5, pages 54 & 102.*

After reviewing the situation, Allison informed the admiral that he did not want to split his forces as a command-and-control nightmare (C&C) could ensue. He suggested that his force be assigned the defense of Tra Vinh and the canals leading in a northeasterly direction across the peninsula from the Bassac to the Mekong.

At this point, CAPT Allison put in calls over the Navy's secure phone system to the commander of Game Warden in Can Tho, CDR Weldon, and the US Coast Guard commander aboard one of the cutters off the coast patrolling in Market Time. The biggest problem was enlisting the cooperation of MACV's logistic support group, known as the J-4 Section. Arrangements for the coordination of their forces, rendezvous points, and times was going to be no small undertaking.

CDR Rodriguez had the aviators on HQ staff in touch with CDR Elliott at Bien Hoa Naval Air Station. HQ took over the relatively easier task of assessing procurement and potential C&C problems arising from having to respond to Army, Ranger, Navy, SEAL, and Coast Guard communications from possibly two different theaters of operation.

What wasn't easy was getting MACV's J-4 Section to respond to any field unit's needs, no less the Navy's.

Somebody had sense enough to order in pizzas and a large bowl of spaghetti and meatballs, and work proceeded well into the night without regard for time. What had to be done, had to be done *now*. There was no tomorrow!

I was reminded of the old baseball bromide of years ago—the Boston Braves of those times had two pitchers, and nobody else who could win a game. The adage was "Spahn and Sain and pray for rain!"

Much like the Braves, we needed bad weather between Rach Gia and Soc Trang in order to buy time and slow down the column of forces advancing south toward Can Tho. We had to coordinate the assembly of these diverse forces under what amounted to very compressed time requirements.

It was sometime late in the evening, the War Room, as it became known that night, looking something like a Chinese fire drill, began to quiet down—especially when our ubiquitous ensign informed Rodriguez and myself that the ole man wanted to see us. Usually, in times such as these . . . that's not a good sign!

As we entered the admiral's office, I observed from both the condition of his desk and his face, he was not his usual self. One could see the pressure manifesting itself in more ways than one. I quickly concluded to allow Ed to do the talking for the time being. People sometimes change radically when under pressure.

Dispensing with the preliminaries, the ole man led off with, "Men, how sure are we of what we're doing here?" Ed and I looked at each other. I outlasted the staring that ensued, after all, fundamentally, this was their show. Finally, he said, "Sir, based on all the information at our disposal, the enemy has come out in the open, and as your discussion with GEN Westmoreland indicated, they may have made a tactical error!"

For me, this was as good a start as any! Under the aegis of not wanting to miss an opportunity, I said, "Sir, I don't see any viable alternative but to meet the enemy head-on. Moreover, if in fact Charlie's aim is to cut off the Navy's ability to enter the Mekong from the South China Sea by cutting off our access in the lower portion of the provinces bordering the area, we cannot tolerate this type of action.

Besides, psychologically, as I'm sure you are aware, sir, war is a series of actions and reactions on the part of the antagonists. In this case, we cannot show weakness by allowing the VC to seize the initiative and control the entrance to these river systems."

Rodriguez nodded his head in agreement, and the admiral pondered what had just been said. The admiral quoted Ariel Sharon, famed Israeli prime minister and warrior, who had stated, "Keep your enemy off balance." He countered, "OK, do we have sufficient assets in place? I don't want to be right and lose this engagement because of a missed assessment of the enemy's strength." Almost in the same voice, Ed and I responded, "We've asked for the force levels we think is necessary to cover all known threats. We are attempting to round up the assets . . . your help with the various parties, especially MACV, could be pivotal in this regard, and in achieving our goal."

I was stunned by something I had suspected, but not experienced. Getting logistical support out of Westmoreland's MACV shop was a nightmare. The USARV's efforts in IV Corps were run entirely separate from the Navy's CTF 116—tactical riverine force-sometimes known as Game Warden

See reference document, "Historical Atlas of the US Navy" for how, by the following year, changes to joint command of these two forces and the role of logistical support of all forces under MACV's control were changed.

In English, this meant, "Admiral, make sure we've got those AirCav Boys!" (Getting MACV to support a joint Army-Navy operation was considered a tall order in those days . . . *a very tall order!*)

The USN had prevailed upon the USARV to loan them the squadron of Hueys being used in the Delta . . . sparingly so, however.

The 101st and the 137th Airborne represented 5,000 of the best and most reliable troops in country. They would have the main responsibility for stopping the main salient of the enemy's thrust toward Can Tho and Soc Trang.

If Charlie made the tactical mistake of splitting his forces, because of his underestimation of the size of the force he was going to be confronted with, this could be the main issue upon which his success or defeat would hinge.

215

The admiral wished us luck on our way out and reminded us his door was open at any time we should need him. I thought to myself, I hope he isn't planning on getting much sleep over the next few days!

As if it were an afterthought, I doubled back to his office and said, "Sir, do you think I might accompany the ACVs on this mission?" "Absolutely not, Wilens, you stay right here where I can see you." An answer, I must admit, that did not came as a shock to me!

Apparently, Ed Rodriguez had overheard me and said, "Don't sweat it, if things go well and are not too hot down there, I can commandeer a ride from one of our chopper pilots for us to go take a look-see—when the time is right!" I thanked him and said, "I'll take you up on that, having just been ordered by an admiral no less, not to do so!"

What the hell, they couldn't court-martial me! Could they?

Just then, Ed and I both got a sickening feeling as we peered out the window only to see it getting light in the early morning orange-streaked sky. I asked Ed if there were some taxis out front this time in the morning. He replied, "I'll get one of the men to run you out to Cholon in one of our cars," which I readily accepted.

As the car had some Navy markings on it and being a bit cautious, I had the driver drop me off a block from the villa, *for in this case*, it did not pay to advertise!

I tried the impossible, sliding into bed, getting under the sheets without wakening Nadine. It didn't work, but there wasn't time enough as she had to leave for work in an hour. Oh, yes, there was talk about a tension reliever!

Once again, Harry had called and wanted to meet for lunch. Later in the day, after I had gotten forty winks, I returned his call only to tell him that I was sorry, and I couldn't make it. He obviously was on a fishing expedition . . . Lunch was the bait, and I was the fish.

I wrote off his being nosy, given I had a few other things on my mind, as wanting to be "the guy" with his cronies as he made the rounds of the PXs.

When I arrived at HQ, having only been away six hours, it was now late morning, and Bronson brought me up-to-date on how things were shaping up. It boiled down to our getting all the personnel we had asked for, with some delay of a few days from the MRF Ninth, 80 percent of the aircraft from Bien Hoa Air Base, and about half the cutters from the Coast Guard this week, and the rest from further up the coast by next week.

Some AirCav personnel from the 137th were to be air-dropped into Vinh Binh province. However, the drop would be in the vicinity of Vinh Long as the drop areas farther down the peninsula presented similar obstacles that our paratroopers experienced in WWII, landing in the canals and flooded areas of Belgium and Holland and drowning. This force had the time to convoy their way down toward Tra Vinh over the next forty-eight hours.

Grummond and Allison were busy coordinating and dividing their intended field positions and supplies requirements, while Rodriguez was assigning members of HQ staff, tasks related to C&C and resupply. This included calling his counterpart with the Seventh Fleet on station in the Gulf of Tonkin, to arrange for the loan of aircraft in order to supplement those available at Bien Hoa Air Base. A communiqué from the combined SEAL-Ranger team inserted into the key canal junction just west of Can Tho forwarded this message to the Game Warden commander stationed there:

TEAM IN PLACE NO SIGN OF CHARLIE, OUT . . .

We had just bought the extra twenty-four hours we needed so badly!

Aside from its meaning, we wouldn't have to pull another all-nighter, it allowed the reassignment of various force elements to be accomplished in a more orderly fashion. It also reduced any exposure we may have been creating by such a massive redeployment of forces in such a short time.

I called La Baccara at 9:00 p.m. Nadine had not yet arrived, and I left a message for her that I was headed for the villa.

As I was leaving HQ, I bumped into Harry of all people! Happy to see him, but mentally exhausted, which he detected, he suggested a nightcap at the Continental Bar. Seeing it assured me an air-conditioned ride to Cholon, I agreed to have "one maybe two." It was still early . . .

Things were thinning out by the time we arrived. Just the nightcappers populated the premises. Harry opted for his favorite table where we could observe, but not easily be overheard. There was no sign of either movie legends—Greenstreet or Lorre!

Harry observed that there appeared to be a scarcity of females at the bar and for that matter, at the usual places around town. I countered that it was probably because of the current buildup of GIs in town, causing the shortage. At any rate, we agreed, if you were a female "round eye" in town, you had the pick of the litter! An unattached embassy or USIA female was a rarity.

It was that time of night when the heat had started to dissipate when Harry started asking his usual questions relating to how things were going. After my first drink, I could hardly stay awake, and I realized I had to be careful . . . sort of.

To my surprise, he knew some aspects of what was going on, better than I did, so we played "I'll trade you for some innocuous info for some of yours."

I offered some tidbits of information that might have been sensitive yesterday, but not today. It appeared to me he was doing the same, so we left it that and *silently called the game a draw.*

Harry spotted an old friend, and before he could get started on another round of drinks and making it a late evening, I asked if his driver *could give me a lift home.* Harry said that unfortunately, his man wasn't an intercontinental jet pilot, but he would have him drive me to Cholon! One for Harry . . .

I climbed into an empty bed and was asleep before my head hit the pillow!

LT Randy Harding, US Ranger Team Zulu, crouched low in the eight-foot grass alongside the main canal leading to Can Tho, fifteen miles west of the base. The combined SEAL-Ranger squad had been flown into Can Tho only two days before. The Rangers were part of the USARV's Ninety-First Airborne Battalion having been brought in for this mission from up north in III Corps.

CDR Grummond, head of the SEALs in IV Corps Zone, had flown in with the team and was overseeing the operation from the nearby base. He had with him another two squads of SEALs ready to be deployed on command, should the need arise.

At first, Harding thought he heard the sound of aircraft in the distance. He alerted his squad to take cover, although there was no record of ever having sighted enemy aircraft this far south.

It only took about five minutes for Harding to realize the sound of engines did not emanate from the sky, but from the canals and the unpaved road that ran parallel to it. He estimated these engines were no more than ten minutes away. He did not rule out the presence of motorized troop carriers traveling along this road, alongside troops being transported on barges and sampans in the canal. He was somewhat relieved that in the short time they had been in the area, this road, and to a lesser extent, the canal, *had been mined.*

Harding called Grummond and advised him of the situation. Since Grummond well knew the team's mission was one of detection and surveillance, sometimes known in the trade as recondo (an unfortunate combination of the words *reconnaissance* and *commando*), he ordered Harding to withdraw to a position where the enemy's advance scouts would not discover their presence.

He also advised Harding that the F-8s and Skyraiders were scrambling at this moment, but was attempting to time their arrival until we knew the column's intentions and possibly their destination. Hopefully, the main body of NVN's finest, the green-uniformed 325th Infantry Division, would alter its course southward, deeper into the peninsula, as the intel boys were betting or perhaps hoping.

Just in case, they were wrong and headed for Can Tho. Grummond advised the base commander to set in motion the plan that already had been worked out for its defense and possible evacuation via the river outlet.

The one advantage CDR Shackelford had was that the base could not be surrounded as the river outlet served as a safety valve, if the situation should worsen to a degree that called for a speedy exit.

Additionally, a few booby traps had been set, more to signal an alert of the enemy's presence than to inflict casualties.

On the other hand, the Viet Cong was known for construction of "pungi pits," which were pits lined at its bottom with sharpened bamboo, charred spikes covered with excrement designed to cause infection. These traps were camouflaged by layers of bamboo covered with dirt! Nice guys!

The perimeter of the base had recently had its defenses reinforced with coiled razor wire barriers, claymore mines, various booby traps, and even a moat-like defense area had been constructed to funnel the enemy into the mine field, giving the enemy a taste of their own meds.

PACV off-cushion searching for "booby traps", Plain of Reeds

CIDG personnel search for grenade "booby traps"

CIDG discovers booby trap—grenade in hand

Close-up of grenade booby trap—Plain of Reeds

It was only a matter of minutes before the sound of engines ceased. LT Harding, realizing the VC accompanying the main NVN force knew the area well and by stopping their advance, was sending out scouting parties to reconnoiter the area. Harding had no alternative but to retreat toward Can Tho.

In an act of bravery, two CIDG personnel elected to stay behind and blend in with the local villagers.

The next three hours seemed longer as Harding and Grummond waited for news from the field as to the enemy's intentions. In the meantime, a message was sent to Bien Hoa putting the aerial strike on hold.

Before long, the CIDG personnel arrived in base with the news that the NVN main element—after reaching the junction of the canal and the road heading south toward Soc Trang—had turned south! But they had left a force of about 500 troops at the junction, the clever bastards. Leaving this force accomplished two things:

1. It pinned down a like number of troops at Can Tho.
2. It acted as a rear guard against the main force being attacked from the rear.

The commander of the 101st Air Cavalry, upon hearing the news, contacted Navy HQ and MACV to clear the redeployment of his group already at Can Tho. They were headed south to the secondary defense position just south of Phung Hiep, about one-third of the way between Can Tho and Soc Trang.

Granted the OK, the 101st left 300 men behind and airlifted the remaining 1,200 troops out of Can Tho, heading for a confrontation with the NVN salient before they reached Soc Trang.

Bien Hoa was put on notice of the change in plans and took the rest of the day off.

On the lower Bassac, Game Warden units being joined by three PACVs, fifteen PBRs, six PCFs, and two ACFs were being aided by four Hueys—two flying downriver while the other two flying in the opposite direction. This force was deployed to interdict any segment of the NVN force making an attempt to cross the Bassac into lower Tra Vinh province. *See map 6, page 127.*

The area around the village of Phung Hiep formed the eastern terminus of a major canal running in an east-west direction, forming a junction with a canal coming up from the southwest. This major canal headed in a northeasterly direction toward the lower Bassac. Not only did the junction of these two canals afford an excellent defense position for the 101st to maintain, but also served as a logical point for the enemy force to divide, with one column heading for the Bassac and the other for Soc Trang.

The commander of the 325th NVN Infantry Division, having basically bypassed Can Tho and heading south, bivouacked for the rest of the day, perhaps not wanting such a large force to be detected from the air in the daylight, or just to rest.

For either reason, it was a mistake!

The interval, which was afforded to the redeployed 101st, was used to set up more effective defensive positions and afforded the MRF to get some of their assets in position at the mouth of the river and into Soc Trang.

Of course, the NVN commander had no idea the entire tactical riverine force in the Delta was awaiting him.

Daylight was breaking, and sentries began reporting of movement on the other side of the canal. The first elements of the NVN force attempting to cross the canal were annihilated in a blistering fusillade of machine gun and mortar fire.

Harding was in touch with the commander at Bien Hoa and estimated it would be no more than thirty minutes before the enemy would make some major attempt to cross the canal. For the second time in twenty-four hours, a naval aerial armada was readied for general quarters.

It would be no more than half an hour before the skies around Trung Hiep would be filled with Navy fighter planes and helicopter gunships whining and chopping their way through the thick sky-blue yonder.

To a foot soldier in battle, there was no more welcomed sight!

The captain of the 101st hunkered down, as GEN Schwarzkopf of Desert Storm fame would say, not wanting to expose his strength to the enemy on the chance they had not yet suspected they were encountering a significant force.

LT Harding and CAPT Hughes of the 101st had redeployed south to an area near the village of Thung Hiep, about twenty miles northwest of Soc Trang. When almost thirty minutes had elapsed since the NVN's initial attempt to cross the canal had failed, Harding and Hughes recommended the Ranger and SEAL teams explore both flanks of the defensive line without crossing the safety of the canal system. The idea was to draw the main NVN force out into the open. Ten minutes after these teams left on their mission, CAPT Hughes received a message from the helos coming into the area from Bien Hoa Air Base.

FORCE APPROXIMATING 2,000 NVN TROOPS HEADING FOR SHORES OF BASSAC HEADING ZERO THREE ZERO, OUT.

This message changed everything; simple arithmetic told Harding and Hughes that the NVN force level, originally estimated at 5,000 plus, had now been cut in half. When nothing more transpired over the next twenty minutes, Hughes decided to send one-third of his force, about 750 men, behind the NVN positions in order to encircle them.

Leaving the SEAL and Ranger teams in place to protect the defensive line's flanks, the 101st began to move out on the NVN eastern flank, avoiding having to cross the main canal. Accomplishing this without being detected, a force of 600 AirCav crack troops arrived in behind the NVN force and completed the encirclement. At that point, CAPT Hughes, having taken care of giving the C&C people at Bien Hoa the exact coordinates and the enemy's positions in relation to the main canal, ordered the aerial bombardment of the NVN force.

The reasoning being simple: faced with total annihilation, this action would force the enemy out of the enclave they had formed, and allied forces would be waiting for them to exit in any direction they had chosen.

We watched the Navy fighters approaching the fire zone, wave after wave, firing rockets and heavy-caliber machine guns, wrecking havoc on anyone or anything that looked like a target, becoming the object of their wrath.

It put the Fourth of July ceremonies on the Capitol Mall in Washington, DC, to shame, but it had some similarities.

However, CAPT Hughes's plan didn't seem to be working until the crackle of a message from the Ranger platoon leader, LT Allison, who was anchoring the eastern flank, was received. NVN troops in company strength were attempting to break out. Hughes immediately started shifting his own troops on the defensive line, to the point of attack, while redirecting the "boys upstairs" to a new set of coordinates.

In some of the fiercest fighting of the Delta campaign to date, the main body of the NVN force was chewed to pieces! Reports were coming in from the group of 600 completing the encirclement. They were encountering squad-size engagements as the enemy probed to determine what was behind them, and they were not happy with what they found.

In less than an hour, it was all over. The NVN column headed for Soc Trang would never get there! Our casualties were light!

VC outposts being destroyed

VC Ammo station destroyed

VC hut discovered near Cambodian border.
ACV's on horizon set it afire.

CDR Fleming and the Game Warden force commander patrolling the lower Bassac lay in waiting near the western bank of the river. Messages being received from the gunships above indicated that the NVN forces headed their way would be arriving within the hour. Force strength was estimated at 1,000 men.

The biggest single combined Naval Surface and Air Force assembled south of Saigon, and now a part of Game Warden operations awaited them.

When news spread of the enemy defeat in the area leading toward Soc Trang in Saigon, NAVY HQ and MACV were jubilant.

CDR Grummond ordered his forces in Can Tho to move out and engage the enemy force left behind by the main column as a rearguard force. Before launching an attack, which now had grown to outnumber the NVN's 135th troops left behind, by almost a two-to-one margin. But first, Grummond called for an aerial attack on their positions to soften them up!

In almost a repeat performance, the enemy was forced to come out in the open, due to aerial bombardment of their position, and was cut down in the flat, open topography of this part of the Delta.

Just about the same time our forces were launching an attack against the Can Tho perimeter, the other salient of NVN forces were sighted heading for the lower Bassac, about five miles upriver from the last crossing attempt. Smart . . . smart, but sometimes, armies never learn.

Everyone that was anyone was at Navy HQ hanging out, awaiting message traffic coming in from Game Warden forces, located at both Can Tho and the lower Bassac.

Rodriguez was ecstatic, receiving the news from the base commander and CDR Grummond relating the successful defense of Can Tho, coming on the heels of the news regarding the destruction of advance units of the NVN 325th approaching Soc Trang, it almost seemed too good to be true.

I approached Ed with a half "I told you so" expression, and half mischievous look. He knew what they both meant. Without my asking, he said, "Not yet . . . but soon. I've made preparations."

I interpreted that to mean our flight out of Bien Hoa was ready to go—a thirty-minute official car ride away. But Rodriguez was waiting for official confirmation from someone on site, of higher rank than his, that it was all clear to conduct a flyover. I responded, "I can wait . . . There's *no* rush!"

There was no entrapment or hiding scheme available to our forces patrolling the river, although Charlie's advance recon (reconnaissance) units couldn't determine the strength of Game Warden forces in the area. Nor did he know what awaited him from above, with enough firepower to sink a battleship on alert, as close by as Vinh Long.

CDR Fleming was in hiding a few clicks upriver from what appeared to be a logical river crossing point. CAPT Allison had elements of his Mobile Riverine Force, complete with about one hundred troops, in two ATCs sequestered down river to the south.

As the afternoon faded to dusk over the river and visibility became more and more margin able, all our forces were alerted as to the possibility of an attempted night crossing.

Jack Fleming and Kip Kumler, remembering the night attack at Cat Lo only a few weeks ago, contacted Game Warden CDR Weldon, and a call was sent to Vinh Long and immediately referred to Bien Hoa, that a night crossing was imminent and parachute flares were going to be needed to light up the river.

That done, everyone waited on alert for *"the enemy's other shoe to drop!"*

The last sliver of the sun's crescent was just about to disappear in the direction of the marshy grasslands and rice paddies of Ba Xuyen province. Suddenly, Kip Kumler remembered that the Japanese attack on the morning of December 7, 1941, at Pearl Harbor, Hawaii, came out of the east so as to momentarily blind anyone looking in that direction.

In this case, the attack, late in the day, would come out of the sun at dusk!

Kip sounded the alert to the other PACVs to start their engines and contacted the other commanders over a prearranged radio frequency. His bet came to him like a thunderbolt of clairvoyance. This terrain being flat as a pancake lent itself to attacking out of the sun at dusk to give them an edge and a valuable few minutes for the enemy to disperse along the west bank of the river.

Their objective being to get partially across the river before being detected, seeking refuge on a small island in midriver, and that was exactly what was under way!

CAPT Allison contacted the F-8s based at Vinh Long and repeated the coordinates of the small island in question. His request—like a Southern mama cookin' up some fried chicken and some freshly baked apple pie—was ready, and it said, "Come and get it!"

The open expanse of water between the west bank of the Bassac and the island, a distance of 1,500 yards at most, began to give off the appearance similar to that of piranha attacking someone or something that had just been offered to them for dinner.

The water erupted, bubbled, sprayed, churned, and swallowed men, boats, equipment, and river debris in a mercilessness display of carnage and mayhem.

After the F-8 fighters made four passes up and down river, and almost as an act of mercy, Huey gunships supported by heavy machine gun fire from the surface craft in the area, mopped up those that remained in the river struggling to make the far shore.

Not to leave a job partially done, the F-8s rocketed an area for a click along the west bank of the river and 300 yards inland. Shackelford conferred with other officers having different vantage points on the river and estimated that two-thirds to three-quarters of the enemy force had been disabled or destroyed!

A platoon of the MRF's Ninth Mobile River Division began to land just south of the attempted river crossing while a company of the 101st airborne from the defense of Soc Trang along with a platoon of LT Harding's SEALs and a like amount of LT Allison's Ninety-First Rangers moved into the area from the north.

Like baseball, if the Viet Cong hadn't already learned how to play it, a squeeze play was being put on the remaining NVN forces, somewhat in a state of disarray, on the west bank of the Bassac.

Ed Rodriguez was getting this news while we were speeding out to Bien Hoa Air Base to board a Huey for a flight to the battle zone, for at worst, we were entering the ninth inning of a game whose outcome the VC was rapidly finding out and which was no longer in doubt!

Airborne in a matter of minutes as Ed had called ahead, we approached the battle scene and witnessed what appeared to have been equivalent to feeding time for the tigers at the coliseum in ancient Roman times. Our over flight was a once-in-a-lifetime experience.

To begin with, we were witnessing the tail end of a victorious operation firsthand, without exposing ourselves to any danger. Just listening to the message traffic between the various air units vectoring the ground forces was worth the price of admission!

John Wayne, Harrison Ford, and Tom Cruise in all their theatrical endeavors would have a hard time to replicate the scene we were witnessing.

Needless to say, good news travels fast—from Saigon to Washington, DC—from Navy HQ in Saigon to the Center for Naval Analyses in Arlington, Virginia, the success of the Game Warden operation carried out with the assistance and resources of several different service organizations, combining to defeat a regiment-size force was truly big news!

Dr. Bothwell, upon being informed by CAPT Savadkin, moved swiftly to set in motion a formal request to have me repatriated as soon as it was feasible for me to be debriefed and put on the next plane heading east.

Despite his determination to get me home ASAP, Bothwell knew he had one more aspect of his decision to check. George Benson was summoned to the boss's office to see what had to be done in order for me to return home, even though Bothwell had his mind made up as to what course of action he wished to take.

That was, what was best for CNA, namely putting me out on tour, the so-called rubber chicken circuit.

The commandant of the Marine Corps and the Air Force Academy, plus various lower-level operatives at the Defense Intelligence Agency (DIA) and the Navy's operation centers at the Pentagon had already asked for briefings.

George Benson had informed Bothwell that the computer programs could maintain itself as long as someone in Saigon could keep feeding us data relating to the enemy's whereabouts, that CNA would be OK. Game Warden, Operation Steam Shovel, and CNA's "man in the Delta" were hot! For CNA, it was time to cash in their chips! Sometimes known as, *"quitting while you're ahead."*

Satisfied, Bothwell placed a call to Savadkin *asking for my return. It was mid-December!*

Ap Ba'c is five miles east of Cai Lay, which today sits on Route 30, the main road along the eastern shore of the upper Mekong (Song Tien Giang), and guards the approach to the village of My Tho, a Game Warden naval base at the entrance to the southeastern corner of the Plain of Reeds. *See map 4, page 93.*

The attack on My Tho had started when the main element of the NVN had overrun Ap Ba'c, a lightly defended village for which was there was no prior history or interest on the part of the Viet Cong.

Word reached Vinh Long's commander about the same time the battle for Soc Trang had commenced. GEN Eckhardt, in conjunction with elements of the 137th Air Cavalry, made a beeline for My Tho. Most of the MRFs (CTF 117) armored assets, including four monitors and a like amount of armored troop carriers (ATCs) and a company of men, whereas the rest of his force was tied down at the mouth of the Bassac, were dispatched to this entrance to the Plain of Reeds.

Most importantly, to buy time until these forces were in place in defensive positions, the call went out to Bien Hoa Air Base for immediate air support.

Elements of the NVN 304th Infantry Division, supported by platoon-size Viet Cong units, advanced and took control of the highway connecting Phnom Penh, the capital city of Cambodia, and the strong-point city of Svay Rieng in the "parrot's beak area" pointing threateningly at nearby Saigon.

Central to cutting all river and vehicular traffic along the lower Mekong and the My Tho rivers was the US naval base at My Tho. This small river village, twelve miles east, southeast of Ap Ba'c, lie directly in the enemy's path to Saigon and the southern approaches to this city. Loss of this base afforded the enemy not only the ability to both choke off Mekong and My Tho river traffic, but also set up the encirclement of Saigon from the south.

GEN Eckhardt and Admirals Ward and Veth knew full well the importance of maintaining control of the My Tho base. Plans were set in motion to meet the enemy force head-on at My Tho, as they too welcomed the NVN and VC forces coming out in the open to fight!

Not having any significant advantage in the number of ground troops, which historically one requires when combat takes place on the enemy's home turf, our command structure ordered the field commanders to draw the NVN force into the open, making them vulnerable to attack from the air.

CAPT Scott Thompson, a hoopster from Iowa, received orders at Bien Hoa Naval Air Station to make available every strike force aircraft for this purpose. Led by the A-37 Skyraiders with their phosphorus rocket armament capability and the USN A-7 Corsairs, reinforced by the "helicopter attack light" 3 (Huey gunship squadron), an alert was sounded that amassed the largest single air strike of the war in IV Corps Zone to date.

MRF's task force, 117 ATCs, landed a company of troops from the MY Tho river just west of the village. Furnishing fire support were both Monitors and the armored troop carriers. An airborne insertion of the 137th AirCav was readied to drop in behind the main elements of the enemy force once their point of attack became known.

The road and the river ran parallel to each other, in almost a direct west to east heading, in the immediate vicinity of My Tho. Predictably, the attack came at dusk out of the west one day after our main forces had arrived at My Tho. Not much time for preparation of a plan of defense, no less implementing it.

Our ace in the hole was the USN air strikes. The unknown was how the enemy had prepared for it as it was not a new disadvantage for them to face.

Navy HQ in Saigon looked like a three-ring circus. *Busy* was not the operative word. No one was still. There were no small talks going on at the water cooler! The admiral's door was shut, with movement in or out limited to flying ensigns with papers in their hand, entering, then leaving almost as quickly as they had arrived.

Ed and I arrived at HQ in the midst of this scene! Ed was going to leave the explanation for our disappearance 'il later. Tensions were running too high at the moment, and to enter into an explanation that had absolutely no bearing on the implementation of the plan ahead for the defense of My Tho appeared foolish.

Once again, we were invited in to see the ole man. Oh! Oh! Again!

Like, "Where have you gentlemen been?" But if you're an admiral, one must avoid being predictable . . . ergo. "Good job, men, but what do you make of the NVN 304th at My Tho? And are there more surprises coming? Is this all you think they've got?" I let Ed lead as I had no idea what other elements of the North Vietnamese Army might be hanging around, and some of this attack might be a feint or decoy.

Rodriguez offered that there were no other reports from CIDG Special Forces in the border area and certainly nothing division, or for that matter, regiment size, sighted by aerial recon out of either our shop at Bien Hoa or MACV's corner of the world at Tan Son Nhut. Then, in order to break some of the news gently to the admiral, Ed said, "Marty and I just came from Bien Hoa where we had a little look-see for ourselves and stopped in to see CAPT Thompson."

"He's flying recons up to the Cambodian border and back daily and in touch with his counterpart at CIDG Special Forces group commander. With the exception of this enemy force, which had made its way across the Plain of Reeds, where we had that small PACV squadron stationed at Muc Hoa, we have not seen any sizable enemy force movement." That is, with the exception of indigenous Viet Cong units already here, and Charlie seems to be holding his commitment down to platoon and company strength—almost as if they are reluctant to throw their full support behind this offensive!

CIDG discover VC rice station—Plain of Reeds

PACV foreground—CIDG destroys ammunition dump

I made my first contribution and said, "I concur, sir. It's almost as if the VC either doesn't think the time is right for this type and size action or do not wish to open themselves up to our air power, or some combination of both."

Ed quickly added, "However, we are stretched a little thin at the moment, and with the exception of 1,500 101st AirCav troops on hold at Tan Son Nhut, we are totally committed for the near term. Other than this contingent, we have *no more reserves!* I'm sure you appreciate we have to hold My Tho at all costs." The ole man, matter of factly, nodded affirmatively.

The phone rang. It was the Bien Hoa commander, CAPT Thompson. After listening intently to the captain, ADM Veth said, "I want to furnish our forces at My Tho any and all our assets as requested. Don't hold back, except for the most minimal coverage, for emergency purposes. After all, My Tho is only a few minutes flying time away from your base. I want you to

239

furnish them all the firepower we have at our disposal." The captain basically responded with an "Aye, aye, sir," and hung up.

As Ed and I got up to leave, for once through some of these briefings, with the most important and busiest people in the entire theater of operations, you can sense when it's time to leave.

On the way out, the admiral said, "Oh, yes, gentlemen, this time, stick around, and don't go off on any more jaunts. Things may get hot around here at any time, and if you don't mind, I'd like to be able to have the pleasure of both your company, should I desire it!"

That was that. We were stuck until further notice! Where's that ensign? "I'm hungry again". I blurted out, "I called the villa and left a message for Nadine, again!" We were on call until further notice, but this time from the admiral, in no uncertain terms.

Something began to bother me. I worried that things were not going to be so easy. Perhaps because we didn't have time as we did at Can Tho and Soc Trang to develop a coherent plan of defense and were waiting for the enemy strike force.

Russian-made SA-2s, sometimes known as SAMs, an acronym for surface-to-air missiles, were used extensively in the north around Hanoi and Haiphong. Sporting a 2,000 lb. warhead and traveling at a speed of Mach 3.5 (3.5 times the speed of sound, or about 2,500 mph), wrecking havoc upon our aircraft, particularly our jet aircraft, as they were heat-seeking missiles, and honed in on the jet engine's exhaust. They were not seen in the south . . . until now!

That's what bothered me about Charlie's apparent disdain for our air dominance. They had brought the SAMs with them this time!

On the first day of engaging the enemy's forces just west of My Tho, we lost two Hueys—one with no survivors. As these missiles could be launched from a soldier's shoulder in typical VC fashion, the origin of these firings were never in the same place twice. This was going to be a bitch of a problem!

Rodriguez called CAPT Thompson at Bien Hoa to see if we could acquire just a few fighter aircraft from Yankee Station up north that were equipped with electronic countermeasures (ECMs).

Installed on the wings of our aircraft, the ECMs could receive the signal of an incoming missile, lock in on it, and not only destroy the missile in midflight, but also trace out the flight trajectory of the missile back to its origin, sending an outbound missile directed at its launcher! Hello!

A delay ensued in obtaining any help of this kind, and with our propjet and jet aircraft temporarily grounded, Charlie advanced on My Tho! Preparations were made to evacuate the base via the river, meaning boats—lots of personnel carrying boats!

The next bit of good news was that elements of the NVN 325th were seen on the eastern approaches to My Tho, which meant in English, the base was about to be surrounded with the only exit remaining via the river! That was, if providing help didn't arrive soon.

From WWII, a little Dunkirk, an escape route only via the My Tho River rather than the English Channel, was developing! (Advancing German armies having broken through the French and Belgian defenses had a British division pinned down on the Belgian coast necessitating an evacuation by sea—the English Channel—of an entire division. Churchill appealed to the British people to take to the Channel, open to strafing by the Luftwaffe, in boats down to sailboat size to aid in the evacuation.)

Despite our hopes to the contrary, this type of scenario was developing. BGEN William S. DeSobrey did, calling upon his position as senior advisor, IV Corps, Delta, MACV and his relationship with GEN Eckhardt and GEN Westmoreland, and reinforced by requests of Admirals Ward and Veth, he had the Seventh Fleet Carrier Task Force at Yankee Station come to our aid.

Assets of the 481st Tactical Fighter Squadron were temporarily assigned to the Battle of My Tho. Equipped with ECMs and bull-pup missiles, they were joined by six F-100 Super Sabres from the Seventh Fleet to form a destructive force this area of the country had not yet witnessed, but Charlie was about to!

The terrain in the vicinity of the village of My Tho was typical of that found in the Mekong Delta. Situated on one of the Mekong's tributaries, its flat marshy grasslands harbored rice paddy fields and little else. There was no place or general terrain for any sizable contingent of the enemy force to hide!

As our forces fought a retreating action, they gradually gave up ground in their retreat toward My Tho. Advance units of the NVN units had closed to within a few miles of the village, but were out in the open—their SAMs ready.

Approaching this battlefield at a steep angle of descent, so enemy forces were not aware of their presence until the last moment, A-37s and A7s, Skyraiders and Corsairs caught close to 1,000 of the NVN and VC forces out in the open where they could be easily targeted.

Equipped with ECMs, these aircraft did their thing, to no one's surprise, but the enemy's. The second pass became more tenuous than the first, but 50 percent of the enemy ground forces were killed or disabled. This action was augmented by light 105 mm Howitzer artillery fire, and at close range, a mortar barrage from forces dug in on the perimeter of the village, causing the attacking forces on both sides of the village to retreat.

CTF 117's ATCs performed their function by furnishing support fire from the river, causing the enemy to retreat inland.

Like always, our forces knew they would be back!

But now, the defenders had bought time, at least twenty-four hours of it, time enough to set up defenses similar to those constructed at Can Tho, complete with minefields, barbed wired booby traps and a few claymore mined, antipersonnel carrier ditches and traps.

CDR Ray Dickson, from the west village of New York City, sent a message to HQ in Saigon that the first assault on My Tho had been repulsed! One had to be cautious about celebrating as the VC's first attempt at breaching your defenses was usually a probing action—with another larger attack to follow soon thereafter.

As night approached, the admiral sent the early shift home for a quick six hours, with the late shift to follow upon their return. I took the early shift.

Upon arriving at the villa, I was surprised to see Nadine hanging out at the house but, upon reflection, realized it was too early for her to go to the club.

I guess I spilled the beans a little in order to get her to stay, but she said she would only be gone a few hours and would return well before I had to leave. That meant, in lovers' talk, "don't leave until I get home." I understood!

In Navy parlance, "I shot the shit" with some of the SEALs sitting around a poor excuse for a kitchen, but it had a fridge, a sink, and a table and chairs, so I guess it was a kitchen. Two Ba Muoi Bas (local 33 beers), and I hit the sack.

If Nadine came home on time, I was going to need my rest!

I was at the desk Rodriguez had "borrowed" for me eight, not six hours later, as Nadine had made me—in more ways than one—to be late. I wasn't complaining.

Bronson was already on his second cup of Java when he spotted me. His good-morning smile told me he knew why I was late. At worst, what could it mean? No promotion for me? Hardly a problem, given the circumstances, I'll take it every time.

The news from My Tho, which at first was worsening with each message, markedly began to improve. The admirals were prevailing upon the generals to commit more resources, namely a battalion of the 101st AirCav being held in reserve at Tan Son Nhut.

The powers that be were playing chess with the NVN commander, waiting for him to make his move on My Tho with his main force, before committing their reserves. The commander at My Tho wanted to deliver a knock-out blow with these reserves as there was no immediate assistance if the 101st failed, and as I've said before, they were some of our best.

The day passed with no word from My Tho, but the news from west of the Bassac couldn't have been better. The NVN force trying to cross the river failed, and remnants of some five hundred enemy troops were caught in a proverbial squeeze play that was slowly, but inexorably, reducing their force strength, with minimal casualties on our side.

There still remained the NVN-VC force of about three hundred troops who were left behind at Can Tho acting as a rearguard for the main force. After CDR Weldon's contingent had attacked them, supported by an aerial strike force out of Bien Hoa Air Base, the enemy had scattered "from whence they came"!

A platoon of SEALs and Rangers acted together in a mopping-up operation as that was all that remained to bring this phase of the battle to a close.

As the day passed by, we began to wonder what Charlie had up his sleeve at My Tho. Suddenly, it became clear—Katyusha rockets mounted on the rear of tracked artillery vehicles came into play.

Designed in 1942 by the Russians, used extensively in Korea and Afghanistan by the Taliban, and most recently by insurgents in Iraq and by the Islamic militant groups—the Hezbollah and Hamas in the Israel-Lebanon theater of operations in 2006.

The BM-13 rocket system, designated RS-132 (for rocket propelled shells) had a limited range of eleven miles[*] and, except for a finned tail section, were devoid of guidance systems, sometimes resulting in the destruction of nonmilitary targets and inflicting casualties upon civilians.

Sometimes mounted on the back of vehicles as small as a pickup truck, in a parallel array of tubes about six inches in diameter, they resembled the arrangement of organ pipes.

The Russians had nicknamed the system the Stalin Organ. In fact, the name Katyusha originated from the popular Russian wartime song "Katyusha" loosely interpreted from the female name, Katherine.

These rockets were 5.75 feet long, 5.2 inches in diameter, weighed 92 pounds, propelled by a solid chemical propellant and had a warhead consisting of fragmentation or explosive charges weighing 48 pounds.

---

[*] Recently, the Hezbollah have modified this rocket system to extend their range to 60-70 miles. In the year 2000, the US Army Space and Missile Defense Command, White Sands, New Mexico, developed an antidote to the Katyushas called the Tactical High Energy Laser (THEL), a radar-based antimissile system. The United State has handed over this system to the State of Israel.

Their principal utility was close in support of insurgency forces where broadly defined targets, over a relatively short range, was their principal military use. Because of this, the *Katyushas* were sometimes used in guerrilla warfare.

The absence of any reliable guidance system limited their utility to large or concentrated targets or installing fear in the general populace. However, because of their limited range, they are usually airborne for less than thirty seconds. Even today, these missiles are extremely difficult to intercept or shoot down in flight.

The first salvo of Katyushas hit the village of My Tho creating the same effect as if they were being bombed. Several of the rockets were duds, with another few landing aimlessly in open fields inflicting little or no damage.

However, one of the rockets hit barracks' housing locals working at the base. Poorly constructed, they afforded little defense against flying metal and glass. As a result, casualties ran as high as 70 percent.

It was time for the 101st!

Having experienced Katyusha raids in the north, in both I Corps and II Corps zones, we knew immediately that the launch sites were mobile, therefore ground forces would have to bring the fight to the enemy. Inevitably, this meant higher casualties.

The Game Warden commander at My Tho, CDR Weldon, sent out squad-size patrols to probe the enemy's defenses. His initial objective was to fix the coordinates of the NVN positions for the Navy fly boys, who had used the last twenty-four hours to reload.

Within a matter of hours, the squad leaders began to report contact with enemy sentries positioned on the outer limits of the NVN-VC main force. Probing enemy lines in squad-size units is not my idea of the safest job in the military. Casualty rates are usually high, and Weldon couldn't afford the loss of any sizable number of men, so as a result, he called the units back to base after they made initial contact with Charlie.

CAPT Thompson scrambled six A-37 Skyhawks, assigning these aircraft to join three F4U-5 Corsair Phantoms flying south from the Seventh Fleet's carrier *Franklin D. Roosevelt* (CVA-42) in the Gulf of Tonkin. Their mission: sweep in on enemy positions just west of My Tho. Their mission was designed to draw enemy ground fire and retaliate. Equipped with ECMs on each wing, they were ready for ground-launched SAMs.

Accompanying this joint squadron was the deployment of four UH-1(B) gunships, Squadron HC-1 to Tan Son Nhut airbase from the carrier Coral Sea (CVA-43). It was at this point the NVN command had to make a crucial judgment: to use the SAM missiles and disclose his position or not, that was the question. Unlike Shakespeare, he chose incorrectly, not quite up on the latest intelligence relating to our ECM capability. The result was disastrous for the enemy. Not only did he expose the position of his main force, but his rocket launchers were greeted with a hello from the F-100's wing-mounted rockets. Coming in right behind the first pass of the 100s were the A-37's firing phosphorus rockets at the enemy positions.

The NVN forces had no alternative to open with automatic weapons fire with their Russian-made AK-47s, M-1 rifles, and Chinese-made 90 mm recoilless rifles and mortars, from their previously concealed positions. Their coordinates were compared to those furnished by the squads that went probing earlier, and CDR Weldon ordered his forces to attack.

The commander of 101st, having heard by radio of the enemy's position from Forward Air Controllers (FAC Spotters), decided to land half of his paratroopers behind the NVN, flying the rest of his group into My Tho to join the frontal assault.

At this point, I imagine the NVN command were sorry to have ventured out in the open, as with no air cover in relatively flat terrain, his forces were going to appear like ducks in that boardwalk shooting gallery with no place to hide.

At this point, the enemy had no more cover than a bullfighter in the middle of the corrida (bullring), with wave after wave of bulls charging at him with no place to retreat and someone high in the stands shooting rockets at him! Not good . . . for the toreador!

As everyone had expected, the attack was led by the Air Cav troopers from the 101st, supported by Huey gunships, which tore the enemy units to pieces!

Rockets and .50 caliber machine guns fire from above, M-16 assault rifles and M-60 and M-79 mm grenades from the ground caused advancing elements of the NVN's 305th to take on the appearance of rag dolls being chewed to pieces by attack dogs.

Charlie's use of Katyushas versus our ground units had little effect, and their launching of SAMs against our aircraft likewise failed to find their mark. To the contrary, the ECM's antimissile systems had a field day retaliating against the origin of the VC's launchings.

Communication between our ground forces and the attacking aircraft had left something to be desired as it slowed our men on the ground from advancing too quickly, lest they become the target rather than the enemy.

CDR Dickson radioed Navy HQ that My Tho was holding its own—the main wave of enemy attackers had been repulsed—having inflicted heavy losses upon the enemy! The admirals called the generals and thanked them while the men in the field did the work and took the risk! *Some things never change*! ADM Veth appeared from the relative seclusion of his office with a smile on his face as broad as the Delta itself! The men in the office responded with a celebratory war whoop that transcended normal military decorum!

Ed Rodriguez grabbed the nearest ensign and instructed him to go the nearby PX and bring back four cases of cold Becks! No Ba Mui Bas for this occasion.

Upon his return, a group of us walked into the ole man's office and gave him a good ole Navy hip, hip hooray and placed a cold one in his hand!

Next!

The Delta has been quiet as long as the USN slept, but when they awakened and carried the fight inland to interdict the VC convoys on the canals leading to the Mekong—Charlie stepped up their activity and came out in force.

The North's foray into the Delta had been thoroughly defeated in a joint Army-Navy operation melding air and ground units from several diverse combat elements. It turned out to be the first major Command and Control success in the conduct of the war in the Delta south of Saigon.

For the first time in weeks, I seriously gave thought to getting the hell home! Of course, this was not the time . . . not now! But maybe, tomorrow!

And there was the no small matter of . . . Nadine.

But first, there was another "no small matter," getting the admiral to OK it. I had already laid the groundwork, knowing this day would come. It was another thing to bring home the bacon!

After a good night's sleep in which I pondered my next move, I concluded the best way to secure the ole man's blessing on returning to the land of the puzzle palace was to find a substitute to continue with my role in Operation Steam Shovel. Simultaneously, I had to make clear to him that my touring the States in the months ahead, briefing the brass, would be in his best interest.

With Dr. Bothwell pushing from the other end, it was a plan.

If at the beginning, the powers that be had decided the correct slot for me was the Navy research office in Saigon, then who better could take my place—CDR Bronson—the head of that office! Logical? I thought so . . . and told the ole man just that.

In a meeting, which I rehearsed in my mind ad nauseam, I explained that I had worked closely with Bruce on a daily basis and assured him that he could collate the necessary data coming in from the field to keep things going back at CNA's computer room.

I thought I had the admiral convinced on this point, so I launched into my song and dance on how my superiors back in DC, at the behest of CNO's office, had me scheduled to make the rounds of various congressional committees and assorted influential people. (Little did I know that they had me scheduled or committed to make presentations to VIPs for what turned out to be the better part of a year.)

The admiral agreed, after rubbing his chin a few times as if he were pondering the logic of my reasoning, to what I'm sure he had already decided upon before I arrived in his office. He asked that I see Ed Rodriguez to be debriefed and thanked me for my service. I figured he had also heard from Dr. Bothwell.

I rose, shook his hand, no saluting nonsense, and told him it was an honor to have been of service under his command—and left his office—before he changed his mind!

Yow! My heart was beating a mile a minute!

For those of you who have never been in a similar circumstance, the relief that is experienced knowing that you have just been released from serving further and free to go home is an exhilarating feeling not often felt, at least in my lifetime.

Now, I was overcome by the other feeling or sensation I had encountered on my arrival that first day at Tan Son Nhut, how many days, and whatever you do, don't take any unnecessary chances . . . The ball game was over!

It was a feeling, as if I had thought all along, that this day might never come! Now that it was here, I couldn't wait for it to happen fast enough.

I scheduled a debriefing session with Rodriguez and went home early.

It was on the way to Cholon that I began to figure out the sequence of events that was remaining before I left town. There was Harry . . . and Nadine!

There was also no small issue in making sure Bruce Bronson would carry out the liaison duties with the computer effort back in Arlington, which I had promised the admiral I was going to take care of.

I estimated a couple of days for this effort, and of course, I was wrong!

Rodriguez, after we spent an entire day going over everything that I knew or learned since my arrival, threw me the curveball about obtaining an exit visa! Where and how do I get one of those? Ed replied, to my astonishment, at the Saigon Post Office! You're a civilian . . . That's the procedure. In a flash, I had gone from a rank just below a rear admiral to a civilian trying to secure an exit visa at the local PO! Holy Toledo!

What was some local yokel going to do, check to see if I had paid all my parking tickets? I was not a happy camper as I do not "wait well".

The entire scene flashed in front of my eyes, and I could see a bespectacled bureaucrat wearing brown-tinted sunglasses like those of the desk clerk at the Embassy Hotel when I first arrived in town, not being able to find my reservation and so on! Only this time, it was going to be my parking tickets, fines, or some other bullshit.

Doc Colladay and I had planned on this from day one. That is precisely why I had insisted upon return airline tickets on a commercial plane. We hadn't been smart enough to anticipate this twist of obtaining a visa to clear customs.

Rodriguez's reassurance only served to elevate my apprehensions about this whole undertaking. Roadblocks were one of my single most feared and hated obstacles to getting along in life, and this one was turning out to be an anathema to me.

Just the thought of going to a Vietnamese post office had me shuddering in my boots, and the reason was simple: I shudder just to go to one of our own POs in the States! Did you ever see anything like those clerks?

And in this case, I wasn't going to mail a package or get some stamps! Oh no, this one had trouble stamped all over it! No pun intended.

I don't have to tell you I waited in line for almost an hour, only to be told that my passport was not in order and needed some stamps from the place I had been employed, and of all places . . . at my hotel! The sleazy brown-tinted, bespectacled desk clerk, who I had to "schmeer" to find my hotel reservation, immediately came to mind.

252

I just knew this exit visa bullshit was not going to be easy.

After some consideration of what I was facing, I returned to Navy HQ and confronted Rodriguez with the fiasco that was unfolding. He smiled, apparently getting a chuckle out of what he easily could see was frosting me, and said that he would see what he could do about it.

The last thing I wanted to do was return to the post office!

In the meantime, I continued to wrap things up with both Ed and Bruce Bronson. The next day, Rodriguez asked that I come over to HQ as he had found a solution to my conundrum. I couldn't get over there fast enough!

Ed had written a short letter on COMNAVFORV stationary for the admiral's signature, stating I had been an exemplary employee, and made a call over to the Embassy Hotel. I would have no problem securing a pass from our friendly desk clerk stating there were no unpaid balances due to the hotel.

I breathed a sigh of relief—one last trip to the post office.

If I ran into another roadblock, I was going to strangle someone. After waiting the obligatory time in line, I approached a new version of a municipal bureaucrat, who smiled, took my passport for someone to review, and upon returning said, "No problem, Mr. Wilens, we can process your exit visa now, and would you please return tomorrow to pick it up?"

If you think I was leaving my passport with this wacko, think again! I replied I couldn't do that. I would wait for them to process it now and stared at him as if I was about to explode. He got the message and disappeared into the back room, again.

What seemed like an eternity, our friendly clerk returned, apparently defeated in his endeavor to see how frustrated he could make me or resigned to the fact that I wasn't going to bribe him to get that passport stamped.

God help an ordinary unconnected civilian trying to exit this country.

The exit visa in hand . . . Nadine was next!

I came up with at least three different explanations of how to say good-bye, none of them entirely true, nor in any sense directly to the point. I was gettin' outta Dodge, and that was it. How do you say that to someone you are most likely never going to see again? Not easy!

Of course, the answer is, quickly and unemotionally! Something like some of the docs that tell you, "That you are not going to make it." As my mind wandered, troubled by what might lay ahead of me, I thought,

In combat, death is something that happens to someone else. Yet for such a cataclysmic event of finality, we detach ourselves from it—thinking it both hopeless and useless to worry about. We are rendered defenseless against its ramifications and effects upon us. To see it manifest itself close-up in war magnifies this aspect of finality, observing how quickly and simply it comes upon us. We shake our heads in dismay when contemplating how drastic and rapidly a fellowman is morphed into a lifeless corpse, when a brief moment before he had been so full of potential and promise. Either a soldier becomes hardened to this aspect of death in battle, or is inexorably destined, and often permanently, to be psychologically affected by it.

To some returning veterans, the experiences of the war were so horrific and mentally disturbing, they never wanted to recall or relive them. Consequently, it was not unusual that once at home—to leave Vietnam—was to leave it in Vietnam.

Snapping out of it, I returned to the present and made my way to the villa in Cholon, half-hoping Nadine wouldn't be there. We never want to confront a difficult issue in the present—of course, procrastinate, and maybe the problem will go away. It never does . . . It only gets worse!

She was home . . . Wouldn't you know it? After the usual small talk about both of our days and what to do this evening, I pussyfooted around, discussing how everything had been going so well at work and how things seemed to be winding down, almost running themselves.

With that, apparently Nadine couldn't stand it any longer, having allowed me to pay the penalty of being such a cad—sort of like Nixon when he instructed Atty. GEN Mitchell to allow Haldeman and Ehrlichman *to swing in the wind* during the Watergate affair of the early seventies.

She smiled, hugged, kissed me, and said, "I know you're leaving!"

"Let's stay home tonight," she said and poured us both a stiff drink. "Harry told me—everyone knows." I was relieved as Nadine clearly was taking it in stride for that matter better than I was.

I suggested a little quiet place in the neighborhood, which we compromised on, as Nadine wanted to stay at the villa, and we belted down another round. This was going to a long, tough night!

It was difficult to explain, but I was taking it harder than she was. In fact, Nadine seemed to be handling the reality of the s ituation that this part of our story was quickly coming to an end.

It was as if life was telling us that all our experiences are zero-sum games. No matter how much joy and happiness you experience in a given time frame, there is always a price to pay. Happiness and luck even out over a lifetime, and for the average person, happiness and luck even out over the space of one's lifetime. "There is no free lunch!" At least here on earth! Perhaps when transiting a black hole from one galaxy to another, where one may be able to retrace one's footsteps in time, the situation is different. And for some reason, it didn't bother me in the least that Harry had spilled the beans. I guessed just about everybody that knew me . . . knew!

We finished dinner quietly and quickly and headed toward the villa, walking aimlessly through the streets of Cholon, with our arms wrapped around each other's shoulders, just enjoying the evening, not saying much.

Even though it seemed that we both knew the old middle Eastern proverb of "This too shall pass" prevailed, it wasn't passing tonight!

It was a night that I was to long remember, and I was reminded, not for the first time, it was better to have loved and lost than not to have loved at all. Neither of us could find the right words, and as our eyes met, the love and the sadness we were sharing was apparent. Nadine held on to me like it was for the last time. As I tried to comfort her, I realized in fact I was comforting myself. The night passed slowly, but quickly.

Not being able to sleep, I left for my office early, determined to bring matters to a close and clear the decks for my departure. It seemed that now that I had made my peace with Nadine, I wanted to leave Saigon as quickly as possible.

No luck, Harry called about ten o'clock and told me keep the decks clear for tonight as he muddled incoherently about a group of us going to dinner to sort of celebrate.

The last day in our office on "nondescript street" was a lost day with staff and visitors coming in all day long to say good-bye. Bruce Bronson had lunch brought in from the Navy PX, and I was presented with a Nikon single-lens reflex (SLR) camera, one of the world's best lenses and therefore cameras of its day.

The card, signed by everyone, including the local sweep and clean lady (*lau chu'i*) who among her other duties, used her overused broom to sweep the sidewalk in front of our building. That is, if the ever-present group of unemployed men, sitting on their haunches in the middle of the sidewalk, condescended to being interrupted in their three-hour card game.

When I arrived at the villa that night, I found Nadine getting ready for our night out with Harry, who was due to pick us up in about an hour.

That left no time for anything but a shave, shower, and a little smooching. Besides, Nadine was giving me that "later look," which all men know how to recognize, and the smart ones agree to before they get the "I'm too tired tonight" or "I've got a headache" look!

Harry arrived on time, only fifteen minutes late, and he was, for him, dressed to the nines. I wrote it off as a coincidence as we were headed for dinner at a fairly swanky operation at the Continental Hotel. I'm sure it included a few cocktails at the bar in the lobby, where we last looked for Sydney Greenstreet and his sidekick, Peter Lorre!

Not to be disappointed, we arrived at the city's busiest before-dinner bar, the place humming with the usual cast of characters, along with a few European contractor types looking to pick up someone, but more likely to pick up something.

Before long, we were joined by some of the staff from Navy HQ, including Ed Rodriguez, with a cute blond round eye from the office on his arm. You were lost with this crowd if you didn't drink!

As a rule, we avoided shoptalk, particularly in a place such as this, so after patting ourselves on the back a few times, talking in what amounted to our own private code, the conversation drifted over to looking me up when any of them got to Washington. I half-tried to discourage it as I didn't want to dwell on a subject that had not been discussed with Nadine. Moreover, most of the "promises to look you up back in the States" was just cocktail-hour talk anyway.

After about an hour and a half of celebrating, which seemed longer, we made our way upstairs to the restaurant overlooking the city. Nadine and Harry sort of hung behind and allowed me to lead them into the restaurant. I was not getting it.

You guessed it! As I entered the restaurant, to my surprise, the place erupted. It was a surprise party, which I was completely surprised by. What do you think of that?

If the Viet Cong only knew, this would have been a good time to attack some nearby naval installation, for I think everyone from HQ was there, even the admiral! I must admit, although the whole thing being a surprise worked, I was a bit embarrassed. Harry had that look on his face, which indicated to me among other things, he had a hand in its arranging.

Once again I should have known something was up, the way both Nadine and Harry had dolled up for dinner. I was my normal dress-down and comfortable self. It didn't matter.

I must have had my picture taken with forty different people, some of whom I barely knew, but it was an enormously gratifying gesture. Now my mind tried to clear, alcoholic as it was, for the few words I surely was going to be asked to say, as all these shindigs seemed to call for. I was trying to think of something funny to kid the ole man about, and at first, I couldn't come up with a damn thing.

The admiral opened the festivities with the expected statement on how much he appreciated all the hard work and long hours the staff had put in, particularly over the past few weeks. Then there was a toast for a job well done! And a few hip, hip hoorays. Everyone in the place was pretty well gassed! I could feel the pressure mounting, as it could not be much longer before I was to be called upon to say a few words. I had to think of something, anything . . . quick!

The admiral clinked his glass with his knife as I started to choke on absolutely nothing but air or the lack of it.

He uttered a few nice words of introduction about me, something to the effect that I had been called back to CNA in Arlington, Virginia, and he thanked me for all my help and that I would be missed. Standard stuff.

As I rose to speak, it came to me. First, I raised my glass and proposed a toast to ADM Veth and his entire staff for all their hard work and cooperation.

I also said some nice words for Bruce Bronson and Ed Rodriguez and what a great help they had been and in particular the wonderful hospitality that had been afforded me during my "brief stay." A little false modesty never hurts.

It was then that I launched into my put-on for the admiral.

I said, "that I had been taking copious notes since my arrival in anticipation to writing a book about my trip and all that ensued up until tonight's party! I had completed a draft of it and sent it to some of my friends in Hollywood to see if they might be able to find a producer for the movie or any such similar undertaking."

Central casting had decided to make our boss, Admiral Veth, the central figure, and I had just received a wire that the Tinseltown moguls had decided upon producing the movie, but first wished me to consult with our boss to see if it was OK to cast Gary Cooper to play the admiral!"

The place roared, I think, half in courtesy to me and recognition that the ole man was getting a kick out of it.

And there was another problem . . . They couldn't as yet find anyone to play my part! The place roared, again! I went down the list of principle characters in my world: Harry (Bruce Dern), Bronson (George Clooney), Rodriguez (James Wood), Kip Kumler (Matt Damon), Mr. Bernard (Adolphe Menjou), Nadine (Gene Tierney) with black hair . . . and so on into the night, one toast after another.

I finished by singling out Harry for keeping a close eye out for "this civilian" and what a great help he had been to me. In conclusion, I offered that my office door in Washington was open to any who might come that way—all would be welcome!

I raised my glass again to toast the United States Navy and all those that serve and sat down, and I might add, to quite a gratifying applause.

As I went to sit down, Nadine rose and "laid one on me," just to let everyone know who she was as if they didn't know.

Mentally, that was it. I was out of here . . . most likely never to return.

X

Hong Kong and Tokyo – On the Way Home

My plane to Washington, through Hong Kong, Tokyo, entering the United States in Anchorage, Alaska, was scheduled to leave the next afternoon, and there was the issue of packing and spending the rest of tomorrow with Nadine.

After dinner, a few of us returned to the bar downstairs, and it was there, in private, that I said my good-byes to Harry. I knew then that I would never forget him. I think he understood that. Of course, we kidded ourselves about my returning to the Orient somehow, somewhere, to make money in what had to be the place, worldwide, where the most business potential existed.

We were right—just about thirty years too early!

The next day, Nadine stayed at the villa and helped me pack. Harry's driver was taking me to Tan Son Nhut around 4:00 p.m. It was a sad day as much as I wanted to get home; leaving was gut-wrenching, especially that last day with Nadine.

Nadine had given me the name of her brother Jeffrey, who lived in Hong Kong, and she had called him and asked him to meet my plane and show me around town.

I said good-bye to her at the villa as she wished to skip the ride to the airport. I kissed her good-bye out in the street by Harry's Mercedes and didn't look back as we drove away.

My plane from Saigon landed in the early part of the afternoon at Kai Tak Airport in Hong Kong. Landing at Kai Tak was always an experience as the short runway, since lengthened, brings the flight path in steeply overtall tenement houses and is bounded at the end of the runway by the sea. Landing there was always an experience!

Clearing customs was easy as these officials knew who or what they were looking for. It reminded me of the easy access at Schiphol Airport in Amsterdam in which there was self-chosen entranceways for passengers to choose to enter Holland. One was marked "Nothing to Declare"; the other, the opposite.

Once inside the airport, I easily found Nadine's brother Jeffrey—a tall, skinny Asian, no more than twenty-five years old, holding a cardboard sign marked Wilens. He spoke perfect English.

He very politely introduced himself and his two friends, who together didn't weigh much over two hundred pounds. He indicated that we didn't need to rent a car as he would be happy to drive me to my hotel, and the island was replete with Mercedes taxicabs, and almost everything was concentrated downtown along De Veaux Road where I was staying.

Seeing it was my first night in town, he invited me to an offbeat restaurant once I had indicated that I had no particular plans for the evening and liked Chinese food. I added that I intended to go shopping tomorrow at the China Fleet Club to which he raised his eyebrows.

Jeffrey said, "You have to be a US naval officer to shop there." I responded, "Don't worry, Jeff, I've got it covered."

After checking into my room on the Hong Kong Hilton's nineteenth floor, with a glorious view of the harbor and mainland China across the way, known as the Kowloon side, I showered and breathed a deep sigh of relief. I was coming down from the past six months in 'am . . . slowly . . . quickly.

On the way out of the lobby, I stopped to ask the concierge to have the maid take all my clothes, no exceptions, to the cleaners. He smiled approvingly and said, that he would be happy to!

Jeffrey was waiting for me out in front of the hotel, which was across the street from Hong Kong's supposedly best place to stay—the Mandarin Hotel.

We drove a short distance up De Veaux Road, the main drag, and got out of the car. "Where's the restaurant?" I asked. "Up there," Jeffery responded. We walked up a stairway street, climbing at least thirty steps, then turned left into an alleyway. Another alleyway!

There we entered an undecorated, no-frills restaurant, without a Caucasian customer in attendance. Looked great to me. And we settled down to one of the most genuine Chinese meals I had ever had the pleasure to eat, complete with dog soup, which wasn't so bad either!

I picked up the tab after a marathon-eating session and was ready for my first good night's sleep in months!

Jeffrey offered a few suggestions for shopping along De Veaux Road, for jade and ivory in particular, and he drove me to the Hilton.

Before turning in, I threw open the curtains to their full width and took in the breathtaking sight of the Hong Kong harbor. It was a kaleidoscope of flashing lights reflecting off the traffic moving in different directions as it seemed like New York. This city never slept.

Rising early the next day, I was excited as I had awaited this shopping spree that was about to take place for months. I had refined my shopping list time and time again as there was no limit to the advice I was offered as to what camera, hi-fidelity amplifier and speakers, tape recorder (reel to reel), watches, etc., I was to buy.

First place to stop was the USN-sponsored China Fleet Club as there were many cleared vendors there all under one roof. In four hours, not counting lunch, and being a quick shopper, I spent almost $7,500 on about 80 percent of my list.

Feeling satisfied, having broken the back of the spree, I returned to the hotel as Christmas was only two days away. I had some phone calls to make and a nap to take.

Passing my friend, the concierge, in the middle of the lobby, I inquired as to the status of my cleaning. He said, "I'll look into it and call you."

"Incidentally, where can I have some suits made?" I asked.

"George Chen's over on the Kowloon side. Just take the Star Ferry and go to the Peninsula Court building next to the Peninsula Court Hotel. The ferry costs five HK cents first class!" (One cent US!) I was afraid to ask what steerage cost!

"And another thing, Mr. Concierge," I said, seeing this guy obviously knew his way around, "would it be possible to send a woman up to my room?"

"Do you wish Chinese?" he said? Liking Chinese food, I said, "Yes, please!"

It was about thirty minutes later, and I was about to get into the shower. The phone rang, and it was the concierge indicating that he was sending a young lady up to the room. Service with a smile, I thought.

Perhaps it was the maid with my cleaned clothes . . . I hoped I was wrong!

The bell rang, and I moved with anticipation across the room to open the door. I opened the door, and for the first time in my life, I froze, dumbfounded . . . speechless . . . It was Nadine!

In somewhat of a state of shock, I invited her in. Just minutes before, I was reveling in surprising relief and easing of pent-up tension accumulated over almost six months' time . . . that it was over and I had made it! Now my mind was spinning with irrational thoughts and bewilderment.

The last thing I needed was to take Nadine home!

She asked me to pour her a drink, and I joined her as quickly as I could manage it. We sat down next to each other on the couch where we could see the lights flashing in one of the world's most beautiful harbors. It was quite a romantic setting with a most attractive woman, but my thoughts weren't running in that direction—for once in my life.

"Marty, first let me say that our relationship got out of hand. At first it was all business. It was my job. I hadn't planned for it to go as far as it did. I'm sorry!" Here we go again, another *sin loi*.

I thought, *Where had I heard that before? Surely somewhere, sometime.*

"OK, but who are you, and who do you work for?" I could hardly wait for the answer. I was dying with anticipation!

"I work for the company, out of Langley, assigned to Saigon permanently. My job was to infiltrate local VC intelligence for the CIA . . . a mole! My relationship with you enhanced my credentials to the VC hierarchy!" I began to sweat.

"OK, but I don't get it . . . why me?"

"At first, nothing, but you came into town, and I was assigned to both use you, to make it look to the VC like I was well connected, while simultaneously looking after you . . . For as long as you were with me, our relationship became useful to their intel people.

"Hanging out with you fit perfectly into this undertaking and enabled me to create the appearance to the VC that I was getting somewhere!"

My sweating had now reached the point where I was beginning to feel uncomfortable . . . and pissed!

"In that way, you were safe, except perhaps from the Saigon cowboys."

"What did you tell them? What did you know?"

"That was easy. Whatever the local CIA office, in conjunction with Navy HQ, wanted them to know! Don't worry, nothing important."

"And how did you know who I was and where to contact me and what I was in the country for?"

"That was easy too. Harry briefed me!"

"Harry? Oh no, not Harry too," I blurted out like the dummy I was beginning to feel like.

Nadine embarrassingly said, "I reported to Harry. He was deputy chief of the CIA desk in Saigon . . . and had been for two years!"

I belted down the remainder of my drink and poured another . . . Neat!

"And why are you here?" I stammered? "And how did you know where I was staying? Oh, I see, I guess Jeffrey isn't your brother, either!"

"The boys at Langley wanted me to debrief them on this whole operation in person and felt it was a good time for me to leave, with your exiting the country . . . for all I know I may be reassigned."

I thought, but did not say, "I hope not to Bethesda, Maryland, or anywhere close by."

Nadine offered, unsolicited, "It may be with all that's ready to break loose in the Delta, this operation of yours. The company wants me the hell out of the country. The VC weren't too happy about that last operation."

In less than a minute, the events of the past months flashed across my mind like a comet careening across the sky, and it quickly burned itself out fading into oblivion and finality.

In that minute, I remembered Harry's more-than-expected knowledge of naval affairs, the procurement of the captured Chinese shotgun, the introduction to Rashid—the money exchanger, his ability to get things done not normally accomplished easily, the "arranged weekend" in Bangkok with Nadine, and his relationships at important places in Saigon—to say nothing of his chauffeur-driven Mercedes.

In the last half of the minute's reflection, I recalled my "chance meeting" with Nadine at La Baccara, the arrangement for the villa in Cholon, the familiarity with the VC at the gas station we stopped at on the picnic, her conversations with the SEALs staying at the villa and the Marines in Bangkok, Harry's insistence on blowing my cover at Van Caan's while I attempted to make Nadine his date for the evening, and her dinners alone with Harry!

"Marty, for the time being, both of our jobs are over. Everything I could get from the local VC operatives has been turned over to Harry, and Navy HQ is incorporating the info, where appropriate, into your operation.

"No harm's been done! Quite to the contrary, my sense is this new SEAL Team-CIDG force operation in the canals, leading to the main tributaries, is going to be very successful!"

I guess we had covered it all, or should I say Nadine had just covered it all. She said, "Let's clean up, and I'll treat you to dinner. I owe you, and I know a great place on the other side of the island."

I know it's crazy, and despite feeling a bit foolish and used—but Nadine was stunning. As we left the hotel, the concierge gave me the eye, and so we asked him to call a cab for us to go over to Aberdeen.

It turned out we were heading for the world-famous floating restaurants, where dinner was served on board one of the junks that berthed in the little fishing village of Aberdeen, located completely around the other side of Hong Kong island from "the Kowloon or mainland side."

After a three-hour dinner by candlelight and seafood fit for a king and Queen and two bottles of wine, we weaved our way back to the Hilton in what we both knew would be our last night together.

At one point during the evening, we stood together embracing, looking out over the majestic harbor, with the dominating blue Seiko sign reflecting on its placid waters, knowing this episode was coming to a bittersweet ending.

I don't have to tell you we didn't get much sleep as our plane was scheduled to leave for the States at 10:00 a.m. In fact, I don't remember sleeping at all! It was a night to remember . . . our last hurrah.

Nadine and I would share the long plane ride to the States through Tokyo, entering the United States via Anchorage, Alaska. There, the customs lady, after taking a peek at both my six pieces of luggage and the military stamps all over my passport, and seeing the Nikon camera slung around my neck, to say nothing of the Yamaha skis teetering over my shoulder, smiled. Needless to say, Nadine had no trouble with customs either.

The customs lady sailed me through, chalking "OK" on my bags, while asking me, "Was Vietnam rough, son?" Glancing over at Nadine and reflecting briefly, I replied, "Not so bad, ma'am!"

*   *   * THE END *   *   *

Epilogue

The conflict in Vietnam was essentially comprised of three wars.

One aspect of which we never had a chance to win, being fought daily against the time-honored adage "not to fight a land war on the continent of Asia."

Secondly, the war's progress, being reported back to the Pentagon by the military brass in country, was designed to appease their superiors while biding their time, hoping that things would change for the better or a deal could be struck along the lines of the Korean settlement.

Thirdly, the war being reported to the president, his cabinet, and the media by the Joint Chiefs and the MACV was designed to place a spin on its true status. Public demonstrations against the war turned out to be correct, but were for the wrong reasons. I leave it to the reader to draw their parallels in history, both past and present.

At the crux of the problem was that we hadn't any ally. A case certainly could be made that we had chosen the wrong side. To this day, no determination has been made as to the responsibility for the assassination of South Vietnam's president Ngo Dinh Diem in November 1963.

Many felt his regime authoritarian and that the military coup that deposed him was inspired by the United States. No proof of this was ever presented to support this, however. Similar assertions were made about his wife, Madame Nhu.

It has been reported publicly that President Kennedy had instructed his secretary of defense, Robert McNamara, and Defense Intelligence Agency (DIA) chief, GEN Maxwell Taylor, to reduce the number of "advisors" in Vietnam from about 13,800 to 12,800 by the end of the year 1963.

In Robert Dallek's book, *An Unfinished Life*, published in 2003, he refers to this JFK directive but also notes that on October 11, 1963, slightly over one month before President Kennedy's assassination, an NSA memo was issued "that no formal withdrawal" was being planned . . .

No confirmation of this report or similar assertions relating to a phased withdrawal made by subsequent government officials were ever made.

That there was no intention under JFK to pursue the eventual massive buildup of troop levels asked for by presidents Johnson and Nixon was ever confirmed.

The South was clearly the less industrious of the two populaces and was mainly agrarian in nature, lacking the resources of the North. Under the threat that the North Vietnamese had designs on spreading their brand of Communism throughout Southeast Asia, known as the domino theory, our policy, correct or not, drove us in the direction of using South Vietnam for a containment action—not that they were the preferred side to ally with. Also working against our achieving our intervention in Vietnam, as a limited action, was the South Vietnamese business establishment. For that matter, the general populace located in the southern half of the country (III and IV Corps zones)[*] was prospering as they never had during the years under French rule, especially in Saigon.

Additionally, insisting on fighting mainly a defensive action limited our ground forces to actions within the borders of South Vietnam, except for sporadic raids that generally failed to achieve their objective and hamstrung our overall strategy from the

---

[*]   III Corps were comprised of twelve provinces, just immediately north of Saigon.

beginning. It was a war of position and maneuver, one that we were neither qualified nor prepared to fight.

In mid to late 1967, a controversy developed between the CIA and the Department of Defense (DOD). It centered upon the issue of whether the corridor that existed along Cambodia's eastern border, particularly as it related to access to War Zones III and IV, immediately above and below Saigon, were the staging areas from which the VC infiltrated contraband into those regions of the country.

The agency took the position that it didn't form such a staging area or repository for enemy weapons, ammunition, and medical supplies. DOD contended that it did. The controversy was classified top secret under the code name Sunshine Park. After the war reached its final stages, circa 1970-71, the CIA investigated the adjacent border areas in question and uncovered twenty-two tons of contraband, proving their position to be incorrect. (This amount of supplies could not in any way have represented a maximum amount, as at this point, the war was not only winding down, but other avenues of infiltration now had become available to both the VC and the NVN as the concept of Vietnamization was in a state of collapse.)

When President Kennedy took office in 1960, there were 900 military advisors in country, which increased to 15,000 by November 1963 when Lyndon Johnson assumed the presidency. By June 1965, this number had increased to 23,000 combat soldiers, and by year-end, this force numbered 184,000 troops and advisors. At the peak of our involvement, under a third president (Nixon) during 1968-69, had committed 525,000 combat and support personnel to Vietnam. Instead of gaining progress through this buildup of forces, not counting Australian, Korean, and Philippine participation, and the bare survival of the Tet Offensive in January to February 1968, the die had been cast, and the North's forces along with the Viet Cong had gained the upper hand.

The Swift Boats were also a part of the patrol force contingent in Operation Game Warden (Task Force-TF 116). Senator John Kerry, who was assigned to duty aboard these boats, was known for his four-month tour of duty in which he was awarded three Purple Hearts and was never admitted to a hospital for any of his wounds "incurred in battle"!

Once involved in analyzing the Game Warden operations, the Swift Boat (PCFs), along with the water-jet propelled PBRs in Game Warden as having limited use, for the time being, and dismissed them from any utility in solving ADM Veth's problem. Desperate for assets, the PBRs were used for patrolling in certain areas consistent with their light armor and spotty reliability.

Given the shortage of assets in 1966-68, these boats were nevertheless used extensively. The formation during this period of the Mobile Riverine Force (MRF), designated CTF-117, with its armored troop carriers (ATCs) and armored support patrol boats were initially under the command of Maj. GEN George S. Eckhardt. This force did not become completely operational until mid-1967.

Craig Symonds, in his accounting of Game Warden Operations during this time, described them this way in his *Historical Atlas of the US Navy*:

> In addition to the lightly armored PBR's, the Navy also employed monitors, armored troop carriers (ATC's), and armored support patrol boats . . . were built atop the hulls of old landing craft (LCM's converted to armored fire-support vessels) . . . and equipped with bar armor designed to detonate heavy ordnance, especially rockets before it could penetrate. Heavy, slow, and ungainly, ... the ATC's was the exact opposite of the speedy little PBR's. Their function was to carry soldiers to enemy strong points and provide fire support during ground operations.

The joke around HQ, where Market Time (Task Force-TF 115) and Game Warden were nominally administered, was that the Swift Boats "weren't too swift." Many years later, Senator Kerry's account of his heroics on patrol in the Delta was even funnier.

GEN Vo Nguyen Giap, NVN. Viet Minh planned Tet Offensive of '68, known for siege at Dien Bien Phu, commanded by French GEN Jacques Leclerc. Located in northwest part of North Vietnam, it was besieged by the NVN (Viet Minh Army), surrounded, and through a maze of tunnels, tightened the noose around the fortress until its collapse and surrender on May 5, 1954. This culminated the long-standing (1863) French involvement in the region.

North Vietnamese torpedo boats reportedly attacked two US destroyers at 2035 hours, in the Gulf of Tonkin, in NVN waters, just west of Hainan Island, on August 2, 1964.

Congress voted for a Gulf of Tonkin resolution a few days later, which authorized President Johnson "to take all necessary measures" to win the war. Johnson retaliates with air strikes in the North.

Extracted from the US Department of the Army Report:

Vietnam Studies, Command and Control (1950-1969), Department of the Army, by Major General George S. Eckhardt[*]. Library of Congress Catalog Card No: 72-600186. From Chapter 4, "The Continuing Buildup," July 1966-July 1969, pages 77-80, entitled "Naval Forces—Vietnam."

Mobile Riverine Force

In 1966, a concept was developed for extending US combat power into the Mekong Delta area where the enemy was strong and where the United States had lacked the resources to assist the Vietnamese Army in achieving control. MACV headquarters organized what was originally called the Mekong Delta Mobile Afloat Force, soon to be known as the Mobile Riverine Force. The original plan called for basing one US Army division in a location where it could operate along the Mekong and Bassac Rivers. Army troops were to be supported by US Navy river assault groups, and one brigade of the division would be stationed aboard converted LSTs (landing ships, tank). This concept required new and unusual command relationships.

General Westmoreland proposed that one brigade of the arriving Ninth Infantry Division be the Army component of a mobile joint task force. The Navy component would consist of tactical and logistic ships and craft to support the brigade afloat on riverine operations. General Westmoreland further proposed that the joint task force be commanded by the assistant commander of the Ninth Division, who would have a small joint staff of operations, logistics, and communications personnel.

---

[*] In January 1968, GEN Eckhardt became commanding general of the Delta Military Assistance Command, and senior advisor, IV Corps Tactical Zone, headquartered in Can Tho.

In Honolulu, General Waters, commander in chief, US Army, Pacific, concurred with General Westmoreland's proposal. Admiral Sharp and the commander in chief of the Pacific Fleet, however, favored a command arrangement in which the naval force would be under the operational control of the commander of the River Patrol Force (a task force, CTF 116, which was already conducting operations in the Mekong Delta) and would operate in support of the ground forces involved. A compromise solution ultimately developed, which placed US Army units conducting riverine operations in the III and IV Corps Tactical Zones under the operational control of the commanding general of II Field Force. He could exercise control through a designated subordinate headquarters, such as the Ninth Infantry Division. According to this arrangement, Navy units would be under the operational control of Admiral Ward, who could also operate through a designated subordinate Navy commander. (Another task force, CTF 117, was established to control Navy riverine forces.) Finally, riverine operations would be conducted with Army and Navy units commanded separately, but the Navy would provide close support through procedures of mutual coordination *(Chart 9)*.

The Mobile Riverine Force began operations on June 1, 1967, with Operation Coronado in Dinh Tuong province. The Second Brigade of the Ninth Infantry Division and the Mobile Riverine Force conducted a two-month offensive in the vast waterways of the Mekong Delta with extraordinary success. The force continued aggressive operations until August 25, 1969, when the riverine force was deactivated and its mission and equipment were taken over by the Vietnamese Navy Amphibious Task Force 211.

The Army will provide the base commander both ashore and afloat. The Navy will provide its appropriate share of personnel for local base defense and primary efforts directed toward provision of gunfire support and protection against waterborne threats.

*   *   * END of EXTRACTION *   *   *

Epilogue (*cont'd.*)

The North Vietnamese Army (NVA) refused to be drawn into the open by our search-and-destroy tactics. These probing tactics were designed to make contact with large numbers of enemy forces in an effort to use our superior ordinance and air power to inflict casualties by drawing the NVA into major encounters. On the other hand, the NVA, and to a greater extent, the Viet Cong, employed hit-and-run tactics while attacking on their frequency and schedule.

These tactics relegated us to fighting defensive battles, the most visible being the long siege by our First Marine Division in I Corps, just south and inside the demilitarized zone (DMZ), separating North and South Vietnam at the Seventeenth Parallel north of the equator. The world followed the yearlong siege of a company of Marines at Khe Sanh, just south of the DMZ.

The Viet Cong employed a guerrilla-type insurgency battle strategy. Moving in squad-size units of fifteen to twenty men, they used ambush and booby trap tactics as part of a strategy to slowly weaken our resolve to continue fighting.

Often the supply and infiltration of small units in close proximity to our lines, or within our sphere of influence, was accomplished by tunneling, much like the Cu Chi tunnels connecting VC sanctuaries near the Cambodian border thirty miles away from Saigon. Purported to contain medical facilities, arms and ammunition caches, and sleeping rooms, these tunnels had three levels and enabled the VC to tunnel to the northwest outskirts of Saigon. They were in existence at war's end.

American forces were usually not prepared to respond or counterattack this type of warfare, constantly keeping our forces off balance. Some larger battles eventually took place in II Corps, in the Itrang and Ashau Valleys, and near Hue and Danang, coastal cities far to the north. These encounters never met with any marked success and often in defeat.

Whether better intelligence as to the enemy's intentions and capabilities, would have improved the final outcome, will forever remain in question.

Central to our failure to win was the absurd tenet that we fight a limited defensive action within South Vietnam.

As in any sporting contest, it is paramount to play to win. This could not have been accomplished without physically interdicting the enemy's supply lines emanating from the city of Vinh in the North, and raiding enemy sanctuaries in Vietnam and parts of eastern Cambodia, *we were doomed to failure.*

Some critics would say this would have brought the Chinese into the war. To them, I counter in two ways: (1) not if we limited our insurgence to the lower half of the North, up to and including the northern terminal of the Ho Chi Minh Trail at Vinh near the Nineteenth Parallel, and (2) if that action drew the Chinese into the North, we would have had plenty of time to withdraw, leaving the problem of Ho for the Chinese to resolve as we never entertained, even remotely, occupying that region contiguous to the Chinese border.

It appeared that the feared Cambodian Communist forces, intent on overthrowing the incumbent regime in Phnom Penh, had made an accommodation with the Viet Minh forces to allow the VC to operate freely within about fifty miles of the SVN border.

A little-known secret operation was conducted as we placed forces in very limited numbers into southeast Laos, in the vicinity of the Ho Trail.

Apparently, it met with limited success, and I suspect because its existence being designated top secret, was undermanned and undersupported for fear of detection.

The parallels between then and now are inescapable. Although our military has been downsized and made more effective with the advent of laser-guided missiles, GPS-guided bombs, global surveillance through "spy in the sky" systems, drones (unmanned aircraft), and more effective firearms and ammunition, and the development of highly trained strike forces like the Delta forces and Army Rangers teams, we still are at our weakest fighting a guerrilla-like force, using counter-insurgency tactics.

Terrorism, and its tactics, adds another negative dimension to this picture.

Today, developments are under way for an anecdotal system using ground positioning radar (GPR) to counter IEDs[*], and their development is being fast-tracked by the military. To the extent these remote-controlled devices are set alongside roadways or out in the open where they can be detected using the GPR concept, they will be removed from our enemy's arsenal of remote activation explosives devices.

However, the Pentagon reacts to new threats rather than forecasting them, and unfortunately, American lives are lost while our military's planning and ability to forecast new guerrilla or terrorist threats are playing catch-up!

In Vietnam, whether it was a lack of understanding as to the nature of the war we were engaged in or our inability to change or alter its course, we failed at both.

In 1971, the US Congress voted to bar the use of combat troops in Laos and Cambodia, limiting our military action in those countries to air strikes. Secretary of State Kissinger's "enclave strategy and Vietnamization" of the war failed. Fatalities swelled to

---

[*] *Improvised explosive devices.* Their position will be marked in the roadway by fast-moving, heavily armored, modular-designed vehicles equipped with these antidetection devices.

280

58,000 Americans killed in action, and plans were set in motion in Washington to withdraw.

A tripartite peace conference was convened in Paris consisting of both representatives of North and South Vietnam and the National Liberation Front (the Viet Cong). A number of western countries, including the United States, participated as observers. A peace settlement was signed in January 1973. As fighting continued between North and South during the prolonged maneuverings at the conference, Northern forces reached within forty miles of Saigon, and with the downfall of the capital imminent, President Van Thieu resigned on April 21, 1975. The reduction of our forces had been under way since mid-1971, with the withdrawal completed on April 30, 1975, as the last American forces and civilians left the country, ending the longest war in American history, sixteen years.

In 1976, both North and South were unified through an election by the national assembly in Hanoi, under Ho Chi Minh as premier.

After my return to Washington in 1967, I was asked to debrief some of the most powerful military advisors in the United States. Among them were GEN Maxwell Taylor, Defense Intelligence Agency; the commandant of the Marine Corps and at least a half a dozen of his top advisors; Herman Kahn, of the Hudson Institute (author of a popular book of the time, *On Thermonuclear War*); the commandant of the Air Force Academy; the brass at the Navy's postgraduate officers school at Monterrey, California; the Navy's CNO; the submarine-base brass at Groton, Connecticut; and various senior naval officers in the Pentagon including those of OP-93.

The essential theme and observations of this book were clearly made known to them in no uncertain terms, often in private. It is incomprehensible to me that the truth of the actual conduct and status of the war was not conveyed up the chain of command to the highest level. We will never know whether it was a case of being unable to figure out a way to extricate ourselves from the conflict sooner, or that an attempt was made, but like a battleship's momentum was difficult to turn around—either quickly or gracefully.

The Vietnam conflict will remain a blot on the history of this country for time in memoriam.

*   *   * END of EPILOGUE *   *   *

The CIDG Program Begins to Mature

In the early years, the Civilian Irregular Defense Group program was essentially a defensive effort characterized by the overriding goal of securing control over the indigenous minorities and winning their allegiance so that they would not fall to the Communists. The missions were to control the Viet Cong, either through area development or border surveillance or combinations of the two. The civilian irregulars and the US Special Forces were not hunting the Viet Cong in the beginning. The buildup of conventional US forces in Vietnam changed all that and opened the door to the next stage in the evolution of the Special Forces CIDG program—a stage in which the Special Forces and the irregulars would find themselves cast in a distinctly offensive role. They were to become hunters with the mission of finding and destroying the enemy.

In January 1965, just before the beginning of the massive US commitment of conventional forces to South Vietnam, the US Special Forces counterinsurgency program was defined in a letter from headquarters, Fifth Special Forces Group (airborne), to the commanders of all operational A, B, and C detachments:

Definition: The SF Counterinsurgency Program is a phased and combined military-civil counterinsurgency effort designed to accomplish the following objectives: (a) destroy the Viet Cong and create a secure environment, (b) establish firm governmental control over the population, and (c) enlist the population's active and willing support of and participation in the government's programs.

These objectives are accomplished while executing any one of three possible assigned missions: (1) border surveillance and control, (2) operations against infiltration routes, or (3) operations against VC war zones and bases.

Concept of the operation: This is essentially a clear, secure, and developed operation. A fundamental point in the counterinsurgency program is that, where possible, the strike force personnel should be locally recruited in order to provide an exploitable entry to the populace, which in turn, facilitates military-civil relations.

The letter goes on to state that no population area which is "uncommitted" or which has been dominated by the Viet Cong can be considered won to the government until the Viet Cong have been cleared from the area, the local Viet Cong underground organization has been eliminated, and the government of the Republic of Vietnam has firmly replaced that of the Viet Cong. The letter also points out that in remote areas, the task is often to introduce the government representatives for the first time.

While the new offensive role of the CIDG under the US Special Forces is reflected in the letter, its operations statement reveals that the old area development concepts were still operative to a large extent. As the number of conventional US forces began to grow, however, the use of the Special Forces and CIDG troops in a straightforward, offensive combat role became the norm—both in theory and in practice. In these middle years, the civilian irregulars under the Special Forces assumed a fully offensive, though not always fully conventional, role. They became hunters of the Viet Cong and the North Vietnamese Army.

US forces were there to defeat the enemy. Their presence and the presence of conventional North Vietnamese units changed the nature of the entire war. Before 1965, there was principally a guerrilla insurgency. After 1965, the conflict became more conventional, with the major qualification that guerrilla tactics were used heavily by the enemy. At any rate, the "conventionalization" of the war led to the "conventionalization" of the civilian irregulars, who were no longer fighting for their own protection but instead were fighting to defeat the enemy.

The emergence of the Special Forces Civilian Irregular Defense Group project as an offensive effort is not surprising. For the most part, the American soldier arriving in Vietnam found himself in an environment totally different from anything he had ever experienced. He was not used to the heat, the rain, the jungle. He did not know the Vietnamese people and their culture. He did not speak the language. And most significantly, he did not know who or where the enemy was or how to find out. On the other hand, the US Special Forces and their civilian irregular troops were accustomed to the heat, rain, and jungle, and they could communicate. Special Forces men had come to know the people and their culture. Participation by the Special Forces in tribal ceremonial functions was not uncommon, and the Montagnard bracelet worn by many Green Berets was a token of Montagnard respect and involved a ceremony for its presentation.

And finally, if they did not know who or where the Viet Cong were, they could find out.

Besides causing the shift to the offensive in the Special Forces CIDG role, the large number of American troops had other effects on the CIDG program, both good and bad. For example, new American commanders often misjudged or misunderstood the capabilities of the Civilian Irregular Defense Group units present in their tactical areas of responsibility. As a result, a company of irregulars would occasionally be requested for a job which a US infantry company could handle but for which the irregulars were neither trained nor prepared. Another mistake US commanders made was to propose splitting a CIDG company, with the idea of sending one platoon here and another there. This practice, standard procedure for an American unit, was hard on the CIDG troops for whom unit integrity was extremely important. The civilian irregulars did not think of themselves as battalions, brigades, or divisions. They were companies, strike forces, tied together not only by their Vietnamese Special Forces commanders and US Special Forces advisers, but also by their common homelands and tribal bonds. It is not surprising then that a CIDG platoon would be in over its head trying to work with a US infantry platoon on its flanks. On the whole, US commanders never really became familiar with the civilian irregulars and their capabilities.

The US buildup also had good effects. Most important of these was in the area of camp defense and security—two major concerns in the early years. The chief difficulty had been to reinforce a camp rapidly and effectively when it came under imminent or actual enemy attack. The buildup of US forces not only provided powerful US reaction forces, but it also promoted further development, particularly from 1966 to 1967, of indigenous reaction forces, known as mobile strike units, in numbers, dispersion, and strength.

The advent of US Air Force support along with the helicopter and its availability to the CIDG reaction forces made rapid and effective response a reality. Command and operational control structures were reorganized and streamlined in order to provide rapid reaction forces with reserves. Eventually, these developments would make it possible for the Special Forces and civilian irregulars to reinforce camps under attack that would otherwise have been lost. Similar positive effects were achieved in other combat operations. For example, in the early 1960s, the irregulars had run into enemy units which were too big for them to handle. In the latter years, such contacts could be and were exploited. In fact, one of the major functions of the CIDG came to be precisely that of finding the enemy in force so that he could be engaged.

Along these lines, it is not surprising that the ability to gather intelligence that was inherent in the Special Forces CIDG effort came to be heavily used. The CIDG troops and their US and Vietnamese Special Forces leaders were ideally suited for the task of finding and fixing enemy forces. Their camps were dispersed from one end of the country to the other, usually in Viet Cong territory. Further, the civilian irregulars and the Special Forces were themselves trained guerrillas, capable of meeting the enemy on his own terms. Military Assistance Command, Vietnam, estimates indicate that in the course of this period, almost 50 percent of the command's ground combat intelligence came from Special Forces and civilian irregulars.

Again, this new role as intelligence gatherers had both good and bad effects on the Special Forces CIDG program. On the positive side, the CIDG program was revitalized and strengthened when its value as a source of intelligence was realized and exploited. In the early years, plans had been formulated for the discontinuance of the program as such and its integration into the conventional Vietnamese military structure. In fact, the opposite happened. The program continued to expand vigorously as new missions like the production of intelligence were devised.

On the other hand, the emphasis on producing reliable intelligence for use by conventional forces necessarily led to the decline of what may be termed "local" intelligence. Under the area development concept, emphasis had been placed on intelligence covering the local Viet Cong underground organization in the area of operation of each camp. The aim was to destroy the Viet Cong organization in each tactical area of responsibility. Later, when priority was given to intelligence for conventional forces, local intelligence efforts deteriorated, with a corresponding decrease in the effectiveness of local area development. Finding and destroying the Viet Cong countrywide by conventional military methods took precedence over the more subtle tactic of systematically rooting out the Viet Cong structure in each of the areas surrounding the CIDG camps. This is not to say that the expanded and unified intelligence mission given the Special Forces and civilian irregulars was not effective. On the contrary, it was effective. But the talents of the Special Forces in area development came to be exploited only to a minimal degree.

Finally, the demand for intelligence was the primary factor influencing the development of the so-called unconventional operations carried out by the Special Forces during this period. The mission of finding the enemy led to the establishment of such special operations as Projects Delta, Omega, and Sigma, which proved to be significant contributions of the US Special Forces to the war in Vietnam. The intelligence these projects produced was invaluable, and their deadly effectiveness against the enemy proved their worth as methods of offensive counterinsurgency.

In the course of these middle years, the Special Forces troops also were given new missions, which, while related to the CIDG program, were in addition to their CIDG mission. Included among these were the subsector advisory mission and the recondo (reconnaissance-commando) school mission.

Combat actions during this period fell into three categories. First, there were actions connected with the opening, closing, or defense of CIDG camps, especially along the border, including the battles at A Shau, Lang Vei, Con Thien, Loc Ninh, Thuong Thoi, and Bu Dop. The pattern seems to have been that when a camp became a real nuisance to the enemy, he was very likely to attack in great strength in an effort to overrun and destroy it. Otherwise, the camps were left alone, and any contacts made were, for the most part, the result of sending out patrols from the camp.

Second, there were combat actions that grew out of the special operations, including Project Delta operations in I Corps; Blackjack 33 operations in III Corps under Project Sigma—the first operation in which mobile guerrilla forces were employed in conjunction with a project force; Blackjack 41, in which two mobile strike force companies conducted a parachute assault in the Seven Mountains region of IV Corps, and a mobile strike force carried out an operation in III Corps around Soui Da, in which the force was credited with rendering a Viet Cong battalion ineffective and which eventually developed into Operation Attleboro.

Finally, the third type of combat action took place when CIDG troops were employed in conjunction with conventional forces in conventional combat operations. Among these were Operation Nathan Hale, jointly conducted by CIDG forces, First Cavalry Division (Airmobile), and 101st Airborne Division; Operations Henry Clay and Thayer; Operation Rio Blanco in I Corps, involving CIDG troops, Regional Forces, Vietnam Army troops, Vietnam Rangers, Korean Marines, and US Marines; and Operation Sam Houston in II Corps, conducted by the Fourth Infantry Division and the CIDG troops. The CIDG troops also fought in the cities during the enemy Tet Offensive of 1968. Contacts made by mobile strike forces and mobile guerrilla forces often developed into significant combat actions.

The introduction of large numbers of US forces to the conflict in Vietnam brought drastic changes in the role of the US Special Forces, in the Civilian Irregular Defense Group program, and in the war itself. The effects were felt almost immediately in the assignment of new subordinate missions, including that of assisting in the introduction of US forces into remote areas.

Initially the US troop buildup had its greatest impact on the CIDG program in the II and III Corps Tactical Zones because conventional operations were, in the beginning, conducted there on a much larger scale geographically than they were in IV Corps or I Corps. In II and III Corps, tactical areas of responsibility of the CIDG camps repeatedly intersected or were included in the operational areas of conventional US forces, with the result that camp strike forces came more and more under indirect US operational control.

US unit commanders soon realized that a Civilian Irregular Defense camp was an excellent source of local information. They learned quickly that guides, interpreters, scouts, or trackers, and fairly proficient prisoner-of-war interrogators were to be found in the camps, and that the strike force companies—provided that their special aptitudes were exploited and they were not expected to perform in all respects like US infantry companies—could be useful adjuncts to US search-and-destroy operations.

In I Corps, conventional operations by the III Marine Amphibious Force were concentrated near the coast and therefore did not become operationally involved with the Civilian Irregular Defense Group. It was not until the spring of 1967, with the introduction of Task Force Oregon, that this situation changed. In IV Corps, the US buildup had no impact on operations in the beginning, although good effects were felt, for example, in more helicopter and tactical air support.

The buildup benefited the Civilian Irregular Defense Group program itself in many ways. US Army engineers were brought in to assist in the construction of camps. US ground forces could now be used as security forces when areas were being explored to select new campsites. A combination of US combat forces and civilian irregulars would make it possible to establish CIDG camps in areas where enemy strength had previously made it unfeasible. There was now increased helicopter support for CIDG air mobile operations. US combat forces could now be employed as reaction forces to exploit opportunities developed by CIDG operations and to relieve CIDG troops or camps under attack.

The camps of the civilian irregulars were small isolated strong points, without any inherent capability for mutual support. The organic mobile strike forces did not attain significant strength until late in 1966. Vietnamese Army reaction forces were usually available but could seldom be committed quickly. Actually, until the US infantry arrived in strength, there was no force available to exploit such a target of opportunity as a multibattalion concentration of Viet Cong preparing to attack a Special Forces camp or to justify penetration of the war zones by CIDG reconnaissance patrols to locate enemy units. Especially during 1965 and 1966, many of the more productive US operations in II and III Corps began as reactions to CIDG contacts with the enemy or as attacks against enemy concentrations discovered in their preparations by Special Forces agencies.

The troop buildup also brought difficulties for the Special Forces. These invariably stemmed from a lack of understanding on the part of US commanders at all levels of the nature of the CIDG program and its command structure, of the role of Special Forces operational detachments, and of the capabilities and limitations of irregulars. The most common mistakes of US commanders and staff officers were to equate a strike force company with a regular infantry company and to assume that CIDG camps located in an American unit's assigned area automatically came under its operational command.

In the period from July 1965 to June 1966, the Special Forces continued to grow. No attempts at turnover were made during this year; the emphasis was on expansion and development of CIDG resources in support of the war effort in general. This growth was another effect of the US buildup, one which had not been expected and which came to light when the Fifth Special Forces Group submitted its analysis of the CIDG.

With the deployment of conventional US combat units to RVN in May 1965, it was felt by many that the CIDG effort was no longer required or valid in the face of the increased enemy threat. A study was conducted by the MACV staff to determine the desirability of completely phasing out all USASF and converting the ClDG to Regional Force status by January 1, 1967. The proposed conversion schedule required a specified number of CIDG to convert to RF during a specified time frame.

While being considered for complete phaseout by January 1967, it was found that the CIDG camps provided valuable staging bases from which ARVN and the Free World Military Assistance Forces (FWMAF) could launch offensive operations against the enemy, a role the founders of the program had not foreseen.

Some of the points made by the departing commander of the Fifth Special Forces (airborne) in June 1966 concerning his year of command will bear repeating here.

The "special" about Special Forces is simply that the noncommissioned officers are the finest to be found anywhere in the world. Their multiple skills and individual motivation are exploited to the fullest in the combat environment of the A detachment in VC-dominated areas. If today's Special Forces NCO has ever had any peer, it was probably the tough, self-reliant, combat-tested soldier who fought on the Indian frontier of our own country during the 1870s.

Also, to my surprise, I discovered that the CIDG troops are not the band of unskilled, disorganized, and disgruntled peasants I had envisioned. They are, in fact, closely knit religious or ethnic minority groups with a fierce loyalty to each other and to those who will treat them with respect and consideration.

The addition of an air mobile company (light) has proved to be of particular value. Command and control are greatly enhanced, and the organic capability to stage my own air mobile operations has drastically reduced reaction time, which is so important in this counterinsurgency environment. Similarly, the engineer augmentation has greatly assisted in improving airfields and expediting camp construction.

A few observations should be made in the area of combat operations. First, much of the initiative still rests in the hands of the VC and the NVA. This remains so primarily as a result of the first-rate intelligence system of the VC. In general, most engagements occur when the VC determine that it is to their advantage to fight. Otherwise, they fade into the bush. Operations of larger-than-company size seldom make contact. Small-unit patrolling and ambushes (squad and platoon), backed up by responsive air support and reaction forces, have proven to be a most effective approach. In this manner, we have been able to average 9.7 contacts per day with the enemy during the past year.

Counting operations outside the camp perimeters each day during the past twelve months.

Project Delta continues to be a particularly useful intelligence gathering means. The technique of employment of these reconnaissance teams today differs somewhat in that they are now employed in VC-controlled areas where there are no major friendly actions in progress which might compromise Delta's presence. Currently, these six-man US-Vietnamese teams "work an area" for longer periods (generally thirty days) than heretofore. Repeatedly, they have collected valuable intelligence.

Probably, the single greatest US shortcoming in Vietnam is our lack of timely, accurate intelligence. Soldiers' complaints about their repeated "walks in the woods" without contact give evidence of this problem. SF CIDG camps, however, have helped to fill this vacuum. SF camps are able to establish effective agent nets in the locale of the camp using CIDG who are native to the area. It is a unique capability which accrues to the USASF-CIDG system. MACV J2 states that over 50 percent of all their ground intelligence reports in the country come from Special Forces sources. The First Air Cavalry Division's Operation Crazy Horse during May 1966 in Binh Dinh province is an example of an operation launched solely as a result of intelligence obtained by a CIDG-Special Forces patrol. Another example of success achieved from rapid exploitation of SF battlefield intelligence occurred when Camp Buon Ea Yang, Darlac province, II CTZ, conducted an operation on March 18, 1966, in which a VC company commander was KIA and several documents were captured. Subsequent analysis of the documents indicated the location of four VC companies, approximately twenty-two kilometers from the camp. An operation was planned on the basis of the captured information. Operation Le Hai 21 made contact with a VC battalion located at the coordinates taken from the documents.

The areas of civic action and psychological operations continue to occupy much of our attention. According to USARV records, the Fifth Group Civic Action Program accounted for half of all the civic action projects conducted by USARV units during 1965-66 to date.

In 1964, officials in the United States Mission in Saigon began pressing for more emphasis on providing advice and assistance to the Vietnamese on civil matters. One program which developed and rapidly expanded called for US advisers to assist the Vietnamese government officials in improving the civic and community activities in their local areas. The advice and assistance ranged from large-scale projects such as dam construction, crop development, bridge building, and road improvements to the digging of wells, planning and supervising elementary sanitation systems, the establishment of small businesses, the construction of Montagnard hospitals, and the technical training of medical orderlies, dental technicians, and automotive mechanics.

US Military Assistance Command, Vietnam, advisers were assigned to province or sector officials (roughly equivalent to state officials in the United States), and as the number of American advisers increased, they were assigned to the next lower political level, the subsector (town or village) officials. At the same time, it was recognized that the real focal point for advice and assistance should be the officials of the town or village. The availability of US advisers, civilian and military, did not always stretch to include these grassroots officials.

Since a number of CIDG camps were located near subsector headquarters, the US Army Special Forces was asked in 1964 to study the practicality of assigning the additional mission of advising subsector officials to the US Special Forces commanders in the nearby CIDG camps. At this point in time, the 103 advisers from the Military Assistance Command, Vietnam, had proven their worth in the political structure but had all the responsibility they could manage.

Geographically, they were stretched thin. The US Special Forces headquarters agreed to take on the additional mission of advising the Vietnamese civilian officials with the clear understanding that the CIDG combat mission had priority. One compelling reason for accepting these posts in a select number of locations was that the Special Forces adviser had a built-in defensive capability in the form of the CIDG troops in nearby camps, a resource not available to the Military Assistance Command adviser, especially in insecure districts largely controlled by the Viet Cong.

After a successful test period with an A detachment in this dual role, the Military Assistance Command assigned the subsector mission to appropriately situated A detachments in all four corps tactical zones. In certain provinces in III and IV Corps, where most of the subsector officials were advised by Special Forces A detachment commanders, the control B detachments were assigned the next higher political level requirement—the sector advisory mission. The mission of an A detachment commander in this assignment was to advise and assist the subsector official or district chief in the training and employment of his Regional and Popular Forces troops. As a sector adviser, a B detachment commander had a similar mission in relation to the sector commander or province chief.

By October 1965, five B detachments had coequal missions, and thirty-eight A detachments were assigned the subsector mission. The number of detachments assigned these missions peaked in the first quarter of 1966 at seven B and forty-one A detachments and thereafter declined. At the end of June 1967, there were four B and twenty-three A detachments so assigned. On the whole, the performance in the subsector and sector advisory mission by the Special Forces was very good, but A detachments were clearly better motivated and more effective in carrying out the subsector mission when controlled by a B detachment charged with the sector advisory mission.

The combination of the coequal missions of B detachments and the similarly charged A detachments under them was most productive in the Mekong Delta, where the presence of US troops was not a factor, and the contest, despite presence of the Vietnam Army, was for the most part between government paramilitary forces and local Viet Cong units. In these circumstances, the B detachment commanders were in a position to plan and coordinate the operations of all CIDG, Regional Forces, and Popular Forces units in a province by using an integrated intelligence system. Detachment B-41 at Muc Hoa in Kien Tuong province, B-42 at Chau Doc in the same province, and B-43 at Cao Lanh in Kien Phong province—all in the IV Corps—were able to operate most effectively in this way.

In the area of combat developments, the achievements of Project Delta must be mentioned. Project Delta was the first unit specifically trained to perform special operations. When it first became operational in December 1964, after a long period of training, it consisted of six reconnaissance teams of eight Vietnamese and two US Special Forces men each, and a reaction force, the Vietnam Army's Ninety-First Ranger Battalion (airborne) consisting of three companies. By 1967, Project Delta had expanded to sixteen reconnaissance teams composed of four Vietnamese and two US Special Forces members, eight roadrunner teams, and a reaction force of six companies. The pattern of operations consisted of infiltrating teams, normally by helicopter, at dusk or after dark into a Viet Cong-controlled area, without benefit of lights or ground reception party. At first, the teams were limited to reconnaissance and were withdrawn if discovered. Subsequently, a decision was made to allow them to continue operations provided that contact with the enemy had been safely broken and to attack small targets that they could handle without help. Missions were assigned by Military Assistance Command, Vietnam, or the Vietnamese Joint General Staff and were based on recommendations from the commanding general of the Vietnamese Special Forces and the commanding officer of the Fifth Special Forces Group (airborne).

Besides Project Delta, other combat developments in this period included the creation of the Apache Force and the Eagle Scouts, which were eventually integrated into the combat reconnaissance patrol and mobile strike forces, which also had their beginnings at this time. The full effectiveness and capabilities of the combat reconnaissance patrol and mobile strike forces were not realized until after June 1966.

The Apache Force was conceived as a combined force of Special Forces men and indigenous troops with the primary mission of orienting an American battalion or larger size unit prior to its commitment to combat against Viet Cong or North Vietnamese Army forces. The orientation included terrain walks, map analyses, Viet Cong or North Vietnamese small-unit tactics, a review of lessons learned to date on enemy weaknesses and common mistakes made by US forces when first committed. Finally, the Apache Force usually accompanied the American unit into the field for the first several days of combat. Its secondary mission was to serve as a multipurpose reserve for the Special Forces CIDG program in order to extend intelligence capabilities, conduct offensive operations with Nung companies (which came to be heavily utilized in the mobile strike forces), reinforce threatened areas, or act as a reaction force for camps, outposts, or forward operations bases under attack. The Eagle Scouts, like the Apache Force, were capable of reconnaissance and combat and could be moved by helicopter as well. These two forces, along with others, represented stages in the evolution of an effective reconnaissance and reaction force—the mobile strike force.

The formation of combat reconnaissance platoons of thirty-four men each, one platoon to each camp, began during the first quarter of 1965. It took some time to send all the platoons to Dong Ba Thin to receive special training at the Vietnamese Special Forces training center under Project Delta instructors, but the reconnaissance platoon became the elite unit of each camp and measurably increased the effectiveness of strike force operations. In most camps, there was at least a reconnaissance squad attached to a regular strike force patrol, usually of company strength. The combat reconnaissance platoon was infrequently employed as a unit, but elements were often assigned the task of finding and fixing enemy targets or used for psychological operations and small raids, or to adjust artillery fire and air strikes. In July 1966, the decision was made to increase the strength to two reconnaissance platoons per CIDG camp.

* * * END of EXTRACTION * * *

Note: Extracted from Vietnam Studies (1961-1971). The CIDG Program Begins to Mature. *See reference page 305.*

Errata Sheet

List of City locations:
Saigon
Embassy, Continental & Caravelle hotels
Le Cave and Van Caan Restaurants
La Baccara nightclub
Cholon District (Chinese)
Hong Kong
Mandarin, Peninsula Court, HK Hilton
Aberddeen Fishing Village floating markets and restaurants
Tiger Baum Gardens
USN Fleet Club
Kai Tak Airport
Bangkok
Don Muang Airport
Siam Square District
Nana Plaza
Pratunam Square
Chao Phraya River
Royal Grand Palace
Temple of the Dawn
Temple of the Emerald Buddha
Ploenchit Square
Lumpini Stadium, Sukumvit Road
Dalat
Home of SVN's West Point
Lake Ho Xuian Ha'o'ng
Dalat Palace Golf Course
University of Dalat
South Vietnam Nuclear Research Center (served by Vietnam Airlines)

Senior advisor, IV Corps, Delta, MACV was Brig. GEN Wm. S. DeSobrey, USA. Assumed title, June 3, 1966.

In January 1968, GEN Eckhardt became commanding general of the Delta Military Assistance Command, and senior advisor, IV Corps Tactical Zone, headquartered in Can Tho.

Seventh Fleet Carriers:

Constellation, 60K tons

Enterprise: (CVN 65): 93 - 94 tons, 2 Nuclear Reactors

(Essex Class Carriers):

Ticonderoga

Oriskany, 32K tons;

Coral Sea, 45K tons[*]

Hancock: (CVA - 19): 27 tons.

Ranger: (CVA - 61): 56 tons . . . First "angled landing decks"

Midway: (CV - 41): 45 tons comm'd. to 74 tons decomm'd[**]

Midway in 1963 after SCB-110

---

[*] Department of the Navy—Naval Historical Center, 805 Kidder Breese SE -- Washington Navy Yard, Washington, DC 20374-5060, Online Library of Selected Images: U.S. Navy Ship Types -- Fleet Aircraft Carriers

[**] The first and last air-to-air kills in Vietnam. Illustrative of the major contribution the carrier made to the war was a notable "first" for aviators of her Attack Carrier Wing 2, who on June 17, 1965, downed the first four MiGs credited to U.S. Forces in Southeast Asia. On 12 January 1973, LT V. T. Kovaleski (pilot) and LT J. A. Wise (RIO) of the Midway's VF-161 Chargers downed a North Vietnamese MiG-17 with an AIM-9 Sidewinder launched from their F-4B Phantom II.

UH-1(E)s—Huey; Boeing-Vertol (CH-47s); Chinook helos; USN A-37 Skywolves; F-8 Navy fighter planes; F-4 Phantom jets;

Dalat (Vietnam's West Point), US Special Forces—Green Berets, Operations near Pleiku.

First Cavalry Airborne units. Tough, well-trained, operated in II Corps in highlands 60 km. from Cambodian border and south to Parrot's Beak near Saigon.

Tan Son Nhut Airbase (about 20 km. north of Saigon)

Parrot's Beak (Tay Ninh, 90 km. northwest of Saigon, 40 km. north of Cambodian border)

The Plain of Reeds, Muc Hoa (50 km. due west of Saigon, only 20 km. from Cambodian border in Kien Tuong province), the Parrot's Beak protruding between them. Major supply lines traced from Sihanoukville to this area.

Can Tho, major Game Warden base on the Bassac River, 50 km. southwest of Saigon.

Vinh Long at intersection of Mekong and My Tho Rivers 100 km. southwest of Saigon. (Co Chien is the lower Mekong).

Ca Mau, formerly Quan Long, provincial capital of An Xuyen, VC bastion 240 km. southwest of Saigon, southernmost province adjacent to Ba Xuyen province.

Plain of Reeds, approximately 2,000 sq. mi. swampy area immediately to the west and north of Saigon. Bordered on the west by the Mekong and its tributaries and on the north by the Cambodian border, this desolate area served as "a corridor" for Viet Cong shallow draft sampan convoys to resupply about 70,000 of the enemy south of Saigon.

Cambodian Delta provinces: Kien Giang and An Giang spanning the Mekong and Bassac Rivers. The Soirap River (RSSZ)

Nha Be, naval base on the Saigon River, South of Saigon

The Mekong, My Tho, Bassac, Saigon, and Soirap Rivers. Vinh Long and Sa Dec on the Mekong River. Co Chien River (lower Mekong). Hau Giang (lower Bassac).

Ho Chi Minh Trail, MK-5

Commencing in 1967 and continuing after the Tet Offensive by the North in early '68, an additional bombing campaign was undertaken against the Ho Chi Minh Trail. The trail led from deep in the north's industrial area, south through the key junction point of Vinh, and continuing through the extreme southeastern corner of Laos, and then along the Cambodian side of the border with the South, into the highlands of South Vietnam both south and north of Dalat (the home of the West Point of South Vietnam). *See map 1, page 19.*

Listening devices, known as MK-5s, the existence of which were classified top secret, were dropped along the trail to alert our monitoring stations of impending shipments. Unfortunately for us, the North ran their shipments at night, while the daylight bombings exploded their ordinance in the thick canopy of trees protecting the trail, resulting in little impedance of the trail's traffic. Similarly, when key sections of bridges in the North were bombed out, duplicate or spare sections of the bridge would be floated back in place at night from their hidden locations along the shore. Subsequently, the traffic along the trail would be resumed. Vinh was located about 15 km. inland from the coast and just below the Nineteenth Parallel in lower NVN. I considered this city the northern terminus of the Ho Trail. A severe blow to the

Trail's ability to function efficiently could have been struck by eliminating Vinh as a functioning terminal. The only effective way to accomplish this would be by the introduction of ground forces into the North. Vinh's location being so close to the coast rendered it open to a commando-like amphibious landing, which in fact, I recommended to the powers that be after my return to Washington. In every instance, particularly in my meeting with representatives of the Defense Intelligence Agency (DIA), I was told, in no uncertain terms, to "forget and bury" this idea.

For reference purposes, the DMZ was located just below the Seventeenth parallel and represented the demarcation area between NVN and SVN.

Dr. Bothwell, Chas. Di Bona, past presidents of the Center for Naval Analyses.

Chaplin and Nakonekne, ACV researchers at David Taylor Model Basin (now Naval Research and Development Center, Potomac, MD.-NRDC).

Christians v. Buddhists and Taoists—business and profits were the issues, not the war. Large Chinese populace led to Confucianism being practiced.

Cu Chi tunnels—Surfacing just outside the northwest edge of Saigon were these tunnels, purported to be three levels deep, with its own hospital and weapons-ammunition facilities, originating from as far away as the Parrot's Beak, Cambodia.

References

- *The Summoning of the Trumpet* by Dave R. Palmer

- *Eyewitness Vietnam* by Donald L. Gilmore, with D. M. GianGreco. Published by Sterling Publishing Co. Inc., New York City.

- *Honor Project* by David Connelly and Mike Dolan, Bob Kirk, Marc Honory. Published by First Person Productions, LLC.

- *Historical Atlas of the US Navy* by Craig L. Symonds. Published by the Naval Institute (USNI), Annapolis, Maryland.

- *Vietnam Studies—Command and Control (1950-1969)*, Department of the Army by Maj. GEN George S. Eckhardt. Library of Congress Catalog Card No 72-600186.

- *Vietnam Studies (1961-1971)*, CMH Publication 90-23[*], Department of the Army, Washington, DC, 1989. Chapter 4, *"The CIDG Program Begins to Mature."*

- *TIME Almanac*-2004, published by TIME Inc. ISBN: 1-931933-78-2.

- *Up Country* by Nelson DeMille. Published by Warner Vision Books, an AOL, Time Warner Company.

- *An Unfinished Life* by Robert Dallek. Published by Little, Brown & Co. Boston, Massachusetts. 2003 (Pps. 678-680).

---

[*] On or about October 16, 1966, GEN Westmoreland wrote to Admiral Ward congratulating him on a successful Game Warden Operation just west of My Tho, where 6 PBRs assisted by elements of the SV Navy inflicted heavy casualties upon the NVN's 304th Division. This letter was found in the referenced US Naval Monthly Historical Summary-'66. Discussions of Tet from Westmoreland, Hunt, and the Pentagon papers are presented as well as Seymour Hersh on My Lai.

- *One Percent Solution* by Ron Suskind. Published April 2006.

- *Wikipedia*. Katyusha (through Google, the online search engine).

- US Naval Forces—Vietnam, Monthly Historical Summary, Group 4, Pps. 8-10. (Declassified after twelve years, in three-year intervals). [*]

- Extracted from *Vietnam Studies (1965-1971)*
  CMH Publication 90-23, Part Two, The Middle Years: 1965-1968
  Department of the Army
  Washington, DC, 1989 (First Printed 1973)

---

[*] Secured through the cooperation of the Department of the Navy, Naval Historical Center—Washington Navy Yard, Washington, DC, 20374.

Reviewers

Theodore J. Lowi - professor, American history, Cornell University. Ithaca, New York

CDR Jas. Rooney - USN, copter pilot, retired. Nebo, North Carolina[*]

Christopher Ohly, Esq. - Schiff Hardin, LLC. Washington, DC.

LTCOL Bruce DeWoolfson - USMC, retired. Vienna, Virginia[*]
        - Chairman, EUCLID Visions Systems

Paul Kagan - IT Consultant, Silver Spring, MD.

CAPT Harry Hagerty - Twenty-Fifth US Infantry Division, stationed in Long Binh. US special advisor to SVN, retired. Washington, DC.[*]

Yoav Katz, Israeli Army tank commander. 1967 Six-Day War. Pres., Katz & Latter, P.A. Bethesda, Maryland.

Paul Belford - Central Intelligence Agency, retired. Kensington, Maryland. Author of three novels, one of which, *Notes from a Passage* was about his experiences in Vietnam in the seventies. Written under the name P. D. St. Claire. (Amazon.com).

MGEN Bernard Loeffke[*] - retired, commanding general. Army South Vietnam. PhD, international relations and masters in Russian

---

[*] GEN Loeffke, US Army; CDR Rooney, USN; CAPT Hagerty, US Army; LTCOL DeWoolfson, USMC, all served with distinction in Vietnam.

language. He is a seven-time decorated Vietnam vet, including the Purple Heart.

Mark and Sorcorro Tischer, Katie Glacken, and Marsha Selig (sister).

Raymond Chin, Production Supervisor, Xlibris Corporation *(one of the pioneers of the print-on-demand publishing services industry)*

* * * THE END * * *

Appendix

I. National Front for the Liberation of Vietnam (Redirected from Viet Cong)
From *Wikipedia*, the free encyclopedia

Beginning of Extraction

Viet Cong (NLF) flag

The National Front for the Liberation of Southern Vietnam (Vietnamese Mặt Trận Dân Tộc Giải Phóng Miền Nam), also known as the Viet Cong, VC, or the National Liberation Front (NLF), was an insurgent (partisan) organization fighting the Republic of Vietnam during the Vietnam War.

The NLF was funded, equipped and staffed by both South Vietnamese and the army of North Vietnam. Its military organization was known as the People's Liberation Armed Forces (PLAF).

The PLAF were, according to the official history of the (North) Vietnamese Army, strictly subordinated to the general staff in Hanoi. Their name "Viet Cong," (VC) came from the Vietnamese term for Vietnamese Communist (Việt Nam Cộng Sản). American forces typically referred to members of the NLF as "Charlie," which comes from the US Armed Forces' phonetic pronunciation of VC ("Victor Charlie").

Organization:

The VC was nominally independent of the North Vietnamese armed forces and although the leadership of the group was communist, the NLF was also made up of others who were allied with the Front against the policies of Ngo Dinh Diem.

However, as the war with the Americans escalated North Vietnamese personnel increasingly formed the military staff and officer corps of the VC as well as directly deploying their own forces. People's Army of Vietnam (PAVN) official history refers to the PLAF as "part of the PAVN."

Communist cadres also, from the start, formed the majority of the decision-making strata of the organization, though non-Communists, encouraged by the initial chair, Nguyen Huu Tho, were also involved in this process American soldiers and the South Vietnam government typically referred to their guerrilla Opponents as the Viet Cong or VC.

The VC organization grew out of the Viet Minh organization. By the time the Viet Cong began fighting the ARVN, the insurgency had a national infrastructure in the country. Rather than having to create "liberated zones" as in a classic insurgency, the VC were in control of such zones at the start of the war. The US/ARVN response~involving big-unit, conventional warfare and counter-insurgency was ineffective~in part because it was fighting an insurgency with an infrastructure that in many areas was already 20 years old. The long western border of South Vietnam and the weakness of its reflected the People's War approach of Giap, who modified the writings of Mao for his purposes. But in truth, the People's War approach was abandoned after the Tet Offensive in favor of small-unit conventional warfare led by the army of North Vietnam.

In 1969, the VC formed a Provisional Revolutionary Government—PRG which after the fall of Saigon in 1975 claimed to represent South Vietnam. The provisional government never ruled any territory or exercised the functions of a government.

Its principal role was to sign the instruments of unification with North Vietnam forming the Socialist Republic of Vietnam in 1976.

No non-communists were allowed to take part in the transitory PRG government. VC "minister of justice" Truong Nhu Tang describes how cadres from the north took over the work of his ministry within days of the take-over.

The Tết Offensive and Afterward

During the celebration of Tết in January of 1968, the NLF violated an implicit holiday ceasefire held between themselves and the US-RVN forces and attacked many of the main cities, provincial capitals and villages throughout South Vietnam. The US embassy in Saigon was attacked, and it appeared at first glance that the PLAF could attack anywhere with impunity. The Tết Offensive came as a surprise to the American public, who had gotten constant optimistic appraisals of the war by GEN William Westmoreland. In the wake of Tết, Westmoreland claimed that the NLF failed to achieve any of their strategic goals or hold any of their brief gains and that they achieved a "psychological victory" at best. Westmoreland's assertions have been called into question by Vietnam historians such as David Hunt and Marvin Gettleman, who argue that one of the major aims of Tết was to bring the Americans to the bargaining table. Although the main military forces of the PLAF no doubt suffered tremendous losses due to the Offensive, historians differ on the degree to which the NLF suffered as a result of Tết. However, there is no doubt that after Tết the cadres of the NLF were more and more made up of Vietnamese from the north.

The Tết Offensive is sometimes portrayed as a crushing failure for the US, a military giant humiliated by the NLF. This analysis, however, speaks more to the largely—unanticipated psychological effect the Offensive had on the American public, rather than any military success. The NLF and North Vietnamese had clearly stated goals in launching the Offensive, including a mass uprising of the South Vietnamese citizenry in support of the NLF. These goals were not achieved, but the US military, media and public were all caught very much off guard by the offensive, thanks largely to Westmoreland's rather faulty prognostications.

Walter Cronkite, for example, famously stated on February 27, 1968, that the US was "now mired in a stalemate" in Vietnam. The idea that Vietnam could not be won, and instead should be resolved via "disengagement with honor," animated both the Johnson and Nixon administrations and led to the latter's process of "Vietnamizing" the war. Some academics have pointed out that regardless of the ultimate military success of the US at the end of the Tet offensive, the offensive had shown that three years into the war US intelligence was inept in not being able to even detect a national uprising, that the scale of the offensive showed that the insurgency had not been defeated by the introduction of hundreds of thousands of soldiers from the US, and that those supporting the war could not credibly describe a strategy for victory.

Rather than offering a hope for success, many supporters of the war fell back on patriotic arguments and the idea that the war had to continue on in its current form forever because a lack of success was better than an admission of failure.

In 1969, the NLF formed the Provisional Revolutionary Government which operated until the end of the Vietnam War. But it was a powerless front organization that no real authority and no other function than propaganda. When the North Vietnamese army captured Saigon in 1975, the NLF and the PRG were set up as a legal front as part of the process of unification.

The PRG never functioned as a real government in South Vietnam. After the fall of Saigon, administration was organized by the North Vietnamese Army. The country was unified under the leadership of the Communist Party of Vietnam as the Socialist Republic of Vietnam in 1976.

Retrieved from:

http://en.wikipedia.org/wiki/National_Front_for_the_Liberation_of_Vietnam Categories: Irregular military | Rebellions in Asia | Vietnam War

. . . End of Extraction

Further Reading

1. Marvin Gettleman et al. 1995. *Vietnam and America—a Documented History*. Grove Press. ISBN 0-8021-3362-2. (Especially see part 7, "The Decisive Year.")

2. Truong Nhu Tang. 1985. *A Viet Cong Memoir*. Random House. ISBN 0394743091. (See chapter 7 on the forming of the NLF and chapter 21 on the Communist takeover in 1975.)

3. Frances Fitzgerald. 1972. *Fire in the Lake: The Vietnamese and the Americans in Vietnam*. Boston: Little, Brown and Company. ISBN 0316284238. (See the description in chapter 4, "The National Liberation Front.")

4. Douglas Valentine. 1990. *The Phoenix Program*. New York: William Morrow and Company. ISBN 068809130X.

5. Merle Pribbenow (transl). 2002. *Victory in Vietnam: The Official History of the People's Army of Vietnam*. University Press of Kansas. ISBN 07000611754.

6. *Vietnam: A Complete Photographic History*. Text by Michael Maclear. Photography edited by Hal Buell, Tess Press, NYC.

7. *Vietnam and America: A documented history*, 2nd Edition by M. Gettleman, J. Franklin, M. Young, H.B. Franklin, Growth Press New York Pps. 247-274

8. *Technology for the US Navy and Marine Corps*, 2000-2035, Volume 1 overview, National Academy Press, Washington D.C., 1997

9. *A Bright Shining Lie: John Paul Vann and America in Vietnam* by Neil Sheehan. Vintage Books, September 1989.

10. Edward J. Marolda. *Ready Seapower: A History of the U.S. Seventh Fleet. (Washington, DC: Naval History & Heritage Command, Department of the Navy, 2011.* xv, 195 pp. <u>ISBN 9780945274674</u>).

Suggested Reference Materials

Deployment for Carriers and Carrier-Based Squadrons in the Western Pacific (WestPac) and Vietnam (1964-1975)
http://www.history.navy.mil/avh-1910/APP26.PDF

Carrier, Carrier-Based Squadrons, and Noncarrier-Based Squadrons Deployments to Vietnam. US Naval Aviation 1910-1995. Chronology of Significant Events in American Aviation. The Sixth Decade: 1960-69. Part 9, Pps. 260-263 and Deployments-1966, Pps. 723-725.

Another Vietnam—Pictures of the War from the Other Side by Tim Page. *National Geographic*. Washington, DC.

Historical aircraft
http://www.history.navy.mil/branches/org4-8.htm

Index

A

Aberdeen, 268
ACV (air cushion vehicles), 9, 16-18, 20, 33, 42-43, 46, 49, 52, 56-57, 91, 93-94, 97, 119-20, 126-29, 191-92
ACV-3, 197-98, 201
  Alpha, 141, 145, 147
  Tango, 141, 146-48
  See also PACV
Air Cavalry (also Air Cav), 131, 206, 211, 224, 235, 248
AK-47s, 141, 247, 302
Allied forces, 140
Allison, Captain, 212, 217
Alpha team, 170-71, 184-86, 188, 194
Apache Force, 297-98
Ap Ba'c, 235-36
Army. *See* US Army
ARVN (Army of the Republic of Vietnam), 67, 91, 123, 292
ATC (armed-troop carriers), 28, 207, 231, 235-36, 242, 274

B

Ba Muoi Ba beer, 37, 43, 243
Bangkok, 181
Bao Dai (emperor), 81-82, 200
Bassac River, 18, 53, 59, 78-79, 123, 170-71, 184-86, 188-89, 202, 204, 212, 224, 230, 232-33, 303
Ba Xuyen province, 77, 170, 203, 232, 302
Bell Aerosystems, 17
Benson, George, 68, 157-58, 167-68, 171, 185, 193, 234-35
Ben Tre, 205-6, 208
Bien Hoa Air Base, 89, 119, 121, 136-37, 139-40, 156, 162, 169, 188-89, 193, 217, 223-26, 231, 235-36, 238-39
Binh Dinh province, 294
Blackjack operations, 288-89
BM-13 rocket system, 245
Bothwell, Dr., 17, 20, 45, 106-8, 134, 153-55, 168, 193, 234-35, 250, 304
Bravo team, 171, 185-86, 189-90, 208
Bronson, Bruce, 28, 30, 32-33, 50-52, 55-57, 60-61, 84, 108-9, 118-19, 133, 166-67, 192-93, 201-2, 250-51, 259-60
Burma, 100

C

Cai Lay, 208, 235
Cambodia, 18, 53, 56, 59, 73, 79, 81, 83, 91, 95, 108, 147-48, 150-51, 154, 156
Cam Ranh Bay, 197

D

CPSIA information can be obtained at www.ICGtesting.com
Printed in the USA
LVOW081045210912

299700LV00002B/60/P